AF770457

COMPANY LAW IN PRACTICE

COMPANY LAW IN PRACTICE

Inns of Court School of Law

BLACKSTONE
PRESS LIMITED

First published in Great Britain 1998 by Blackstone Press Limited,
Aldine Place, London W12 8AA. Telephone (020) 8740 2277
www.blackstonepress.com

© Inns of Court School of Law, 1998

First edition 1998
Second edition 1999
Third edition 2000

ISBN: 1 84174 009 8

British Library Cataloguing in Publication Data
A CIP catalogue record for this book is available from the British Library.

Typeset by Style Photosetting Ltd, Mayfield, East Sussex
Printed by Ashford Colour Press, Gosport, Hampshire

All rights reserved. No part of this book may be reproduced or transmitted in any form or by any means, electronic or mechanical including photocopying, recording, or any information storage or retrieval system without prior permission from the publisher.

FOREWORD

These manuals are designed primarily to support training on the Bar Vocational Course, though they are also intended to provide a useful resource for legal practitioners and for anyone undertaking training in legal skills.

The Bar Vocational Course was designed by staff at the Inns of Court School of Law, where it was introduced in 1989. This course is intended to equip students with the practical skills and the procedural and evidential knowledge that they will need to start their legal professional careers. These manuals are written by staff at the Inns of Court School of Law who have helped to develop the course, and by a range of legal practitioners and others involved in legal skills training. The authors of the manuals are very well aware of the practical and professional approach that is central to the Bar Vocational Course.

The range and coverage of the manuals have grown steadily. All the practice manuals are updated every two years, and regular reviews and revisions of the manuals are carried out to ensure that developments in legal skills training and the experience of our staff are fully reflected in them.

This updating and revision is a constant process, and we very much value the comments of practitioners, staff and students. Legal vocational training is advancing rapidly, and it is important that all those concerned work together to achieve and maintain high standards. Please address any comments to the Bar Vocational Course Director at the Inns of Court School of Law.

With the validation of other providers for the Bar Vocational Course it is very much our intention that these manuals will be of equal value to all students wherever they take the course, and we would value comments from tutors and students at other validated institutions.

The enthusiasm of the staff at Blackstone Press Ltd and their efficiency in arranging the production and publication of these manuals is much appreciated.

The Hon. Mr Justice Elias
Chairman of the Board of Governors
Inns of Court School of Law
December 1999

CONTENTS

TABLE OF CASES

TABLE OF STATUTES

ONE

INTRODUCTION

1.1 Company Law Practice

Much of the work in company law at the Bar is connected with corporate insolvency. Many junior practitioners, almost regardless of their chambers' specialisations, will find themselves being instructed to appear on winding-up petitions. Indeed for many practitioners, winding-up petitions are the full extent of their involvement with this area of law.

A small number of practitioners practise exclusively in company law. Many others combine a specialisation in company law with other areas of Chancery practice and commercial law. These practitioners may be instructed in a wide range of company matters, for example:

(a) Drafting a company's articles of association.

(b) Drafting applications and affidavits in miscellaneous matters where a company or its members can apply to the court under the Companies Act 1985.

(c) Advising in writing or in conference where shareholders claim they have been unfairly prejudiced and on innumerable other matters.

(d) Appearing in court on insolvency applications, applications to reduce share capital, in proceedings to disqualify directors from acting as such etc.

1.2 The Course

The following chapters concentrate on a number of areas which are important and commonly met in day-to-day practice. An attempt has been made to preserve a balance between substantive company law and insolvency topics.

Company law is an area where you will need to develop the full range of barristers' skills, from organising the facts of your case, through researching the law and procedure, to drafting the necessary documents or advising the client or appearing in court.

1.3 Sources

You will find that company law is a broad subject, with many areas covered by detailed statutory provisions. Most barristers attend court with their papers, notebook and a copy of *Butterworths Company Law Handbook* (currently in its 13th edition, 1999). The Handbook contains all the relevant legislation (including statutory instruments), and its usefulness cannot be overstated.

1.3.1 LAW REPORTS

Some areas are still governed by case law, and many statutory provisions have been scrutinised many times by the courts. Cases are to be found in most of the main series of law reports, but, in addition, there are now two sets of reports dealing exclusively with company cases, namely:

British Company Cases (BCC), published by CCH.
Butterworths Company Law Cases (BCLC).

1.3.2 PRACTITIONER TEXTS

Atkin's Court Forms, vols 9 and 10.
British Company Law and Practice (CCH).
Gore-Browne on Companies, 44th edn. (Jordans, 1998).
Palmer's Company Law (Stevens).

1.3.3 STUDENT TEXTS

There are many excellent texts on company law. The following is only a selection:

Farrar's Company Law, 4th edn. (Butterworths, 1998).
Mayson, French and Ryan on Company Law, 16th edn. (Blackstone Press, 1999).

For reference:

Gower's Principles of Company Law, 6th edn. (Sweet & Maxwell, 1997).
Pennington's Company Law, 7th edn. (Butterworths, 1995).

1.4 Abbreviations

AGM	annual general meeting
BCC	*British Company Cases*
BCLC	*Butterworths Company Law Cases*
CA 1948	Companies Act 1948
CA 1980	Companies Act 1980
CA 1985	Companies Act 1985
CA 1989	Companies Act 1989
CA	Court of Appeal
CDDA 1986	Company Directors Disqualification Act 1986
CDPD	Chancery Division Practice Direction
ChD	Chancery Division
CJA 1993	Criminal Justice Act 1993
CPR 1998	Civil Procedure Rules 1998
DTI	Department of Trade and Industry
EGM	extraordinary general meeting
FSA 1986	Financial Services Act 1986
HL	House of Lords
IA 1986	Insolvency Act 1986
IPPD	Insolvency Proceedings Practice Direction pursuant to the Civil Procedure Rules 1998
IR 1986	Insolvency Rules 1986 (SI 1986 No. 1925)
PD 49B	Practice Direction 49B to the Civil Procedure Rules 1998
PF	prescribed form (to be found in vol. 2 of the 'White Book')
reg.	regulation
RSC 1965	Rules of the Supreme Court 1965 (as preserved in the CPR, sch. 1)
SCA 1981	Supreme Court Act 1981
SCP	*Supreme Court Practice* (the 'White Book')
Table A	Regulations for management of a company limited by shares, to be found in Companies (Tables A to F) Regulations 1985 (SI 1985 No. 805).

TWO

COMPANIES PROCEEDINGS

2.1 Jurisdiction

Many provisions in the Companies Act 1985 provide for various applications to be made to 'the court'. This expression means the court having jurisdiction to wind up the company (CA 1985, s. 744). The High Court always has such jurisdiction provided the company is registered in England and Wales, and the county courts will have concurrent jurisdiction if the company's paid-up share capital does not exceed £120,000 (IA 1986, s. 117).

2.1.1 COUNTY COURTS

Very few companies have paid-up share capital in excess of £120,000, so most company law applications can be commenced in a county court. However, in practice only a relatively small number of Companies Act cases are brought in the county courts as most practitioners prefer to use the High Court.

Procedure in the county courts basically follows that in the High Court. The same forms of originating process are used, the only difference being the reference to the court in the title. The IA 1986, s. 117(5), provides that where it has jurisdiction, a county court has all the powers of the High Court.

If proceedings are wrongly commenced in a county court they are not invalid and may be retained there or transferred (IA 1986, s. 118).

2.1.2 HIGH COURT

High Court proceedings may be commenced in the Royal Courts of Justice, London, or in any Chancery district registry (Birmingham, Bristol, Cardiff, Leeds, Liverpool, Manchester, Newcastle upon Tyne and Preston: see CDPD 2).

All applications under the CA 1985 and other legislation relating to companies are assigned to the Chancery Division (SCA 1981, sch. 1), and proceed in the Companies Court.

2.1.3 COMPANIES COURT

The Companies Court is part of the Chancery Division. It has a separate General Office for the issuing of originating process pursuant to the CA 1985 and IA 1986, filing affidavits etc. Judicial functions are performed by the Companies Court Registrar and by judges with expertise in company law. The Companies Court, presided over by a puisne judge, hears companies interim applications and petitions adjourned by the Registrar on Mondays (CDPD 5). Matters estimated to exceed two hours are usually stood over to dates fixed by the Chancery Clerk of the Lists.

2.2 Procedural Provisions

A great deal of the litigation in the company law field is brought under Acts of Parliament. Different procedural codes apply depending on the statute governing the case. The general scheme is as follows:

(a) Proceedings under the CA 1985 are governed by PD 49B.

(b) Insolvency proceedings are governed by IR 1986.

(c) Proceedings under the CDDA 1986 are governed by the Directors Disqualification Proceedings Practice Direction pursuant to the CPR 1998.

The above rules often lay down detailed procedural provisions in addition to laying down the appropriate method of commencement. If no specific method of commencement is laid down, the application is commenced by issuing a claim form using the CPR, Part 8 procedure: PD 49B, para. 2(1).

As mentioned above, a great deal of company law litigation is brought under statute. In addition, company law often forms the basis of ordinary civil actions, for example, ordinary actions commenced by claim form against directors for breach of their duties to their companies. Further, failure to comply with various provisions in the CA 1985 can result in criminal proceedings being brought against those in default.

We will now consider the various procedural rules in a little more detail, starting with applications under the CA 1985.

2.3 Applications under the Companies Act 1985

2.3.1 PART 8 PROCEDURE

2.3.1.1 Applications made by Part 8 claim form

Unless contrary provision is made (see **2.3.2** and **2.3.3**) all applications (other than interim applications) under the CA 1985 are begun by issuing a Part 8 claim form. Examples include applications under:

(a) CA 1985, s. 6(2), to extend the time for delivering to the registrar of companies any order made under CA 1985, s. 5, cancelling or confirming a resolution altering a company's objects.

(b) CA 1985, s. 216, for an order imposing transfer and voting restrictions on shares in a company where a person interested in those shares has failed to give the information required by a s. 212 notice served by the company.

(c) CA 1985, s. 318(9), for an order requiring a company to permit its shareholders to inspect its directors' service contracts or the written memoranda of its directors' terms of service.

(d) CA 1985, s. 371, to summon meetings of a company and, if necessary, to declare such meetings quorate even if attended by fewer persons than the minimum number prescribed by the company's articles of association.

(e) CA 1985, s. 383(5), to compel inspection or provision of copies of the minutes of a company's general meetings.

(f) CA 1985, s. 425(1), to order meetings of creditors or members where a compromise or arrangement is proposed.

(g) CA 1985, s. 721, brought by the prosecuting authorities for an order for the production or inspection of a company's books in relation to investigations into offences connected with the management of the company's affairs. An order under this section is rather similar to a search warrant.

2.3.1.2 Title

The general rule is that the title should contain only the parties to the proceedings, and there is no need to mention the statute under which the application is made in the title (CDPD 11). However, this general rule does not apply to companies proceedings, and the title of the claim form (and of any witness statements or affidavits) must be entitled in the matter of the CA 1985 (PD 49B, para. 1(3)). For many applications under the CA 1985, the only party will be the company itself. For these cases it is therefore only necessary to name the company in the title, which will take the following form:

IN THE HIGH COURT OF JUSTICE — No. of 2000

CHANCERY DIVISION

COMPANIES COURT

IN THE MATTER OF [NAME OF COMPANY]

AND IN THE MATTER OF THE COMPANIES ACT 1985

Where the application is adversarial in nature, such as applications under CA 1985, s. 216 (see **2.3.1.1(b)**), the practice is to name the respective parties. The practice in the Companies Court is to term them applicants and respondents. The company involved is often, but not always, named as one of the parties. Any persons responsible for the default, such as directors and other officers of the company, may be joined as respondents. This is particularly so if the applicants intend to apply for an order for costs against such persons.

2.3.1.3 Evidence in support

The Part 8 claim form will invariably be supported by a witness statement or affidavit setting out the relevant facts. It will be entitled in the same way as the Part 8 claim form, and is otherwise drafted and endorsed in the same way as other witness statements and affidavits (see ***Civil Litigation Manual*, chapters 10 and 30**).

In the body of the evidence in support the deponent will explain the nature of the application and give full particulars of the dispute. Relevant documents will be exhibited in the usual way. In addition, it is usual for evidence in support of applications under the CA 1985 to give some or all of the following details of the company in question:

(a) Its date of incorporation, its registered number, and the nature of any limitation of liability.

(b) If it is a company limited by shares, its nominal, issued and paid-up share capital.

(c) The present ownership of its shares.

(d) The present directors.

(e) The address of its registered office.

(f) As an exhibit, a print of its memorandum and articles of association, together with any special resolutions.

(g) The nature of its objects.

2.3.1.4 Subsequent steps

After the Part 8 claim form is issued by the court, it must be served on the company together with the evidence in support and a response pack for acknowledging service. Service must be effected by the applicant (PD 49B, para. 10). A respondent who wishes to rely on written evidence must file it when acknowledging service (CPR, r. 8.5(3)). The applicant then has 14 days to serve further evidence in reply (r. 8.5(5)). A respondent who does not acknowledge service may attend the hearing, but may not take part unless the court grants permission (r. 8.4(2)). Part 8 claims are treated as allocated to the multi-track (r. 8.9(c) and PD 49B, para. 9).

The court may give directions immediately a Part 8 claim form is issued, either on the application of a party or of its own initiative (PD 8, para. 4.1). Directions may include a hearing date if the court considers this to be convenient. This will commonly happen in Part 8 claims under the CA 1985. If the court does fix a hearing date on issue, obviously details of this have to be served with the claim form. At the hearing, depending on the nature of the claim, the Registrar will either determine the application or give directions for the future conduct of the matter. In cases where the court does not fix a hearing date when the claim is issued, it will give directions (either with or without convening a directions hearing) as soon as practicable after the respondents have acknowledged service, or after the period for acknowledging service has expired (PD 8, para. 4.2).

2.3.2 PETITIONS

2.3.2.1 Applications made by petition

PD 49B, para. 4(1), sets out a list of 12 types of application under the CA 1985 which must be commenced by petition. These include applications under:

(a) CA 1985, s. 17, to cancel the alteration of a condition contained in a company's memorandum.

(b) CA 1985, s. 136, to confirm a reduction of the share capital of a company.

(c) CA 1985, s. 425, to sanction a compromise or arrangement between the company and its creditors, its members, or any class of either. Note that applications for orders for meetings of creditors or members under s. 425 are commenced by a Part 8 claim form (**2.3.1.1(f)**).

(d) CA 1985, s. 727, by an officer of the company for relief from liability for any claim in respect of negligence, default, breach of duty or breach of trust (see **7.6.3**).

2.3.2.2 The petition

There is no PF for petitions under the CA 1985, but several precedents can be found in vols 9 and 10 of *Atkin's Court Forms.*

A petition is entitled in the same way as a Part 8 claim form (see **2.3.1.3**). It sets out the grounds of the application and gives short particulars of all relevant facts in numbered paragraphs. The relief sought is set out in the prayer. The contents of any individual petition will be tailored to the facts of the case in hand. As an example, the facts stated in a petition to sanction an arrangement under CA 1985, s. 425 (see **2.3.2.1(c)**) will include:

(a) The date of the company's incorporation.

(b) The address of its registered office.

(c) The company's objects.

(d) A statement that the company has carried on business since its incorporation.

(e) Its nominal, issued and paid-up share capital.

(f) Details of the scheme, including the events leading up to the scheme being proposed. The terms of the scheme must be set out in a schedule to the petition.

(g) Whether creditors' or members' meetings were advertised.

(h) Any court order to summon meetings.

(i) Numbers present at the meetings in person and by proxy.

(j) Results of votes taken at the meetings, and any difficulties encountered in relation to voting.

2.3.2.3 Evidence

The statements of fact contained in the petition must be verified by written evidence. A print of the company's memorandum and articles of association, together with any special resolutions, will normally be exhibited to the witness statement or affidavit.

2.3.2.4 Directions

Unless the case falls within one of four exceptions, the petitioner must apply for directions by filing an application notice immediately after presenting the petition PD 49B, para. 5(1). The application will be heard by the Companies Court Registrar. At the directions hearing the Registrar will give such directions as seem desirable, and will in particular give directions for the publication of notices such as by advertisement and for the making of any inquiry (PD 49B, para. 5(3)).

The four exceptional cases mentioned above are listed in PD 49B, para. 5(2), and include applications under CA 1985, s. 425, to sanction compromises and arrangements (unless the s. 425 application includes an application for an order under s. 427.

2.3.2.5 Inquiries

Where a petition seeks the confirmation of a reduction in a company's capital, the court will be astute to protect the company's present creditors. To this end, the Registrar may give directions for an inquiry into the company's debts and any claims against the company, and may also give directions for settling a list of creditors entitled to object to the reduction.

If such a direction is made, the company must, through a competent officer, file at court written evidence within seven days of the making of the order verifying a list giving the names, addresses and amounts due to all its creditors. Within the next seven days the company must post notices to all the listed creditors stating:

(a) The amount of the reduction sought.

(b) The effect of the direction ordering the inquiry.

(c) The amount specified in the list as due to that creditor.

(d) The time fixed by the court for disputing the amount specified.

The direction will specify a time within which the company must file further evidence dealing with the posting of the above notices and the company's answers to any responses, including responses to newspaper advertisements of the petition and inquiry. Any disputes between the company and individual creditors may be either secured by the company or adjudicated by the court. When all matters have been resolved, the Registrar files a certificate giving full details of the results of the inquiry. The Registrar will usually then direct that details of the hearing date of the petition be published in specified newspapers.

2.3.2.6 The hearing

Petitions to sanction schemes of arrangement are always heard by a judge in open court. Other petitions are first heard by the Companies Court Registrar, usually on the hearing for directions. Although he may determine such petitions himself, he will usually refer them to the judge.

2.4 Applications under the Insolvency Act 1986

Detailed procedural rules for applications under the IA 1986 are laid down in the IR 1986. The essential contents of many forms are specified in the rules, and prescribed forms can be found in sch. 4. Specific provision is made in the IR 1986 for the following types of applications:

(a) Administration orders. Application is by petition supported by an affidavit (IR 1986, part 2, ch. 1).

(b) Winding-up orders. Application is by petition (IR 1986, part 4, ch. 3 and ch. 4). For further details see **Chapters 9** and **10**. Winding-up petitions are heard by the Companies Court Registrar on Wednesdays.

Other types of applications are divided into:

(c) originating applications (to commence insolvency proceedings); and

(d) ordinary applications (made in pending proceedings).

2.4.1 FORM OF GENERAL APPLICATIONS

Every application, whether originating or ordinary, must state the parties' names, the names of persons to be served or notified; the addresses of the applicant, respondents and persons to be notified; the nature of the relief or order applied for or the directions sought from the court; and must be signed by or on behalf of the applicant (IR 1986, r. 7.3). They are intitled 'IN THE MATTER OF (name of company) AND IN THE MATTER OF THE INSOLVENCY ACT 1986': IR 1986, r. 7.26.

Originating applications must in addition set out the grounds on which the applicant claims to be entitled to the relief or order sought.

To be issued an application must be filed at court, where it will be sealed and endorsed with details of where and when it will be heard.

2.4.2 SERVICE

Generally, service must be effected at least 14 days before the date fixed for the hearing: IR 1986, r. 7.4(5). Service is effected in any of the ways governing ordinary service (see ***Civil Litigation Manual*, 3.6**) IR 1986, r. 12.11. Applications may be sent by first- or second-class post: IR 1986, r. 12.10. They are presumed to have been sent on the date shown by the postmark on the envelope, and to have been served on the second business day if sent first-class, or on the fourth business day if sent second-class, after the date of posting. In cases of difficulty orders for substituted service may be obtained: IR 1986, r. 7.4(4)(c).

The provisions of RSC, O. 11 (as preserved in the CPR, sch. 1) relating to service outside the jurisdiction do not apply in insolvency proceedings: IR 1986, r. 12.12. Rule 12.12 gives the court a much wider discretion to order a method of service in the case of a respondent outside the jurisdiction than that provided by RSC, O. 11, and the court is not required to exercise its discretion on grounds analogous to the principles under RSC, O. 11: *Re Busytoday Ltd* [1992] BCC 480, per Mummery J.

2.4.3 GENERAL PROCEDURE

By IR 1986, r. 7.51, the practice of the High Court or county courts apply to insolvency proceedings except to the extent that they are inconsistent with the IR 1986.

2.4.4 EVIDENCE

Evidence in insolvency proceedings may be given by affidavit or witness statement unless any specific provision of the IR 1986 provides otherwise or the court otherwise directs: IR 1986, rr. 7.7 and 7.57(2). Official receivers may file reports instead of affidavits: r. 7.8.

2.4.5 HEARINGS

Applications before the Registrar are heard in chambers. Judges' applications may be heard in open court or in chambers: IR 1986, r. 7.6(1). The general rule is that applications must be made to the Registrar. Applications which must be made to a judge are listed in the IPPD, para. 9 and include applications for urgent interim relief, such as validation orders under the IA 1986, s. 127 (for which, see **9.7**) prior to any winding-up order being made, and applications to restrain the presentation or advertisement of a winding-up petition (for which, see **9.6**).

2.4.6 ORDERS

Generally, the court drafts and engrosses any order made (IPPD, para. 6).

2.5 Applications under the Company Directors Disqualification Act 1986

Procedure under the CDDA 1986 is governed by the Directors Disqualification Proceedings PD. The law is considered at **7.7.3**.

An application for the making of a disqualification order is commenced by issuing a Part 8 claim form in the format set out in the Annex to the Directors Disqualification Proceedings PD supported by an affidavit stating the matters by virtue of which it is alleged that the respondent is unfit to be concerned in the management of a company. The claim form is served together with the evidence in support and an acknowledgment of service form, which the respondent should return to the court within 14 days of service. Within 28 days of service, the respondent may serve on the applicant and file at court affidavit evidence in opposition to the application. If this is done, the applicant has 14 days to serve and file further affidavit evidence in reply.

The initial hearing of the application is before a Registrar in open court, and must be at least eight weeks after the claim form was issued. The Registrar may determine the application on the initial hearing, but is more likely to give directions, such as for the service and filing of further evidence, and to direct whether the case is to be determined by a Registrar or judge. There are also detailed rules dealing with trial (para. 12) and the summary procedure adopted in *Re Carecraft Construction Co. Ltd* [1994] 1 WLR 172 (para. 13).

2.6 Precedents

2.6.1 PART 8 CLAIM FORM SEEKING ORDER CONVENING AN EXTRAORDINARY GENERAL MEETING

Meetings are discussed at **6.4** and **6.5**. Shareholders' meetings are normally convened by the directors, although there is an exceptional power for shareholders to requisition meetings, discussed at **6.5.5**. The application in this precedent is designed to cope with the situation where a company is deadlocked and unable to hold effective, quorate meetings (see **6.6**).

Royal Arms

Claim Form

(CPR Part 8)

In the High Court of Justice

Chancery Division

Companies Court

Claim No. 007914 of 2000

Claimant

CATHERINE ANNE BARTON

6 University Mews,

Cambridge CB4 8RT

SEAL

Defendants

(1) AT YOUR SERVICE LIMITED

(2) AMANDA LOUISE SIMPSON

IN THE MATTER OF THE COMPANIES ACT 1985

Details of Claim (see also overleaf)

The Claimant seeks an Order pursuant to the Companies Act 1985, section 371:

1. that an extraordinary general meeting of the Company may be convened by the Court for the purpose of considering and if thought fit passing as ordinary resolutions:

    (a) that the second respondent Amanda Louise Simpson be removed as a director of the Company;

    (b) that Deborah Welsh of 12 Parkside Road, Cambridge, CB4 3LR be appointed as a director of the Company;

2. that the Court may give directions as to the manner in which the meeting is to be called, held and conducted and all such ancillary and consequential directions as it may think expedient, and in particular, that the Court may direct that one member of the Company present in person be deemed to constitute a meeting;

3. that the costs of this application may be provided for,

Defendants' names and addresses

(1) At Your Service Limited, registered office 53 College Road, Cambridge, CB1 4LN

(2) Amanda Louise Simpson, 4 Sherwood Road, Lincoln, LN5 2WF

£

Court fee

Solicitor's costs

Issue date

The court office at Thomas More Building, Royal Courts of Justice, Strand, London WC2A 2LL is open between 10 am and 4 pm Monday to Friday. When corresponding with the court, please address forms and letters to the Court Manager and quote the claim number.

Statement of Truth

(I believe) (The Claimant believes) that the facts stated in these details of claim are true. I am duly authorised by the Claimant to sign this statement.

Full name

Name of claimant's solicitor's firm Jackson & Hussain.
signed position or office held
(Claimant) (Litigation friend) (if signing on behalf of firm or company)
(Claimant's solicitor) delete as appropriate

49 College Road Cambridge CB1 4LN	Claimant's or claimant's solicitor's address to which documents should be sent if different from overleaf. If you are prepared to accept service by DX, fax or e-mail, please add details.

2.6.2 WITNESS STATEMENT IN SUPPORT OF PART 8 CLAIM FOR AN ORDER CONVENING AN EXTRAORDINARY GENERAL MEETING

Applicant; C.A. Barton; 1st; CAB 1 to CAB 3; 27.3.2000

IN THE HIGH COURT OF JUSTICE No. 007914 of 2000

CHANCERY DIVISION

COMPANIES COURT

IN THE MATTER of At Your Service Limited.

AND IN THE MATTER of the Companies Act 1985

WITNESS STATEMENT OF
CATHERINE ANNE BARTON

1. I am CATHERINE ANNE BARTON, of 6 University Mews, Cambridge, CB4 8RT. I am a recruitment consultant and company director. I am the applicant.

2. I am a member and director of the above-named At Your Service Limited ('the Company'). I make this statement in support of my application under the Companies Act 1985, section 371, for an order of the Court convening an extraordinary general meeting of the Company, or alternatively an order of the Court directing me to convene such a meeting, to consider and if thought fit pass as ordinary resolutions resolutions to remove the second respondent Amanda Louise Simpson as a director of the Company and to appoint Deborah Welsh of 12 Parkside Road, Cambridge CB4 3LR as a director of the Company.

3. The Company was incorporated on 14 September 1984 under the Companies Acts 1948 to 1981 with company number 1334455 as a company limited by shares.

4. The nominal capital of the Company is £100 divided into 100 ordinary shares of £1 each all of which shares have been issued and are fully paid up or are credited as fully paid up.

5. I am the holder of 60 of the issued shares and the second respondent, Amanda Louise Simpson, is the holder of the other 40 issued shares. Amanda Louise Simpson is also the other director and secretary of the Company.

6. The registered office of the Company is situated at 53 College Road, Cambridge, CB1 4LN.

7. There is now shown to me marked 'CAB1' a print of the Memorandum and Articles of Association of the Company containing copies of all special resolutions of the Company which have been passed since the incorporation of the Company.

8. The Company carries on business as a recruitment agency from premises in Cambridge. The business was originally intended to be a joint venture between the second respondent and myself. Indeed, from incorporation of the Company until July 1998 the only people employed by the Company were the second respondent and myself.

9. In the Spring of 1999 differences of opinion on business matters arose between the second respondent and myself, and in July 1999 the second respondent left Cambridge and set up in business in Lincoln. Since that time the second respondent has not attended the Company's premises, or attended any meetings of the Company or board of directors, or undertaken any duties in respect of the Company.

10. The Articles of Association of the Company incorporate part I of Table A in the First Schedule to the Companies Act 1948. Regulation 53 of Table A provides that:

> 'No business shall be transacted at any general meeting unless a quorum of members is present at the time when the meeting proceeds to business; save as herein otherwise provided two members present in person or by proxy shall be a quorum.'

11. Furthermore, regulation 99 of Table A provides as follows:

> 'The quorum necessary for the transaction of the business of the directors may be fixed by the directors and unless so fixed shall be two.'

The quorum for board meetings was never fixed by the second respondent and myself, and I am advised and believe that the necessary quorum is two.

12. On 10 January 2000 I requisitioned the Company in writing to convene a general meeting of the Company for the purpose of considering a resolution for the removal of the second respondent as a director of the Company and called a meeting of the directors for 17 January 2000 to consider the requisition. There is now shown to me marked 'CAB2' a true copy of that requisition and a true copy of a letter to the second respondent dated 10 January 2000 enclosing a copy of the requisition and notice of the board meeting.

13. The second respondent failed to attend the board meeting fixed for 17 January 2000, which was therefore inquorate.

14. On 31 January 2000 I convened an extraordinary general meeting of the Company under the provisions of the Companies Act 1985, section 368(5), for the purpose of considering a resolution for the removal of the second respondent as a director of the Company, such meeting to be held on 28 February 2000. There is now shown to me marked 'CAB3' true copies of the notice of this meeting and of a letter enclosing the notice sent to the second respondent.

15. The second respondent failed to attend the extraordinary general meeting fixed for 28 February 2000, which was therefore inquorate.

16. In the circumstances I am advised and believe that it is not legally possible to hold meetings of the directors or of the Company or indeed for the Company to function without the order and directions sought from this Honourable Court.

17. It is essential in order to enable the Company to function in the ordinary way that an extraordinary general meeting should be held and that the above-named Deborah Welsh (who is now employed by the Company in place of the second respondent) or some other fit and proper person should be appointed a director of the Company. There would then be two directors able and willing to attend board meetings, and who could register transfers of shares so that quorate general meetings would be possible. I accordingly respectfully request this Honourable Court to make the order sought under the Companies Act 1985, section 371.

Statement of Truth

I believe that the facts stated in this witness statement are true.

Signed:

Catherine Anne Barton
Dated: 27th March 2000

2.7 Exercise 1

RE: BRIGHTWELL HOTELS LIMITED

INSTRUCTIONS TO COUNSEL TO
SETTLE PROCEEDINGS

Counsel will find herewith:

(1) Extracts from the company's articles of association;

(2) Relevant correspondence.

Counsel is instructed on behalf of Mrs Eleanor Owen, a financial services adviser. Late last year our client bought a block of 4,000 25p shares in Brightwell Hotels Limited from the present registered holder, Mr Keith Alan Hensley, for £16,500. As may have been appreciated from its name, the Company runs a number of hotels in the West Country.

On 11th December 1999, Mrs Owen sent the share certificate in the name of Mr Hensley and a completed form of transfer in her favour duly stamped in the sum of £82.50 to the Company's registered office. A card acknowledging receipt of these documents by the Company is dated 18th December 1999. However, nothing further was heard from the company, and our client has not been issued with a new share certificate.

Those instructing were consulted in February. On advice our client attended at the registered office on 26th February 2000 in order to inquire about her certificate. She was told by the manager that none of the directors was present and that he knew nothing about the shares. Instructing Solicitors wrote to the company on 28th February saying Mrs Owen would be attending again on 7th March for the purpose of collecting her share certificate. When Mrs Owen attended on 7th March she spoke to a Ms Karen Ruth Allott, who said the directors did not want to have her as a shareholder, and would not register the transfer. Mrs Allott then retreated into the office and our client was shown out by a member of the hotel staff. Subsequent letters to the company have been ignored.

From the particulars registered at Companies House it appears that the Company was incorporated on 18th June 1979. Its present directors are Mr Richard Hall, of 12 Station Road, Exeter EX6, Ms Karen Ruth Allott of 22 Moor Green, Okehampton,

Devon and Mr Gladstone Lincoln Dyer of 31 Hopewell Road, Bristol BS9. Its present share capital is £12,000 divided into 48,000 25p shares. A total of 36,000 shares have been issued, and all appear to be fully paid-up.

Counsel is asked to settle proceedings and evidence in support, which will be signed by Mrs Owen, for the purpose of compelling the Company to register this share transfer.

Counsel is instructed
to settle proceedings

Extracts from articles of association, Brightwell Hotels Limited.

Transfer of shares

22. The instrument of transfer of any share shall be executed by or on behalf of the transferor and transferee, and the transferor shall be deemed to remain a holder of the share until the name of the transferee is entered in the register of members in respect thereof.

23. Subject to such of the restrictions of these regulations as may be applicable, any member may transfer all or any of his shares by instrument in writing in any usual or common form or any other form which the directors may approve.

24. The directors may decline to register the transfer of a share (not being a fully paid share) to a person of whom they shall not approve, and they may also decline to register the transfer of a share on which the Company has a lien.

25. The directors may also decline to recognise any instrument of a transfer unless:—

(a) a fee of £0.13 or such lesser sum as the directors may from time to time require is paid to the company in respect thereof;

(b) the instrument of transfer is accompanied by the certificate of shares to which it relates, and such other evidence as the directors may reasonably require to show the right of the transferor to make the transfer.

---

42 Market Street,
Exeter,
Devon,
EX4 2TD

11 December 1999

The Directors,
Brightwell Hotels Limited,
Brightwell Hotel,
Bodmin Road,
Okehampton,
Devon

Dear Sirs,

I enclose a stock transfer form in my favour in respect of 4,000 shares recently purchased by me from Mr Keith Hensley. I also enclose Mr Hensley's share certificate and a cheque for £0.13 to cover transfer fees. Please register me as the new owner of these shares, and provide me with a new share certificate in my name.

Yours faithfully,

Eleanor Owen

Brightwell Hotels Limited

Regd. Office: Brightwell Hotel, Bodmin Road, Okehampton, Devon

Your ref:

Our ref: KRA

18 December 1999

We acknowledge receipt of your communication (and enclosures) dated 11th December 1999. A full reply will be sent in due course.

Beddoe & MacKenzie

SOLICITORS

25 Haymarket
Exeter
EX1 8BR

Tel: 01392 639051
Fax: 01392 639555

Our ref: CB/Owen
Your ref: KRA

28th February 2000

The Directors,
Brightwell Hotels Limited,
Brightwell Hotel,
Bodmin Road,
Okehampton,
Devon

Dear Sirs,

OUR CLIENT: Mrs ELEANOR OWEN

We are instructed on behalf of Mrs Eleanor Owen. On 11th December 1999 our client sent to you a stamped share transfer form, share certificate and transfer fee and requested that you register her as a shareholder and issue her with a share certificate. Two days ago she attended at your registered office and orally requested her share certificate. To date none has been forthcoming. We have advised our client that she is legally entitled to be issued with a share certificate, and we are sure that you will agree. To this end our client will be attending again at your registered office at the Brightwell Hotel, Okehampton on 7th March 2000 at 2.30 pm to collect her share certificate. We should be grateful if you could make arrangements to ensure that it is available for collection at that time.

Yours faithfully

Beddoe & MacKenzie

Beddoe & MacKenzie

SOLICITORS

25 Haymarket
Exeter
EX1 8BR

Tel: 01392 639051
Fax: 01392 639555

Our ref: CB/Owen
Your ref: KRA

10th March 2000

The Directors,
Brightwell Hotels Limited,
Brightwell Hotel,
Bodmin Road,
Okehampton,
Devon

Dear Sirs,

OUR CLIENT: Mrs ELEANOR OWEN

We refer to our letter to you of 28th February.

Our client has still not been issued with a share certificate. Unless she is provided with one in the next 7 days, proceedings will be commenced to enforce the same. Legal costs will thereby be incurred which may be ordered against the company or its directors.

Yours faithfully,

Beddoe & MacKenzie

Beddoe & MacKenzie

SOLICITORS

25 Haymarket
Exeter
EX1 8BR

Tel: 01392 639051
Fax: 01392 639555

Our ref: CB/Owen
Your ref: KRA

24th March 2000

The Directors,
Brightwell Hotels Limited,
Brightwell Hotel,
Bodmin Road,
Okehampton,
Devon

Dear Sirs,

OUR CLIENT: Mrs ELEANOR OWEN

Take notice pursuant to the Companies Act 1985, s. 185(6) that unless you make good the default in delivering the certificate for the 4,000 shares the subject of the transfer sent to you on the 11th December 1999 within 10 days after service of this notice on you application will be made to the High Court for delivery of such certificate together with legal costs.

Yours faithfully,

Beddoe & MacKenzie

THREE

CONSTITUTION OF COMPANIES

3.1 Formation of a Company

3.1.1 STEPS TO FORM A COMPANY AND COMMENCE TRADING

To form a company the following documents must be filed with the Registrar of Companies:

(a) Memorandum of Association: this is the constitution of the company which by CA 1985, s. 2, must contain specified information (see below **3.2.1**).

(b) Articles of Association: this sets out the internal regulations of the company covering matters such as calling of company meetings; appointment, removal and powers of directors; keeping of accounts; payment of dividends; and issuing new shares and pre-emption rights. For more detail see below **3.2.2**.

(c) Form 10. This form, required by CA 1985, s. 10, states who the first directors are to be, the name of the secretary and the address of the registered office. The intended company must have, if it is a private limited company, at least one director and one secretary (CA 1985, s. 282) i.e. two officers; whereas a public limited company on incorporation must have at least two directors and one secretary. Each officer will sign the form and indicate, in the case of directors, other directorships.

(d) Form 12. This form, required by CA 1985, s. 12, is the statement of compliance with the registration requirements of the Act. It is usually completed by the proposed company secretary.

On registration, a company will receive a certificate of incorporation and a number (which must be quoted on all company correspondence and is useful for tracing company records). On receipt of this certificate a private company may commence trading. A public company requires, in addition, the issue of a Trading Certificate in order to commence business (s. 117). This will only be issued if the Registrar is satisfied the proposed plc satisfies the capital requirements.

3.1.2 LEGAL EFFECTS OF FORMATION

On formation a company becomes a legal person separate and distinct from its members. The principal effect of this is that, in the case of limited liability companies, the members are in general not liable for the company's debts. A company has separate legal capacity, and can therefore contract on its own behalf when conducting business. It therefore has unlimited liability for its debts (which in practical terms is in fact limited to the amount of the company's assets). Unpaid creditors can petition for the winding-up of the company if it fails to pay them what it owes. If creditors are not paid, the liability of its shareholders is limited to whatever sums remain unpaid on their shares. Once shares have been fully paid for, this means the shareholders have no further personal liability if the company becomes unable to pay its debts. Nowadays shares tend to be paid for in full either on issue or very soon after issue, so in practical terms shareholders are not required to contribute anything if their companies become insolvent. Limited liability companies therefore provide a convenient means through which business people can engage in risky business ventures, because if things go wrong they will not be putting their personal financial resources at risk. It should be kept in mind, however, that financial institutions (principally the banks) can usually sidestep this result by requiring directors to enter into personal guarantees and contracts of suretyship as a condition of providing bank finance to limited liability companies. This does not infringe the limited liability principle, as the director's personal liability under a guarantee or surety arises under a separate contract.

There are a number of further matters that arise once a company is incorporated:

(a) *Maintenance of capital rules.* As a result of the fact that the company alone is liable for its debts and members usually have limited liability to contribute to the company to enable it to do this, the capital which has been or is promised to be contributed by the members must be maintained. The rules are aimed at issued share capital and include prohibitions against purchasing shares, giving financial assistance to purchase shares, payment of dividend out of capital etc. (see **4.9**).

(b) *Disclosure rules.* A company is subject to fairly extensive disclosure duties which fall into three categories:

(i) Documents delivered to the Registrar of Companies. On incorporation various documents must be delivered to the Registrar. A file is opened on registration and a number given to the company to identify its file. The registration documents and any other documents filed during the life of the company are kept on this file which is open to public inspection. A company must annually file its accounts and an annual return which will give latest details on members, directors etc. In addition the company must file any changes in directors, capital, registered office, alteration of articles (CA 1985, s. 9), change of objects etc. with Companies House (in Cardiff, with an office in London), where documents may be inspected, for a fee. A check can be run through one of the specialist firms who will, at a cost, provide photocopies of all relevant documents within 24 hours.

(ii) Maintenance of registers and information at the company's registered office. There are statutory registers which the company must maintain and which are, by and large, open to public inspection, e.g. register of members, interests of directors in a company.

(iii) Accounts must be prepared in a set format and audited. The CA 1985 sets out detailed rules for the keeping, auditing and disclosure of company accounts both to members and the public by filing with the Registrar of Companies. Most small private companies with a turnover of £350,000 or less are exempt from the auditing requirements.

(c) *Transferability of shares.* The general rule is that a shareholder has a right to transfer shares whenever and to whomever she or he wishes, unless this right is restricted by the articles. The transferee takes over all the rights of the transferor.

(d) *Perpetual succession.* A company comes into existence on the date stated in its certificate of incorporation and ceases to exist when it is dissolved and the name is removed from the register of companies. Any alteration in the membership between those dates does not alter the character of the company (even if all the members die: *Re Noel Tedman Holdings Pty Ltd* [1967] QdR 561).

(e) *Management.* A company as a legal person must make decisions, but this must be done by the individuals controlling it. It is necessary to determine what decisions are decisions of the company and not just of the individuals. The members, as owners, make decisions collectively by voting in general meeting and such decisions will be decisions of the company. (CA 1985 requires certain formalities for such meetings which in practice many small private companies do not follow. In theory decisions made without following the proper procedures are not valid. The CA 1989 recognises this problem and relaxes the rules for private companies.) As it is impractical for the members to have general meetings to make all the decisions necessary to run the business, much of the decision-making power is delegated to the directors who must also act collectively through decisions at board meetings unless the power to sub-delegate has been given. There are thus two decision-making organs of the company, the general meeting and the board. As a general rule, once members have delegated their decision-making powers to the board, they cannot simultaneously exercise the delegated powers. This can cause problems where there is disagreement over the manner in which the business should be conducted.

(f) *Contractual capacity.* The company as a legal entity can contract in its own name, although there are limits on its capacity. First, it has no capacity before incorporation and any person who purports to contract on its behalf before this date will be personally liable on the contract (CA 1985, s. 36C). Secondly, any contract not authorised by the objects clause is *ultra vires* and void. The effect of this second limitation has been greatly reduced by statute (see **3.2.1.3** below).

(g) *Ownership of property.* A company owns its own property and not the members. This can create problems in small private companies where the owners often treat company property as their own. See *Macaura* v *Northern Assurance Co. Ltd* [1925] AC 619 and *Tunstall* v *Steigmann* [1962] 2 QB 593.

(h) *Company sues for wrongs done to it.* This is known as the rule in *Foss* v *Harbottle* (1843) 2 Hare 461, and means that any decision to sue must be made by the members in general meeting, or the directors, and an individual member may not sue on behalf of the company. This can cause problems where errant directors are also majority shareholders and exceptions have developed to the rule. However, it is a difficult area of law and one where the concept of separate legal personality does not quite work. See **11.5** below.

(i) *Company can create floating charges.* Only a company can create floating charges, which are charges over a class of assets which change from time to time, and which the company can use and sell in the ordinary course of business, and on such sale the charge ceases to attach to the goods sold. One theory is that the charge 'floats above' all those goods in the class owned by the company at any one time and only attaches to the goods, preventing the company from using them, on crystallisation (see **5.4** and **5.5**).

3.1.3 THE VEIL OF INCORPORATION AND LIFTING THE VEIL

The concept that a company is a legal person separate from its members and that the identity and motives of those who form and control the company are irrelevant as the outsider deals with the company and not its members, is often referred to as the veil of incorporation. The concept is that the outsiders deal with the company and are not allowed to go behind the company and get at those who formed or control it. Many of the consequences of formation set out above are often quoted as examples of this veil of incorporation. There are problems with this concept, and exceptions to it, which are referred to as situations where the veil is pierced/lifted, have developed. Such situations include:

(a) *Enforcement of statutory rules.*

(i) The Companies Act 1985, s. 24, provides that where the number of members in a public company is reduced below the statutory minimum of two for six months, any member aware of it is liable with the company for debts contracted after that period.

(ii) By CA 1985, s. 349, any officer who issues orders etc. on which the company's name is incorrectly stated is liable if the company itself defaults.

(iii) By the IA 1986, s. 213, where persons carry on the company with intent to defraud creditors they may be ordered to contribute to the company's assets.

(iv) By IA 1986, s. 214, where a company goes into insolvent liquidation, and a director knew or ought to have known there was no reasonable prospect that insolvent liquidation could be avoided, and did not take every step to minimise loss to creditors, that director may be ordered to contribute to the company's assets.

(b) *Crimes committed.* Where an offence requires *mens rea*, it is necessary to look behind the veil to see whether it was the company which had the necessary guilty mind (i.e. was the decision one of the members, board or senior officer to whom decision-making power has been properly delegated?). See *Tesco Supermarkets Ltd* v *Nattrass* [1972] AC 153.

(c) *Abuse of the company principle.* Where an individual uses a company to evade legal obligations, the court will pierce the veil, e.g. in *Gilford Motor Co. Ltd* v *Horne* [1933] Ch 935, where Horne set up a company to evade a restraint of trade clause in a contract with Gilford Motor Company. The company set up by Horne was declared to be a sham.

3.1.4 WHO IS OR MAY BE A MEMBER?

Anyone may be a member of a company, including another company, although a company may not be a member of itself or its holding company (CA 1985, s. 23). Capacity to be a shareholder is dictated by the ordinary law of contract and the articles, which may restrict membership to particular persons.

The members of a company are the registered holders of the shares (i.e. those persons whose names are on the register of members kept by the company (CA 1985, s. 22)). The company will deal with the named person and, by CA 1985, s. 360, no notice of any trust may be entered on the register. Thus, where there are nominee shareholders (X, the named shareholder, holds for Y on whose instructions X acts) the company must deal with X and not Y, even if X is not acting according to Y's instructions. As such nominee shareholdings have been used to build up voting control in companies, CA 1985, ss. 198–220, provide for disclosure of interests in voting shares in public companies. Failure to disclose any interest of 3% or more in such shares within two days of knowing of the interest is an offence and may result in the rights associated with the shares being frozen.

3.1.5 DIVERGENCE OF PRIVATE AND PUBLIC COMPANIES

In practice there is a great deal of difference between the conduct of a small private (family) company and a large public company. However, this difference is largely ignored in legislation relating to companies and most regulations are applied equally to both types of companies. Although there have been suggestions for a new form of incorporation (see 1981 DTI Report, *A New Form of Incorporation for Small Firms*), none of these have been put into effect. Provisions in CA 1989 show the beginnings of different rules for private and public companies. These are:

(a) Accounting rules. CA 1985 (as amended by CA 1989) requires the accounts to be drawn up in a particular format, audited, laid before members in general meeting (at the AGM) and filed with the Registrar of Companies every year. Some of the rules are relaxed for small and medium-sized private companies (which are defined on the basis of turnover, balance sheet totals and average number of employees).

(b) Dispensing with formalities (CA 1985).

(c) Decisions by written resolutions (see **6.5.9**).

3.2 Constitutional Documents

Every company registered under the CA 1985 will have a memorandum of association and articles of association. In addition, one meets a number of other forms of constitutional document from time to time.

3.2.1 MEMORANDUM OF ASSOCIATION

This is the official constitution of the company, which, by CA 1985, s. 2, must contain the clauses described in the following paragraphs.

3.2.1.1 Name Clause

The name in this clause is the corporate/legal name of the company. All company names are unique. There are restrictions on the choice of a corporate name, contained in CA 1985:

(a) Section 25. The name of a public company must end with the words public limited company (or plc), and of a private company with limited (or Ltd). Section 30 exempts certain private companies limited by guarantee from this requirement.

(b) Section 26. A company shall not be registered with a name:

(i) which is the same as a name appearing in the registrar's index of company names;

(ii) the use of which would, in the opinion of the Secretary of State, constitute a criminal offence, e.g. use of the word 'bank' without Bank of England authority;

(iii) which, in the opinion of the Secretary of State, is offensive.

(c) Section 26(2). Except with the approval of the Secretary of State, a company shall not be registered with a name which suggests a connection with government or local authority, or which is specified in regulations by the Secretary of State.

The CA 1985 requires disclosure of the corporate name outside every office or place of business (s. 348), on all letters, notices, invoices etc. (s. 349) and of the registered number and address of the registered office on all letters and order forms (s. 351). The Business Names Act 1985 contains similar requirements concerning a company's business name if it is not its corporate name.

3.2.1.2 Public Company Clause

A public company must have a clause stating that it is a public company. This clause does not exist in the memorandum of a private company (i.e. there is not a clause stating that it is private).

3.2.1.3 Objects Clause/Contractual Capacity

The objects of a company, which must be lawful, are set out in the objects clause of the memorandum of association and define the business that a company can carry out. The necessity for such objects has a historical basis in that investors could see if a company was in a business which was likely to be profitable and the *ultra vires* rule ensured that the company did not embark on speculative ventures outside those objects.

The Companies Act 1989 made considerable changes in this area of company law; however, an understanding of the history of the law is necessary for an appreciation of the impact of these changes.

The *ultra vires* rule states simply that if a company enters into a contract which is beyond its capacity, i.e. outside the objects, it is *ultra vires* and therefore void. (For a clear illustration of this rule, see *Ashbury Railway Carriage & Iron Co. Ltd* v *Riche* (1875) LR 7 HL 653.) However, the company will be treated as having implied powers to achieve its express objects, e.g., a trading company will have the implied power to borrow money.

The rather harsh *ultra vires* rule involved an even harsher doctrine, namely the doctrine of constructive notice, which provided that since the documents of registration of a company were public documents, outsiders dealing with a company were fixed with constructive notice of the contents of the memorandum and could see that a proposed transaction was *intra* or *ultra vires*.

The obvious solution for a company was to draw up objects clauses which allowed a company to do anything it liked. The courts rejected this idea because a company cannot do everything under the sun: *Re Crown Bank* (1890) 44 ChD 634.

Next, incorporators started listing everything they thought a company would want to do, but in *Attorney-General* v *Great Eastern Railway Co.* (1880) 5 App Cas 473 the court held that these extended lists of objects had to be construed *ejusdem generis* the main object (cl. 1 of the Objects Clauses). Inroads into this particular rule were made in *Cotman* v *Brougham* [1918] AC 514 where an 'independent objects clause' was upheld, i.e. a clause allowing each object to be construed as a separate and independent object. In *Bell Houses Ltd* v *City Wall Properties Ltd* [1966] 2 QB 656 a subjectively worded objects clause, the gist of which was that in addition to the main object, the company could carry on any business which, in the opinion of the directors, may be profitable was upheld. (For the exact wording of both clauses see the cases or the Oyez or Jordan's standard memorandum.)

A distinction was drawn between objects and powers. Objects briefly defined what the company was set up to do, the powers were the means to achieve the objects.

Following *Rolled Steel Products (Holdings) Ltd* v *British Steel Corporation* [1986] Ch 246 the position appeared to be, in brief, that an express power (i.e. stated in the memorandum) could be exercised by the company without *ultra vires* implications; implied powers had usually to be used in connection with the company's objects.

Originally a company could not alter its objects. Until CA 1948 court approval was required for any alteration. Under CA 1948 and CA 1985 they could be altered by special resolution provided the alteration was to enable it to attain one of the grounds specified in the Act. Alternatives were basically restricted to adding to or altering existing objects. Thus, a company was basically confined to those businesses set out in the objects clause on incorporation.

The *ultra vires* rule often operated unfairly against creditors, e.g. see *Re Jon Beaufort (London) Ltd* [1953] Ch 131.

The changes made by CA 1989 came into force on 4 February 1991 and are as follows:

(a) CA 1985, s. 3A (as inserted by CA 1989, s. 110) enables a company to incorporate with a very wide objects clause i.e. '*to carry on business as a general commercial company*'.

(b) A new CA 1985, s. 4, as inserted by CA 1989, s. 110, empowers a company to alter its objects clause by special resolution and removes the requirement that it be for one of the specified grounds.

(c) A new CA 1985, s. 35 as inserted by CA 1989, s. 108, enables both the company and the outsider to enforce an *ultra vires* act. A member may restrain a proposed *ultra vires* act, but not if a legal obligation has already been incurred. Directors will be liable for *ultra vires* acts to which they commit the company, although the members may ratify their actions and excuse them from liability (by separate special resolutions, 75% majority required).

3.2.1.4 Office Clause

This sets out the country in which the registered office is located (England and Wales, Wales or Scotland) and determines the company's nationality and domicile. The clause does not contain the company's registered office.

3.2.1.5 Liability Clause

If the members' liability is limited, there is a clause merely stating this fact.

3.2.1.6 Capital Clause

If the company has share capital this clause will state the amount of authorised share capital (the amount the company can issue) and the division of that capital into shares of fixed amount (e.g. £50,000, being 50,000 £1 shares). If the company is limited by guarantee, this clause will state the amount which each member guarantees to contribute in the event of an insolvent liquidation.

3.2.1.7 Association Clause

This is merely a formal request that a company be formed by the subscribers who must sign it and undertake to take a minimum of one share each on incorporation. There must be a minimum of two subscribers (members) if the company is public (CA 1985, s. 1).

3.2.2 ARTICLES OF ASSOCIATION

The articles are the internal regulations of the company. On incorporation, the subscribers to the memorandum can adopt whatever articles they choose, and are free (subject to some limitations) to draft each regulation in whatever way they like. However, CA 1985, s. 8(2), provides that, in the case of a company limited by shares, if articles are not registered, or, if articles are registered, insofar as they do not exclude or modify Table A, that Table (so far as applicable, and as in force at the date of the company's registration) constitutes the company's articles. By this means some degree of uniformity is found between different companies' articles. The current Table A is found in the Companies (Tables A to F) Regulations 1985 (SI 1985 No. 805). It is subject to periodic minor amendment. It applies, if at all, to companies registered on or after 1 July 1985, the commencement date for the CA 1985. Like provision is made for companies registered before that date, the appropriate Table A being found in the legislation then in force, e.g., CA 1948, sch. 1.

The present Table A contains 118 regulations dealing with numerous matters from accounts to winding up. As they are the articles most frequently met in practice, repeated reference will be made to them on this course.

3.2.3 OTHER CONSTITUTIONAL DOCUMENTS

These can take several forms, but the most common are shareholder agreements. For example, shareholders may, before incorporation of the company, enter into an agreement between themselves about participation in the management of the business, sharing profits and the arrangements for buying each other out. Such an agreement would almost certainly be considered by the court in the event of a 'just and equitable' winding-up petition or unfair prejudice petition being brought by one of the members (see **Chapters 12 and 13**).

Alternatively, the company may by contract confer rights on individual members on matters such as the composition of the board of directors and the payment of dividends. Although such matters can be dealt with in the articles, there are two main differences in their legal effect:

(a) Provisions in the articles run with the shares, so as to bind successive share owners. A contractual obligation, on the other hand, is purely personal and binds only the contracting parties.

(b) Regulations in the articles can always be altered by the company in general meeting, despite the objections of the individual member. Contractual obligations can only be altered by mutual consent.

There may be arguments about the validity of terms in these extra-statutory documents. Possible grounds include being contrary to public policy or illegal, particularly if the agreement is construed as being a bribe. The agreement may be a fetter on the company's power to alter its articles (see **3.3.2**) or, if only some of the shareholders are party to the agreement, may give grounds to the others to apply for minority remedies (see **Chapters 12 and 13**).

In *Russell* v *Northern Bank Development Corporation Ltd* [1992] 1 WLR 588, HL, a shareholders' agreement was entered into by four of the company's shareholders including the claimant, who between them held 40 per cent of its shares, and the company. The agreement provided that its terms should take precedence over the articles of association and that no further share capital would be issued or created without the written consent of all the parties to the agreement. Some years later the board of directors convened an EGM to consider increasing the company's share capital, whereon the claimant applied for injunctions. It was held that the agreement was an unlawful fetter on the company's statutory powers to increase its capital insofar as it purported to bind the company, but was a valid, personal, agreement outside the articles insofar as it bound the individual shareholders. The invalid part of the agreement was severable from the valid part, and a declaration as to the validity of the agreement as between the shareholders was granted.

The interrelation between a shareholders' agreement and a director's service contract was considered by the Court of Appeal in *Morris Angel & Son Ltd* v *Hollande* [1993] 3 All ER 569. The defendant was a party to the shareholders' agreement, and was a director of the company employed on the terms of a service contract entered into on the same date as the shareholders' agreement. The company's business was sold to the claimant. There was a triable issue as to whether the other parties were in breach of a term of the shareholders' agreement not to sell the company's business without his consent. The claimant immediately sacked the defendant, and brought an application for an injunction to restrain an alleged breach of a covenant in his service contract. It was held that the alleged breach of the shareholders' agreement had no bearing on the discretion to grant the proposed interim injunction, which was granted.

3.3 Altering the Memorandum and Articles

With the passage of time, changes in a company's business and personnel may make it desirable to alter its original constitution. The general scheme of the CA 1985 is to permit any changes duly voted on by the shareholders, except where the change is in some way inequitable.

3.3.1 MEMORANDUM

Various provisions in the CA 1985 make allowance for the alteration of the clauses in the memorandum. Some of the provisions are quite complex, and deal with consequential matters, notifying Companies House, and the hearing of objections by dissenting minorities. The main provisions are as follows:

(a) Name. Can be changed by special resolution (CA 1985, s. 28).

(b) From private to public (CA 1985, s. 43, in addition to satisfying the public company minimum capital requirements) and from public to private (CA 1985, s. 53) requires a special resolution.

(c) Situation of registered office. This is unalterable (CA 1985, s. 2(7)).

(d) Address of registered office. Usually this is altered by resolution of the directors, as the management of the company's business is usually delegated to them (see Table A, reg. 70).

(e) Objects. Can be changed by special resolution (CA 1985, s. 4 as substituted by CA 1989, s. 110).

(f) From limited liability to unlimited requires the assent of all the members (CA 1985, s. 49).

(g) From unlimited to limited liability requires a special resolution (CA 1985, s. 51).

(h) Share capital. Increases can usually be sanctioned by ordinary resolution (CA 1985, s. 121). A reduction involves a complex procedure, including special resolutions and court approval (see CA 1985, ss. 135 to 141).

(i) Additional clauses. The matters referred to in paragraphs (a) to (h) above must, by statute, be included in the memorandum. That does not prevent other matters being included. The most common additional matter inserted into the memorandum is the class rights attaching to the various classes of the company's shares. Generally, such additional clauses may be altered by special resolution (CA 1985, s. 17(1)). However, this does not apply where:

   (i) The memorandum itself expressly provides for or prohibits any alteration. If alteration is prohibited, the clause cannot be altered. If the memorandum provides a different procedure for alterations, that must be followed.

   (ii) The clause confers special rights on any class of members. Such a clause may only be altered by following the procedure laid down in the memorandum (if there is one), by unanimous agreement of the members (CA 1985, s. 125(5)) or by the court approving a scheme of arrangement under CA 1985, ss. 425 to 427.

3.3.2 ARTICLES

A company may by special resolution alter its articles (CA 1985, s. 9). Regulations in the articles cannot be made unalterable (*Allen* v *Gold Reefs of West Africa Ltd* [1900] 1 Ch 656, CA). However, the power to alter the articles by special resolution must not be abused by the majority shareholders, and the alteration may be set aside by the court if it is a fraud on the minority.

3.3.2.1 The principle

An alteration to the articles will be set aside if it was not made 'bona fide for the benefit of the company as a whole' (per Lindley MR in *Allen* v *Gold Reefs of West Africa Ltd* [1900] 1 Ch 656, CA). There is a fair amount of case law in this area, and it is not particularly easy to reconcile all the judgments that have been pronounced.

3.3.2.2 The hypothetical member

One of the leading cases in this area is *Greenhalgh* v *Arderne Cinemas Ltd* [1951] Ch 286, CA, in which Evershed MR said:

> Certain principles, I think, can be safely stated as emerging from those authorities. In the first place, I think it is now plain that 'bona fide for the benefit of the company as a whole' means not two things but one thing. It means that the shareholder must proceed upon what, in his honest opinion, is for the benefit of the company as a whole. The second thing is that the phrase, 'the company as a whole', does not (at any rate in such a case as the present) mean the company as a commercial entity, distinct from the corporators: it means the corporators as a general body. That is to say, the case may be taken of an individual hypothetical member and it may be asked whether what is proposed is, in the honest opinion of those who voted in its favour, for that person's benefit.

The hypothetical member contemplated is a member of the company in question. The court therefore considers the effect of the existing articles, how the company's powers are distributed between the directors and members, the rights attaching to different classes of shares etc. Conversely, the hypothetical member does not have any particular number of shares, so the court does not look exclusively at the effect of the alteration on the dissenting minority members.

3.3.2.3 **Discrimination between members**

Immediately after the passage from *Greenhalgh* v *Arderne Cinemas Ltd* [1951] Ch 286 quoted in the previous paragraph, Evershed MR said that, in practice, an alteration 'would be liable to be impeached if the effect of it were to discriminate between the majority shareholders and the minority shareholders, so as to give to the former an advantage of which the latter were deprived'. A similar approach was adopted by Lord Sterndale MR in *Sidebottom* v *Kershaw, Leese & Co. Ltd* [1920] 1 Ch 154, CA, where he quoted from *Buckley on the Companies Acts*, saying that the majority shareholders cannot 'sacrifice the interests of the minority ... without any reasonable prospect of advantage to the company as a whole'. The effect is that an alteration may be valid despite adversely affecting minority interests, provided the overall (and, perhaps, long-term) effect is beneficial to the company as a whole.

3.3.2.4 **Conflict between the approaches**

Dr Sealy in his *Cases and Materials in Company Law* suggests, along with other commentators, that Evershed MR in *Greenhalgh* v *Arderne Cinemas Ltd* [1951] Ch 286 was trying to have the best of both worlds in that, on the one hand, it is the honest opinion of the majority shareholders that determines whether the alteration is valid, and, on the other, it is whether the alteration objectively discriminates between different shareholders.

3.3.2.5 **Business policy**

In this area, like many others in company law, there are occasions when the court considers that what has been done by the company is most properly characterised as a matter of business policy, and the court will not lightly interfere with the business judgment of the people involved. An example of a case where this factor weighed heavily in the court's decision is *Rights & Issues Investment Trust Ltd* v *Stylo Shoes Ltd* [1965] Ch 250.

3.3.2.6 **Some examples**

In *Greenhalgh* v *Arderne Cinemas Ltd* [1951] Ch 286 the original articles gave existing members preemption rights if any of them wished to sell their shares to outsiders. The majority wished to sell their shares to an outsider, but a minority shareholder was not prepared to forego his right of pre-emption. The majority therefore passed a special resolution to alter the articles so that the company could by ordinary resolution override the preemption provision. The court refused to make a declaration that the alteration was invalid, because any shareholder could in theory take advantage of the altered articles, even though, in practical terms, only the majority could pass the requisite ordinary resolution.

In *Rights & Issues Investment Trust Ltd* v *Stylo Shoes Ltd* [1965] Ch 250 the company's issued capital consisted of 4,000,000 shares, 90 per cent of which were ordinary shares carrying one vote per share, and 10 per cent were management shares carrying eight votes each. In practice, the holders of the management shares controlled shareholders' meetings. After taking over another company, a further 8,400,000 ordinary shares were issued. Resolutions were then passed at class and general meetings doubling the voting rights of the management shares. Again a declaration that the alteration was invalid was refused. The management shares' votes were not used at the meetings, the issue was regarded as one of business policy, the judge was satisfied that the resolutions were passed in good faith, and benefited the company as a whole.

Conversely, alterations compelling the minority to sell their shares have on occasion been held to be invalid. For example, in *Dafen Tinplate Co. Ltd* v *Llanelly Steel Co. (1907) Ltd* [1920] 2 Ch 124 the articles were altered to allow the company by ordinary resolution to require any member to sell its shares to the other members at a fair price, but exempted one named member from the provision. Peterson J held that the alteration was not in the interests of the company as a whole as it allowed the expropriation of a member's shares for no reason save the will of the majority. Further, the alteration was bad because it created a privilege for the one named member when the shares had originally been issued on an equal footing. Contrast *Sidebottom* v

Kershaw, Leese & Co. Ltd [1920] 1 Ch 154, CA, where an alteration to allow the expropriation of shares of any member carrying on a business in competition with the company was held to be valid.

3.4 Contractual Effect of the Articles

3.4.1 THE STATUTORY CONTRACT

CA 1985, s. 14(1), provides:

Subject to the provisions of this Act, the memorandum and articles, when registered, bind the company and its members to the same extent as if they respectively had been signed and sealed by each member, and contained covenants on the part of each member to observe all the provisions of the memorandum and of the articles.

The section creates a contract between the company and its members to observe the provisions of the memorandum and articles. It is a rather unusual contract in that:

(a) The remedies for breach are, generally, restricted to declarations and injunctions. Damages may be awarded in situations such as where there are arrears of dividends, but this is exceptional.

(b) There is no jurisdiction to rectify a company's articles of association: *Scott* v *Frank F Scott (London) Ltd* [1940] Ch 794, CA.

(c) There is no jurisdiction to imply terms into the contract constituted by a company's articles of association: *Bratton Seymour Service Co. Ltd* v *Oxborough* [1992] BCC 471, CA.

(d) The section 14 contract can only be enforced by shareholders insofar as they are affected in their capacity as shareholders.

3.4.2 AS SHAREHOLDERS

Buckley LJ in *Bisgood* v *Henderson's Transvaal Estates Ltd* [1908] 1 Ch 743, CA said, 'The purpose of the memorandum and articles is to define the position of the shareholder as shareholder, not to bind him in his capacity as an individual'. So, in the leading case of *Hickman* v *Kent or Romney Marsh Sheep-Breeders' Association* [1915] 1 Ch 881 Astbury J reviewed earlier authorities on the section and said:

> I think this much is clear, first, that no article can constitute a contract between the company and a third person; secondly, that no right merely purporting to be given by an article to a person, whether a member or not, in a capacity other than that of a member, as, for instance, as solicitor, promoter, director, can be enforced against the company; and, thirdly, that articles regulating the rights and obligations of the members generally as such do create rights and obligations between them and the company respectively.

In this case one of the company's articles provided for disputes to be referred to arbitration. Hickman brought an action complaining of various irregularities, and the company applied for a stay (see ***Civil Litigation Manual*, 28.5**) relying on the article. Astbury J granted the stay because the article operated between Hickman and the company in Hickman's capacity as a member, was a general article applying to all members, and so should have been complied with by him.

3.4.3 WHO CAN ENFORCE THE SECTION 14 CONTRACT?

Case law has established that the section 14 contract binds:

(a) Members in their dealings with the company (*Hickman* v *Kent or Romney Marsh Sheep-Breeders' Association* [1915] 1 Ch 881).

(b) The company in its dealings with its members as members (*Oakbank Oil Co.* v *Crum* (1882) 8 App Cas 65, HL).

(c) Members in their dealings with each other as members, without the need to join the company in any action to enforce the contract (*Rayfield* v *Hands* [1960] Ch 1). This latter situation is the most controversial, and it may be that there are further limits on direct enforceability between members.

3.4.4 AUTHORITY OF *HICKMAN'S* CASE

Doubts have been raised against the decision in *Hickman* v *Kent or Romney Marsh Sheep-Breeders' Association* [1915] 1 Ch 881 on a number of grounds:

(a) The actual decisions in some of the earlier cases are not strictly consistent with the principles extracted from them by Astbury J.

(b) Restricting enforcement to rights and obligations of members as members seems contrary to the terms of section 14 itself, which refers to 'all the provisions of the memorandum and articles'.

(c) There are cases where the courts have enforced individual rights contained in the company's articles. An example is *Pulbrook* v *Richmond Consolidated Mining Co.* (1878) 9 ChD 610, where a director obtained an injunction restraining the other directors from excluding him from the board.

Despite the above, *Hickman's* case undoubtedly states the law at the present time, and was accepted by the Court of Appeal in *Beattie* v *E. & F. Beattie Ltd* [1938] Ch 708.

3.4.5 LIMITS ON THE SECTION 14 CONTRACT

There are two main limits on the enforcement of the section 14 contract. First, the courts will not allow shareholders to use it to avoid the rule in *Foss* v *Harbottle* (see **11.5**), particularly where the shareholders are complaining of directors' breaches of fiduciary duty to the company (see *Prudential Assurance Co. Ltd* v *Newman Industries Ltd (No. 2)* [1982] Ch 204). Secondly, many breaches of a company's articles can be ratified by the company in general meeting, and if this has happened, members will be unable to complain.

3.5 Contracts Incorporating Provisions from the Articles

As we have seen above, CA 1985, s. 14, can only be used to enforce 'insider rights' contained in a company's articles. A person undertaking to act as a company's director, solicitor etc. is therefore best advised to enter into a separate contract with the company, rather than relying on provisions in the articles dealing with the terms of service of such post holders. This section deals with the situation where such a separate contract incorporates terms from the articles. If provisions are incorporated expressly into the contract there should be no undue problem and any breach of the terms contained in the articles can be enforced under the external contract.

In the absence of express provision, the court may be prepared to infer that provisions from the articles have been incorporated into the contract. In *Re New British Iron Co., ex parte Beckwith* [1898] 1 Ch 324 the court implied a term fixing the directors' remuneration from the articles on the footing that the directors had been employed by the company and had accepted office. Provisions will not be implied from the articles if the contract deals expressly with the same matters (*Nelson* v *James Nelson & Sons Ltd* [1914] 2 KB 770, CA), but the articles can be used to infer terms on matters where the express terms of the contract are silent (*Read* v *Astoria Garage (Streatham) Ltd* [1952] Ch 637, CA).

However, the courts have on occasions been reluctant to imply contracts incorporating articles solely on the basis of the parties having acted on the provisions of the articles, see *Browne* v *La Trinidad* (1887) 37 ChD 1 and *Newtherapeutics Ltd* v *Katz* [1991] Ch 226.

3.6 Contracts and Alterations to the Articles

3.6.1 ALTERATION CONSTITUTING A BREACH OF CONTRACT

An alteration to a company's articles, or acting on such an alteration, may constitute a breach of contract by the company. Thus, in *Southern Foundries (1926) Ltd* v *Shirlaw* [1940] AC 701, HL, the claimant was appointed managing director for 10 years. Later, an article was added allowing a director to be removed by two directors and a secretary, and the claimant was removed under this provision. Although the company was entitled to alter its articles in this way, by doing so it was in breach of its contract with the claimant and was liable in damages.

3.6.2 ALTERATION TO JUSTIFY A BREACH OF CONTRACT

Where there is an ordinary contract between a person (outsider or member) and the company, the company cannot resile from the agreed terms and justify a breach of the contract by altering its articles (*Baily* v *British Equitable Assurance Co.* [1904] 1 Ch 374, CA). This principle was approved on appeal [1906] AC 35 by Lord Macnaghten, though the House of Lords reversed the decision of the Court of Appeal. The House of Lords construed the contract as incorporating the articles of the company and as being alterable from time to time (see CA 1985, s. 9), so there was no breach of contract when the articles were altered.

FOUR

SHARE CAPITAL

4.1 Introduction

The topic of share capital covers both the rules relating to individual shareholders' rights and duties and the rules requiring the company to maintain its share capital as a whole.

4.2 Issue and Transfer of Shares

The two methods by which a person can become a member of a company are the allotment of shares by the company to the original allottee and the subsequent transfer of shares to another person.

4.2.1 ISSUE

4.2.1.1 General

An original allotment of shares may be by a fresh issue of shares, a rights issue (fresh issue of shares to existing members who may or may not decide to purchase them) or a bonus issue (where profits are capitalised and shares are issued to members in lieu of dividend). Where shares are offered to existing members, they may be offered by way of a renounceable letter of allotment, which enables the existing shareholder to take up the issue or renounce it in favour of someone else either by sale or gift. Whoever wishes to take up the shares will return the relevant document to the company, which will enter the appropriate name in the register of members and issue a share certificate.

4.2.1.2 Rules on the issue of shares

The following is an outline of the rules on the issue of shares:

(a) *Shares may not be issued if there is no unissued authorised share capital.* Thus if shares have been issued up to the amount set out in the capital clause of the memorandum, the authorised capital must be increased by ordinary resolution of the members before further shares are issued (CA 1985, ss. 2, 121).

(b) *If the power to issue has been delegated to the directors* they must check:

(i) That the authority has not lapsed. By CA 1985, s. 80, whether the authority is given by the articles or resolution of the members it lapses after five years, and if the directors issue shares after it has lapsed the allotment is not void but they commit an offence. Further authority may be given by ordinary resolution.

(ii) That the issue is for a proper purpose. The general rule is that shares are issued to raise capital and not, e.g., to defeat a takeover bid. If the issue is for such a purpose the directors must seek approval of the members in general meeting (ordinary resolution).

(c) *Statutory pre-emption rights must be observed.* CA 1985, s. 89 provides that subject to certain exceptions, a company shall not allot equity securities without first offering them on a pro rata basis to existing shareholders at the same or more favourable terms as will be offered to outsiders. A private company may exclude s. 89 in its articles, a public company may exclude it by special resolution when delegating the power to issue to the directors.

(d) *Shares may not be issued at a discount,* i.e. for consideration of less value than the nominal value of the shares. There are special rules for public companies to ensure that where shares are issued for non-cash consideration, it is not less than the nominal value (CA 1985, ss. 99–116).

(e) *Shares may be issued at a premium,* i.e. at more than the nominal value, but the premium is treated as capital and is subject to the maintenance of capital rules (CA 1985, ss. 130–134).

(f) *A return of allotment* must be made to the Registrar of Companies showing the name, address of the allottees, the number and nominal value etc. of the shares (CA 1985, s. 88).

(g) *Issues to the public.* It is an offence for a private company to issue shares to the public (Companies Act 1985, s. 81), thus limiting the pool of potential investors. If a public company does, it must comply with provisions as to form, content, approval and publication of the prospectus or listing particulars.

4.2.2 TRANSFER

4.2.2.1 Shares are saleable investments

The general rule is that a shareholder has the right to transfer shares unless the articles restrict the right. Public companies generally do not restrict the right to transfer fully paid shares and cannot obtain a Stock Exchange listing if they do (see Listing Rules, ch. 3). Before 1980, private companies were required to impose some restriction and still often do in practice. The two most common restrictions are:

(a) Pre-emption rights of other members. The shareholder must first offer the shares to existing shareholders and may only transfer to others if the pre-emption right is not exercised.

(b) Power of directors to refuse to register transfers. This may be a general power giving the directors absolute discretion, or a specific power enabling the directors to refuse to register a transfer only on specified grounds (e.g. Art. 24 of Table A contains such a provision for partly paid shares whether of a public or private company). The power is given in small private companies usually to ensure that shares remain in a family or among a closed group of members.

Any ambiguity or uncertainty in the provisions is construed in favour of the shareholder wishing to transfer. The company must notify the transferee of any refusal to register the shares within two months of the lodging of the transfer with the company (CA 1985, s. 183). The transfer is completed by entering the name of the transferee in the register of members whereby the newly registered member has a fresh s. 14 contract with the company (i.e. he is not an assignee).

In the event of refusal to register, the transferor's name will remain on the register of members as the legal owner of the shares. The transferee will be the equitable owner although his or her interest will not be on the register as CA 1985, s. 360 will not permit any notice of a trust to be entered on the register. The transferor will remain liable for calls on the shares (where a company calls for money to be paid up on unpaid or partly paid shares). He/she will have to account to the transferee for any dividends received and will even have to attend and vote at company meetings at the behest of the transferee. A transferee who considers that the transfer has been wrongfully refused will apply for rectification of the register of members (CA 1985, s. 359).

Transmission of shares occurs when the shareholder dies or is adjudicated bankrupt and the shares fall under the control of his or her personal representatives or trustee in bankruptcy, who may, if they wish and the articles allow, be registered as shareholders or transfer them without being so registered (CA 1985, s. 187).

4.2.2.2 Procedure for transferring shares

It is not lawful for a company to register a transfer of shares unless a proper instrument of transfer has been delivered to it or the transfer is an exempt transfer within the Stock Transfer Act 1982 (CA 1985, s. 183). Most transfers will come within the Stock Transfer Act 1963, which allows a single form of transfer for fully paid shares, or the Stock Transfer Act 1982 which allows a computerised form of transfer.

The existing method of transfer of shares depends on whether or not the shares are listed on the London Stock Exchange.

(a) Shares not on the London Stock Exchange

Shares not listed on the London Stock Exchange are transferred directly from transferor to transferee. The transferor completes a transfer form in the name of the transferee. If the transferor is selling the whole of the shareholding, the transfer form and share certificate are given to the transferee who forwards the transfer form and share certificate to the company. The company enters the name of the transferee on the register of members and enters a note that the transferor is no longer a member. The old share certificate is cancelled and a new one is issued in the name of the transferee.

If the transferor is selling only part of the shareholding, the procedure is more complicated. The completed transfer form and share certificate are sent by the transferor to the company. The company endorses the transfer form 'certificate lodged' and returns the transfer form to the transferor who passes it to the transferee. The share certificate is retained by the company for cancellation. The transferee sends the transfer form to the company which alters the register of members accordingly and issues two new certificates, one in the name of the transferee for the shares transferred and one in the name of the transferor for the shares retained.

(b) Shares on the London Stock Exchange

Since 1979 transfers on the London Stock Exchange have been done through the Talisman system whereby shares are transferred to and from a pool of shares held by a company called Sepon Ltd owned by the Exchange. The transferor completes a 'sold transfer form' transferring shares to Sepon Ltd and supplies this together with the share certificate to the Exchange which in turn forwards it to the company for the appropriate alterations to the register and cancellation of the certificate. A transferee is allocated shares from the pool held by Sepon Ltd which sends a 'bought transfer form' to the company requesting the company to register the buyer's name on the register of members and to issue a share certificate in the buyer's name.

An electronic system for recording and transferring securities (CREST) is now possible under the Uncertified Securities Regulations 1995. It will dispense with paper transmissions and speed up the process. Both Talisman and CREST will run side by side until the Exchange decides that there is no longer a need for the Talisman system for certificated transfers.

4.3 Ceasing to be a Member

A person ceases to be a member when his or her name is removed from the register or she or he dies. The name may be removed for a variety of reasons, e.g., transfer to another whose name is registered, purchase, redemption, forfeiture by the company or surrender to the company of shares which are then cancelled or reissued, or the company being dissolved. In addition, where a share warrant is issued, the company will strike the name of the member off the register and substitute a statement that a warrant has been issued, the shares included in the warrant and the date of issue of the warrant. CA 1985, s. 355, makes it clear that a shareholder with a share warrant is not a member but may be deemed to be so if the articles so provide. Share warrants are negotiable instruments whereby the bearer is entitled to the shares represented by the warrant and legal title is transferred by delivery, so no entry is made in the register of members on transfer. Share warrants are not very common.

4.4 Register of Members

The subscribers to the memorandum will automatically become members on incorporation and their names will be entered in the register of members (CA 1985, s. 22(1)). All other shares will be allotted by the company on an application by a person to become a member of the company. CA 1985, s. 22(2), provides that every other person (i.e., not being an original subscriber) who agrees to become a member of a company and whose name is entered in its register of members, is a member of the company. CA 1985, s. 352, requires every company to keep a register of members containing the following information: the names and addresses of the members, the date on which each person was registered as a member and ceased to be a member, the shares held by each member, the class and number of those shares and the amount paid on each share. CA 1985, s. 353, requires that the register be kept at the company's registered office or at the office of the place where it is made up, in which case notice of that address must be given to the registrar. The register is open to inspection by any member free of charge and any other person who may be required to pay. Copies must be supplied within 10 days of a request for them and a charge may be made for this. If inspection or copies are refused, the court may order them (CA 1985, s. 356).

4.5 Share Certificates

A company must within two months of allotment or transfer issue a share certificate (CA 1985, s. 185). It will state that the named person is the registered holder of a specified number of shares of a particular class which are fully paid or paid up to a stated amount. The share certificate is not a document of title. CA 1985, s. 186, provides that it is prima facie evidence of title to the shares of the person named in it. This presumption may be rebutted. The share certificate operates as a representation by the company that at the time it was issued the person named in it held the specified number of shares and that those shares were paid up to the extent specified. The company may be estopped from denying statements in the certificate against persons who have relied on them. It may be estopped in respect of the statement of the amount paid up on the shares (*Bloomenthal* v *Ford* [1897] AC 156) or in respect of the statement as to title (*Re Bahia & San Francisco Railway Co. Ltd* (1868) LR 3 QB 584).

4.6 Legal and Equitable Interests in Shares

The legal owner of the shares is the person whose name is on the register of members. Equitable interests may arise in a variety of circumstances: a trustee holding shares for beneficiaries under an express trust; a nominee shareholder holding shares for the true controller of the shares; the seller of shares where an unconditional contract has been entered into holding as trustee for the purchaser until the purchaser is registered; on the mortgage of shares.

4.6.1 NOTICE OF EQUITABLE INTERESTS

CA 1985, s. 360, provides that:

> *No notice of any trust, expressed, implied, or constructive, shall be entered on the register, or be receivable by the registrar, in the case of companies registered in England and Wales.*

This almost certainly extends to all equitable interests. Thus, although priority and protection of equitable interests are usually given by notice, this cannot be done in respect of such interests in shares in a company.

4.6.2 STOP NOTICES

A person with a beneficial interest in shares can protect that interest by issuing a stop notice. The procedure for obtaining a stop notice and enforcing it is governed by the Charging Orders Act 1979 and RSC 1965, O. 50, rr. 11 to 15 (as preserved in the CPR, sch 1). Stop notices are issued by the ChD on the filing of a witness statement or affidavit and copies of the notice to be served on the company. The notice informs the company that the applicant has an interest in specified shares and that the notice is to prevent the registration of transfers of the shares and, possibly, the payment of dividends to the registered holder. As long as the stop notice remains in force the company must notify the applicant at least 14 days before any register of transfer or, where applicable, payment of dividend. This is to give the applicant time to apply to the court for an injunction to prevent the transfer being registered (or dividend being paid).

4.6.3 DISCLOSURE OF INTERESTS

The duty to disclose interests in shares under CA 1985, ss. 198 to 220, has been covered briefly in **3.1.4**. You should be aware of this duty as failure to disclose may result in the shares being frozen.

4.7 Rectification of the Register

CA 1985, s. 361, provides:

> *The register of members is prima facie evidence of any matters which are by this Act directed or authorised to be inserted in it.*

It may, therefore, be challenged, and this is done by asking for the register to be rectified. It is unclear whether the company can rectify the register on a request without obtaining a court order first (see, e.g., *Reese River Silver Mining Co.* v *Smith* (1869) LR 4 HL 64).

CA 1985, s. 359(1), provides:

> *If—*
> *(a) the name of any person is, without sufficient cause, entered in or omitted from a company's register of members, or*
> *(b) default is made or unnecessary delay takes place in entering on the register the fact of any person having ceased to be a member,*
> *the person aggrieved, or any member of the company, or the company may apply to the court for rectification of the register.*

An application to rectify the register is usually made by a Part 8 claim form to the Companies Court unless the case is complicated or other relief is sought when it should be begun by ordinary claim form. The summary procedure may be used where the company wrongfully refuses to register a transferee, there is a dispute about title where the facts are agreed or easily ascertained, or where an allotment is void or voidable because of misrepresentation inducing the purchase. Written evidence must be filed setting out the facts supporting the application to rectify.

4.8 Classes of Shares and Variation of Class Rights

4.8.1 CLASSES OF SHARES

A company may have classes of shares i.e. where different shares have different rights, e.g. to vote, to receive dividends in return for their capital contributions. Shareholders receive their share of the profits by way of payment of a dividend. The right to a dividend only arises if there are distributable profits out of which a dividend has been declared. When and how this is done will depend on the articles. Shareholders may receive a return of their capital investment on liquidation of the company or a reduction of capital in accordance with the provisions in CA 1985, ss. 135–141.

These rights to dividend and return of capital will be set out in the articles or terms of issue of the shares. If different shares have different rights there will be classes of shares. The two most common classes of shares are:

(a) Ordinary shares (equity shares) which are the vast majority of shares and will have the usual rights without any special definition.

(b) Preference shares which have preferential rights to dividend and/or return of capital.

There are two general presumptions on these rights:

(a) A presumption of equality, i.e. all shares are presumed to rank equally in the absence of special provisions.

(b) A presumption of priority rights being exhaustive.

Preference shares usually have a preferential dividend measured as a percentage of the nominal value of the share (10% preferential dividend on shares of £1 nominal value). Such dividend is presumed to be cumulative unless otherwise stated. Thus if no dividend is paid one year, a 20% dividend will be paid the next year. The priority on the dividend means that although dividends will be paid more regularly, they will always be exactly the same and will not increase if, e.g., substantial profits are made. Ordinary shares on the other hand have less of a guarantee of payment of dividend regularly but stand to benefit where a large profit has been made.

Preference shares will also usually be given priority in the return of capital in a liquidation although, given the presumption of equality, this is not necessarily so just because they have a preference to dividend. If given priority to return of capital, the preference shares again are a more secure investment than ordinary shares, as they are more likely to have capital returned even where there is insufficient to pay all shareholders. However, they are also potentially less profitable as they will not share in any surplus.

Note that there are also participating preference shares which combine the benefits of priority of preference shares and of sharing in the remaining profits or surplus of capital of ordinary shares.

4.8.2 WHAT IS A VARIATION OF CLASS RIGHTS?

There will be a variation of class rights where the rights attached to the shares have been varied. This will not include actions which do not alter those rights but nevertheless affect the commercial value of the shares. Many of the cases on this point are concerned with the grant or increase of rights to other members which reduces the value of existing rights without actually altering them. Thus it has been held that a subdivision of ordinary shares which reduces the voting powers of preference shares was not a variation of the rights of the preference shareholders (*Greenhalgh* v *Arderne Cinemas Ltd* [1946] 1 All ER 512). Also, a reduction of capital by which the amount of dividend payable on preference shares was reduced was not a variation of class rights (*Re Mackenzie & Co. Ltd* [1916] 2 Ch 450).

4.8.3 PROCEDURE

When a variation in the rights attaching to a class of shares is proposed, it is necessary to obtain the approval of the members holding the shares in the affected class. Exactly how that approval is obtained depends on the subject matter of the variation, where the class rights are set out, and whether the company has a set procedure for such variations (CA 1985, ss. 125 and 126).

If the variation concerns the directors' powers to allot shares, or a reduction of share capital, it will require the written consent of the holders of three quarters in nominal value of the issued shares of that class or an extraordinary resolution passed at a separate meeting of that class. In addition, the procedure must comply with any other procedural requirements in the memorandum or articles. Once the class approval has been given the company in general meeting passes a resolution to effect the change.

Other types of variation may be made simply by complying with the procedure in the memorandum or articles. Where the class rights are set out in the memorandum (rare) they may only be varied in accordance with the procedure contained in the memorandum or in the articles as originally registered. If no such procedure is prescribed, class rights may be varied if all the members of the company agree. Where class rights are contained otherwise than in the memorandum (e.g., in the articles or terms of issue) they may be varied in accordance with the procedure contained in the articles. The articles may be amended to include or alter the procedure for varying the class rights. Such an amendment of the articles is itself a variation of class rights. Note that if the rights are contained in the articles they will also have to be altered by special resolution in general meeting. Where the class rights are contained other than in the memorandum but no variation procedure is prescribed (Table A does not contain one) they may be varied by three-quarters of the class consenting in writing or by an extraordinary resolution in a separate class meeting. Again if the rights are contained in the articles they will have to be altered by special resolution in general meeting.

CA 1985, s. 127, provides that the holders of at least 15 per cent of the class of affected shares who did not consent to the variation may within 21 days apply to the court to disallow the variation. The variation does not then take effect until the court confirms it. The most usual ground for complaint is that the majority who consented did not act in the interests of the class but to secure some other advantage, e.g., they held shares of another class which would benefit by the variation (see *Re Holders Investment Trust Ltd* [1971] 1 WLR 583).

4.9 Maintenance of Share Capital

It is important to differentiate between:

(a) Authorised share capital — the amount which a company is authorised by its memorandum to issue.

(b) Issued or allotted share capital — the nominal amount actually issued to shareholders at any time.

(c) Paid-up share capital — the amount so far paid on shares which have been issued.

(d) Uncalled share capital — the amount which the company is entitled to call on shareholders to contribute.

Most shares are now issued as fully paid shares: it is rare to have partly paid shares with the resulting uncalled capital.

The members together provide the company with its share capital. The money or assets so contributed become the property of the company. If the company does well, it will have assets worth more than the nominal value of its issued share capital. If it does poorly the sum total of the assets may be less. Thus the capital may be dissipated through trading losses. However, there are stringent rules on not returning to the shareholders the share capital which they have contributed. These rules extend to ensuring that the consideration given by each shareholder in exchange for shares is at least equal in value to the nominal value of the shares. The rules have developed in recognition of the fact that the share capital is the 'creditors' buffer' in that it is the company which is their debtor and whose assets must be used to pay their debts.

Thus a company may not:

(a) Issue shares at a discount (see **4.9.4**).

(b) Provide financial assistance for the purchase of its shares except as provided in CA 1985, ss. 151–158 (see **4.10**).

(c) Reduce its issued share capital without following the procedure set out in CA 1985, ss. 135–141, which includes obtaining a special resolution of members and court approval (see **4.12**).

(d) Purchase its own shares except as provided in CA 1985, ss. 159–181.

(e) Pay a dividend except out of distributable profits, defined in CA 1985, s. 263, as accumulated realised profits less accumulated realised losses. Further restrictions on distributions are contained in CA 1985, ss. 263–281 and, by CA 1985, s. 277, a recipient of an unlawful dividend is liable to repay it if she or he knew or had reasonable grounds to know that it was unlawful (see **4.15**).

4.9.1 NOMINAL VALUE AND PREMIUM AND NO PAR SHARES

All shares issued in the UK have a nominal or par value. This is the face value which appears on the share certificate and in the capital clause of the memorandum of association. It is not usually more than £1. No par shares are used in other countries, e.g., Canada and the USA but not yet in this country. The principal reason for this is that the measure of a shareholder's liability to contribute to the company is the nominal value of the shares.

The nominal value of all the issued shares of the company is its share capital which must be maintained. However, companies frequently issue shares for more than their nominal value. Any amount over and above the nominal value is a premium. The premium obtained is treated as the equivalent of share capital. It must be credited to the share premium account which is subject to the rules on reduction of capital and can only be applied for certain purposes: to pay up bonus shares to be issued as fully paid to members; in writing off preliminary expenses or expenses, commission or discount incurred in the issue of shares or debentures; in paying the premium on redemption of debentures or redeemable preference shares issued before 15 June 1982 (CA 1985, s. 180).

4.9.2 MINIMUM CAPITAL REQUIREMENTS

There is no minimum share capital requirement for private companies. However, public companies must have a minimum of £50,000 issued share capital on which at least one quarter of the value and all the premium has been paid (CA 1985, ss. 117 and 118). Where the issued share capital of a public company falls below that minimum it must re-register as a private company.

4.9.3 PARTLY PAID SHARES

The issue of shares creates a debt due from the allottee to the company. It need not be paid at once. However, a public company must not allot shares unless at least a quarter of the nominal value and the whole of the premium has been paid (CA 1985, s. 101). Shares may be issued as partly paid on the basis that the remainder will be paid by instalments on fixed dates or when demanded by the company. Alternatively a company may by special resolution create reserve capital by deciding that part of the amount payable on the shares shall only be called up for payment on liquidation of the company (CA 1985, s. 120). Most shares are now issued fully paid.

4.9.4 ISSUE AT A DISCOUNT

A company may not allot shares for a consideration which is less than the nominal value of the shares. Any allotment in contravention of this provision results in the allottee being liable to pay the discount (i.e., the shares are treated as partly paid) plus interest on that amount at 5 per cent a year (CA 1985, s. 100).

4.9.5 PAYMENT IN CASH OR KIND

Shares allotted by a company and any premium on them may be paid up in money or money's worth (including goodwill and know-how) (CA 1985, s. 99). Where the company receives non-cash consideration for shares it must be of a value at least equal to the nominal value of the shares. If it is of a value which is more than the nominal value of the shares there will be a premium which must be credited to the share premium account (*Henry Head & Co. Ltd* v *Ropner Holdings Ltd* [1952] Ch 124).

The allotment of shares for a non-cash consideration may result in shares being issued at a discount where the value of the non-cash consideration is less than the nominal value of the shares. Private companies enjoy substantial freedom to determine the value of what is received. The court will only interfere with such valuation where it is patently inadequate, illusory or fraudulent (*Re Wragg Ltd* [1897] 1 Ch 796).

There are a number of statutory restrictions on public companies to ensure that shares are not in fact issued at a discount. Public companies may not:

(a) allot shares for a non-cash consideration unless the consideration has been independently valued in accordance with CA 1985, ss. 103 and 108; or

(b) accept in payment for their shares an undertaking to perform services for the company (CA 1985, s. 99); or

(c) allot shares for a consideration which includes an undertaking which may be performed more than five years after the allotment (CA 1985, s. 102).

If a public company does issue shares in contravention of these rules, the allotment is valid but the allottee is liable to pay the nominal value and the whole of the premium (or so much of that aggregate as is treated as paid up by the consideration) with interest at 5 per cent a year. Any person so liable may apply under CA 1985, s. 133, for relief from liability.

4.10 Financial Assistance by a Company for Purchase of Its Own Shares

4.10.1 THE PROHIBITION

CA 1985, s. 151, provides:

> *(1) . . . where a person is acquiring or is proposing to acquire shares in a company, it is not lawful for the company or any of its subsidiaries to give financial assistance directly or indirectly for the purpose of that acquisition before or at the same time as the acquisition takes place.*
> *(2) . . . where a person has acquired shares in a company and any liability has been incurred (by that or any other person), for the purpose of that acquisition, it is not lawful for the company or any of its subsidiaries to give financial assistance directly or indirectly for the purpose of reducing or discharging the liability so incurred.*

Thus, subject to a number of exceptions, it is unlawful to give financial assistance before, at the same time as or after the acquisition if it is given for the purpose of the acquisition of shares in the company or its holding company. Note that it is not unlawful for a holding company to give financial assistance for purchase of shares in a subsidiary.

4.10.2 FINANCIAL ASSISTANCE

Financial assistance is widely defined in CA 1985, s. 152, to include assistance by way of: gift; guarantee or indemnity; release or waiver of a right or obligation; loan or any other agreement under which the obligations of the person giving the assistance are to be fulfilled at a time when in accordance with the agreement any obligation of another party to the agreement remains unfulfilled; novation or assignment of the rights arising under a loan or such other agreement; any other financial assistance given by a company which reduces the net assets of the company to a material extent or by a company with no net assets. Thus it would cover, for example, the situation whereby a takeover bidder borrows money to buy shares in a company and having acquired the shares uses company money or assets to repay the loan. The definition has been widely drafted on purpose. However, the precise meaning, in particular of the last provision (assistance reducing the net assets) is not clear, see *Belmont Finance Corporation Ltd* v *Williams Furniture Ltd (No. 2)* [1980] 1 All ER 393 and *Charterhouse Investment Trust Ltd* v *Tempest Diesels Ltd* [1986] BCLC 1 on the interpretation of CA 1948, s. 54 (the predecessor to s. 152).

4.10.3 EXCEPTIONS

The provisions of CA 1985, s. 151, are subject to a number of technical exceptions to be found in s. 153, which apply to all companies. For example, distributions by way of dividends lawfully made, in the course of a company's winding up, are not prohibited (s. 153(3)(a)). Private companies may benefit from a relaxation of the rule in s. 151 by following the procedure in ss. 155 to 158.

4.11 Alterations in Capital

4.11.1 INCREASE OF CAPITAL

The authorised share capital, i.e., the amount stated in the capital clause of the memorandum, may be increased by ordinary resolution where the articles so authorise (see CA 1985, s. 121 and Table A, reg. 32). Such increase merely increases the share capital available for issue. Issued share capital may be increased by allotment of available unissued shares. The power to allot is usually delegated to the directors.

4.11.2 CONSOLIDATION AND DIVISION

Consolidation is the combining of a number of shares into one new share of commensurate value, thus five 20p shares may be consolidated into one £1 share. Division is the opposite. If the articles authorise such alterations (see Table A, reg. 32), they may be done by passing ordinary resolutions.

4.11.3 DIMINUTION OR CANCELLATION OF CAPITAL

This is the cancelling of unissued shares by altering the capital clause of the memorandum to reduce the authorised capital. It may be done by ordinary resolution if so authorised by the articles. This is not a reduction of capital as it is merely lowering the amount of shares which the company has the power to issue and in no way reduces the capital available to the company.

4.11.4 REDUCTION OF CAPITAL

This is the reducing of the company's issued capital and is subject to general maintenance of capital rules. Such reduction needs court approval. The formal procedure and requirements are set out in CA 1985, ss. 135 to 141, which are covered at **4.12**.

The court also has power to reduce the company's share capital when ordering the company to purchase a member's shares on a petition under CA 1985, s. 459 (unfair prejudice, see **13.6**).

In addition, the company may reduce its share capital without confirmation of the court where it redeems redeemable shares (see CA 1985, s. 159); purchases its own shares (see CA 1985, s. 162); or forfeits or accepts surrender in lieu of forfeiture of shares.

4.12 Reduction of Share Capital

The general maintenance of capital rule restricts the return of share capital to members or the reduction of liability on shares. However, a reduction of share capital is allowed provided the procedures and precautions set out in CA 1985, ss. 135 to 141, are fulfilled. Although s. 135(1) provides a general power to sanction schemes of reduction, the three most common types of cases are identified by s. 135(2) and are discussed below.

4.12.1 EXTINGUISHING OR REDUCING THE LIABILITY ON SHARES NOT FULLY PAID

For example, a company with issued capital of 1,000 £1 shares partly paid (50p per share) cancels the unpaid sum on each share. This would reduce the nominal value of each share to 50p and the issued share capital of the company to £500. The capital available to pay the company's debts is therefore reduced. This type of reduction of capital is not now very common as most shares are issued fully paid.

4.12.2 CANCELLING PAID-UP SHARE CAPITAL WHICH IS LOST OR UNREPRESENTED BY AVAILABLE ASSETS

For example, a company with issued capital of 1,000 £1 shares fully paid has assets worth only £500 because of depreciation or trading losses. The company wishes to alter its share capital to reflect the true financial position of the company. It therefore cancels 50p per share leaving the shareholders with 50p shares. Its issued share capital is then £500.

This is the most frequent type of reduction. Depreciation and trading losses are facts of business life. In *Re Jupiter House Investments (Cambridge) Ltd* [1985] 1 WLR 975, it was held that 'loss' meant permanent loss, but where it could not be proved to be so the court would in exceptional circumstances confirm the reduction if the company gave an undertaking that if the loss was recovered it would not be distributed as dividends. In *Re Grosvenor Press plc* [1985] 1 WLR 980, it was held that there was no need for a reserve to be set aside indefinitely, as future creditors were protected by the various statutory provisions. An undertaking was given to treat any recovery of the loss as an undistributable reserve for so long as there remained outstanding any liabilities admissible to proof in a winding up commencing on the date the reduction of capital took effect.

4.12.3 RETURNING PAID-UP CAPITAL WHICH IS IN EXCESS OF THE COMPANY'S WANTS

For example, a company with issued capital of 1,000 £1 shares fully paid returns 50p per share to its shareholders. The shares now have a nominal value of 50p and the issued share capital of the company is £500. The capital available to pay the company's debts is therefore reduced. This method of reduction will usually arise where the company has reduced its business by selling off part of it or where it can obtain finance more cheaply from other sources. The repayment can be in cash or in kind, e.g., the company may offer the option of taking debentures or preference shares instead of cash.

4.12.4 PROCEDURE

(a) The company must have the power to reduce in its articles (Table A, reg. 34). If necessary the articles may be altered by special resolution to include such power.

(b) The company must pass a special resolution setting out the terms of the reduction (CA 1985, s. 135). Although there is a general rule that a resolution can be treated as validly passed if all the members entitled to attend the meeting agree to treat it as binding, it would appear that the court requires a special resolution to be passed at a general meeting for a reduction of capital and will not treat unanimous consent as an adequate substitute (*Re Barry Artist Ltd* [1985] 1 WLR 1305).

(c) Once the resolution has been passed the company applies by petition to the Companies Court to confirm the reduction. Written evidence must be filed with the petition, usually made by one of the directors, setting out the reasons and circumstances of the reduction and submitting a statement of assets and liabilities. If possible the position of creditors will be safeguarded in advance by obtaining bank guarantees that all creditors will be paid in full.

(d) An application for directions is taken out and at the hearing before the registrar directions for the publication of notices and steps to protect creditors are given (see **2.3.2.4**). Where the reduction involves the reducing of liability on unpaid shares or the repayment of capital to shareholders, the creditors are entitled to object to the reduction (CA 1985, s. 136(2) and (3)).

The court will therefore direct that a list of creditors be settled. If a creditor on the list does not consent to the reduction the court may dispense with that creditor's consent on the company securing the full amount or an amount fixed by the court where the company disputes the full amount (see **2.3.2.5**). Where the reduction does not reduce shareholders' liability or return capital to them, the creditors have no right to object unless the court so directs.

(e) At the full hearing the court, if satisfied that every creditor entitled to object under s. 136 has either consented to the reduction or has been paid or secured, may make an order confirming the reduction on such terms and conditions as it thinks fit (CA 1985, s. 137).

In addition to considering the position of creditors, the court will also ensure that the reduction is fair between classes of shareholders. Where there are ordinary and preference shares the right to return of capital on liquidation is considered in determining what is fair as a reduction of capital is really a 'mini-liquidation'. If the preference shares carry no priority for repayment of capital they are likely to suffer a reduction of capital rateably with ordinary shares. This may result in a reduction of dividend payable on the preference shares, as preference dividends are calculated as a fixed percentage of the paid-up or nominal value. Such a variation is not a variation of class rights and requires no separate class consent (*Re Mackenzie & Co. Ltd* [1916] 2 Ch 450). If the preference shares do carry a right to repayment of capital in priority to ordinary shares and surplus cash is returned, it will normally be returned to the preference shareholders first. Although such a reduction may eliminate a class entirely, in the absence of a provision in the articles no class consent is required for the reduction as this again is not a variation of their rights but a satisfaction or fulfilment of rights which then cease to exist (*House of Fraser plc* v *ACGE Investments Ltd* [1987] AC 387). If preference shares do carry a right to repayment of capital in priority to ordinary shares, and capital is lost, the ordinary shares should bear the loss first. The court is reluctant to confirm a reduction which cancels the ordinary shareholding entirely.

Where the court confirms the reduction, it may direct the company to add to its name the words 'and reduced' and require the company to publish the reasons for the reduction (CA 1985, s. 137(2)). Such directions are very unusual.

(f) A copy of the order and a minute approved by the court showing the altered share capital, in particular, the amount of the share capital, the number of shares and amount of each share and the amount deemed to be paid on each share, must be registered with the registrar of companies.

The resolution takes effect on registration (CA 1985, s. 138). Where a public company has reduced its capital below the required minimum, the registrar will not register the order until the company has re-registered as a private company (CA 1985, s. 139). On registration the registrar issues a certificate, which is conclusive evidence that the requirements of the Act have been fulfilled and that the company's capital is as stated in the minute.

4.13 Serious Loss of Capital by Public Company

Where a public company suffers a serious loss of capital there is an obligation on the directors to call an extraordinary general meeting within 28 days from the earliest date on which any director knew of that fact (CA 1985, s. 142). Such loss is defined as where the net assets of the company are half or less of its called-up share capital. The purpose of the meeting is to notify the shareholders of the situation and to discuss what measures should be taken. One obvious measure is a reduction of capital (see **4.12**).

4.14 Companies Act 1985, section 425

The Companies Act 1985, ss. 425–7, enables a company to enter into a compromise or arrangement with its creditors or any class of them, or its members or any class of them, which, if approved by the requisite majority of creditors and members and sanctioned by the court, becomes binding on the company, members and creditors. The provisions may be used for a wide variety of purposes from mergers of two or more companies to altering rights attached to debentures and/or shares.

The procedure is as follows:

(a) An application is made to the court setting out the proposed scheme.

(b) If the court is satisfied that the documents are in order and the scheme is not *ultra vires* or being used improperly it will order meetings to be held of each affected class of creditor or member. The notice of the meeting must include a statement explaining the effect of the proposed compromise or arrangement and any material interests of the directors in the proposal.

(c) If the scheme is approved at each of the meetings by a majority representing at least three-quarters in value of those who attend and vote, a further application is made to court. The court will ensure that the procedure has been properly followed, the requisite meetings and majority votes have been obtained, and that the proposal is such that an intelligent and honest person (being a member of the class concerned and acting in his own interests) might reasonably approve.

(d) If sanctioned by the court, the scheme becomes binding on the company, creditors and members.

(e) Where the compromise or arrangement is for the reconstruction of a company or the merger of two or more companies and involves the transfer of some or all of the property from one company to another the court has additional powers to make provision for, *inter alia*, the transfer of property or liabilities, the allotment of shares, or the dissolution of the transferor company.

The court order is ineffective until a copy is received by the registrar. A copy must be annexed to the memorandum.

4.15 Payment of Dividends out of Profits

A basic aspect of the maintenance of capital rule is that the company cannot make a distribution (e.g., pay dividends) out of capital. It can only pay a dividend if there are distributable profits out of which it may be declared (CA 1985, s. 263).

4.15.1 DISTRIBUTABLE PROFITS

Distributable profits are defined as the accumulated, realised profits, so far as not previously utilised by distribution or capitalisation, less the accumulated, realised losses, so far as not previously written off in a reduction or reorganisation of capital duly made. (There are special rules for investment companies and insurance companies.)

The definition does not distinguish between capital and revenue profits. However, it does require the profits and losses to be accumulated. Thus the balance of profit or loss from previous years must be brought into account in the current period. In addition, it requires the profits and losses to be realised. The term 'realised' is not defined in the Act. However, various accounting guidelines have been issued setting out criteria and standards for determining what is and is not a realised profit or loss. The Act itself also makes some detailed provisions, e.g., on the treatment of development costs.

4.15.2 ACCOUNTS

The amount of the distribution which may be made is determined by reference to the last audited annual accounts or, where the figures derived from the latest annual accounts would preclude the payment of a dividend, interim accounts may be used but they must be such as are necessary to enable a reasonable judgment to be made. In addition, if the company has not yet produced its first annual accounts, 'initial' accounts may be prepared for the purpose of declaring a dividend, subject to the same qualification as applies to interim accounts.

4.15.3 DIVIDENDS BY PUBLIC COMPANIES

There are additional rules for public companies under CA 1985, s. 264, which prohibits a public company making a distribution unless its net assets are at least equal to the aggregate amount of its called-up share capital and undistributable reserves and the distribution would not reduce the amount of those assets to less than that aggregate. Thus this takes into account unrealised losses. Undistributable reserves are defined in the section as the share premium account, the capital redemption reserve, unrealised profits less unrealised losses unless previously written off, and any other reserve which the company is prohibited from distributing by any statute or by its memorandum or articles.

4.15.4 UNLAWFUL DISTRIBUTIONS

A member who receives a dividend which is wholly or partly in breach of the rules, knowing, or having reason to believe, that it is paid in breach of the rules, is liable to repay to the company all or so much of it as is paid in breach of the rules (CA 1985, s. 277). In addition, directors who authorise or recommend a dividend in breach of the rules are in breach of their duty to the company and can be required to make good the breach (*Re Exchange Banking Co., Flitcroft's Case* (1882) 21 ChD 519).

4.15.5 PAYMENT OF DIVIDENDS

Dividends are only due when they have been declared. Under Table A, reg. 102, the general meeting declares the final dividend although the directors have the power to declare interim dividends. Also under reg. 102 the final dividend cannot be higher than that recommended by the directors. Payment of a dividend must be in cash unless the articles allow payment in some other form such as bonus shares. Bonus shares may be issued where the company has the power to capitalise its profits and apply the amount so capitalised in the issue of bonus shares issued to members in the same proportion as a cash dividend would have been distributed: see reg. 110.

FIVE

DEBENTURES

5.1 Introduction

5.1.1 GENERAL

Most companies are unable to finance their activities solely from their paid-up share capital. Companies with share capital under £100 and £1,000 are very common, and few businesses can be run without considerably more funds. Most companies raise further finance by borrowing. A company will often be given express powers in its memorandum to borrow for the purposes of its undertaking and to give security to the lender. Even if such powers are not given expressly, they will be implied at common law if the company is a trading or commercial one.

In the past it was quite common for companies to raise finance by borrowing small amounts, often about £100 each, from a large number of private investors. This is now extremely unusual. It is far more common today for companies to borrow, either long or medium term, or on overdraft, from a bank, or for money to be lent by persons or companies connected with the borrowing company (such as shareholders or directors).

5.1.2 DEBENTURE HOLDERS AND SHAREHOLDERS COMPARED

A long-term loan to a company is a form of investment whereby the creditor's return is the interest (as opposed to the dividend paid to shareholders). The loan contract is called a debenture and the lender/creditor, a debentureholder. Although debentures and shares are both forms of investment in a company there are substantial differences.

(a) Position of shareholder/debentureholder. A shareholder is a part owner, whose rights will be set out in the articles or terms of issue. Shareholders may only be paid dividends if there are distributable profits, and dividends only become due if and when declared. A debentureholder is a creditor whose rights are set out in the debenture and whose interest is a debt due from the company, payable even if there are no profits.

(b) Treatment of share/loan capital. The maintenance of capital rules apply only to share capital and thus debentures may be issued at a discount, purchased freely by the company, and interest may be paid out of capital as an expense of the business which will reduce profits.

There are, however, also similarities in that s. 80 (directors' authority to issue), s. 89 (pre-emption rights) apply to shares and debentures convertible into shares and the rules on issue to the public in FSA 1986 apply to both. In addition, the procedure for transfer is the same for both.

There may be a single debenture (e.g. to a bank to secure an overdraft), a series of debentures in identical form all ranking for repayment *pari passu* (e.g. a number of individual loans to the company), or debenture stock which is a single debt in which each lender has a holding of specified value (e.g. through an offer to the public a loan is raised from a large number of lenders). The loan contract must (for debenture stock) and may (for a series of debentures) take the form of a debenture trust deed whereby trustees are appointed who are, in effect, the creditors of the company, but who hold as such for the true lenders, the beneficiaries of the trust, with the duty of enforcing the terms of the contract with the company and protecting the lenders' interests.

5.1.3 STANDARD TERMS OF A DEBENTURE

The most important terms of any debenture will include the following:

(a) That the company pay capital and/or interest as specified.

(b) That if the company defaults in payment, the whole amount becomes repayable immediately.

(c) Giving the lender a fixed charge over fixed assets (see **5.3.1**).

(d) Giving the lender a floating charge over other assets, or a floating charge over the whole of the company's undertakings (note that the company can create a number of charges over the same property; see below for priority of such charges) (see **5.4**).

(e) That the company maintain the property subject to the charge (e.g. keep it repaired and insured).

(f) That the company maintain the value of the class of assets over which the floating charge has been granted at or above a certain level (to ensure there are sufficient assets to use to pay the debt if the company defaults).

(g) Specify the events which will cause crystallisation of the floating charge, e.g., failure to pay or keep the value of the assets at the level promised (see **5.5**).

(h) Specify the events which will entitle the chargee to enforce the charge and the methods by which this may be done. The two most common methods of enforcement are selling the assets subject to the charge, and appointing a receiver.

5.1.4 RETURN ON CAPITAL

Loan capital gives a fixed return (interest) on the investment, payable even if no profits are made. Share capital gives an entitlement to return (dividends) only if there are sufficient profits. The higher the risk of the investment, the greater the return required to attract investors. The equity shareholders will require a greater return than lenders as they risk a decline of profits or insolvency. Thus a company may rely more heavily on loan capital. The ratio between fixed return capital (e.g. loans) and variable return capital (e.g. shares) is called gearing. The greater the proportion of fixed return capital, the higher the gearing. Gearing at too high a level will result in investors requiring a higher return to compensate for the risk of insolvency.

At the Bar, company borrowing on debentures is most commonly met in the context of the provision of security, although other issues can arise from time to time.

5.2 What are Debentures?

The term 'debenture' is defined in the following way by the CA 1985, s. 744:

> *'debenture' includes debenture stock, bonds and other securities of a company whether constituting a charge on the assets of the company or not.*

Obviously, this is an inclusive definition. It covers both secured and unsecured loans, the word 'securities' in the definition being used in its commercial sense of a document evidencing a loan. In *Levy* v *Abercorris Slate & Slab Co.* (1887) 37 ChD 260, a case on the Bills of Sale Act (1878) Amendment Act 1882, Chitty J said:

> In my opinion a debenture means a document which either creates a debt or acknowledges it, and any document which fulfils either of these conditions is a 'debenture'.

In fact, the word 'debenture' is used in two senses. One is the wide meaning considered above, and encompasses the loan securities called debentures in the second, narrower, sense considered at **5.3.2** below, and their derivatives, which are considered at **5.3.3** to **5.3.8**.

5.3 Categories of Loan Securities

5.3.1 SPECIFIC LEGAL AND EQUITABLE MORTGAGES

Such mortgages, if created by companies as security for their debts, have the same effect as like mortgages created by individuals. The usual formalities on execution must be observed (see Law of Property Act 1925, ss. 95, 86 and 136). A specific charge or mortgage gives the lender recourse against identified land or other assets owned by the company in the event of default on the loan, such as if payment of interest falls into arrears. Therefore, the terms of the mortgage will usually prohibit the company from dealing with the charged assets without the lender's permission, and will require the company to maintain and insure those assets.

5.3.2 DEBENTURES

Here we are considering the term 'debentures' in its narrower sense. They encompass all forms of loan contract between companies and lenders. They may be secured or unsecured. Security may be by fixed or floating (see **5.4**) charge. A company may issue either single debentures, for example, to its bank, or a series of debentures. If a series of debentures is issued, it is usual for them to be issued on terms that they all rank *pari passu* (that is, equally) in their rights to interest and repayment. An issue of debentures may sometimes be listed on the Stock Exchange.

Often when a series of debentures is issued, the company will enter into a trust deed whereby the interests of the debenture holders are represented by trustees. In this way the company can negotiate minor alterations in the terms of the debentures with the trustees, rather than having to negotiate with all the debenture holders individually. However, debenture certificates will be issued to all the debenture holders, in which the company will covenant to pay the loan and interest, so the debenture holders are creditors of the company in their own right.

5.3.3 DEBENTURE STOCK

This is a development from the debenture trust deed. Here, the company covenants to repay the total loan with the trustees, with the effect that the trustees, and not the individual stockholders, are the creditors of the company. Any rights against the company are enforced by the trustees, the stockholders being restricted to having remedies against the trustees.

5.3.4 LOAN STOCK AND LOAN NOTES

These are rather like debenture stock, but whereas issues of debenture stock will be secured by fixed and/or floating charges, loan stock and loan notes are unsecured loans. Such unsecured loans are sometimes called unsecured notes or naked debentures. The difference between loan stock and loan notes is that loan notes are shorter term investments than loan stock, usually for periods up to 10 years.

5.3.5 INCOME BONDS

Generally, debentures provide for the payment of interest at a fixed rate, or at a stated rate above base or other fluctuating rate, regardless of whether profits are earned by the company. Income bonds are usually issued by companies in straitened financial circumstances, and provide for interest to be payable only out of profits.

5.3.6 BEARER DEBENTURES

Most debentures are issued in registrable form, and are transferable on sale by instrument of transfer in the same way as shares. Although very rare, a company may issue debentures in bearer form, which are negotiable instruments which may be transferred simply by delivery of the debentures. The holder of bearer debentures usually claims interest by sending coupons, which accompany the debentures, to the company on the due dates.

5.3.7 CONVERTIBLES

These are debentures which include in their terms a right to be surrendered to the company in return for shares. Unlike shares, debentures may be issued at a discount (e.g., debentures with a nominal value of £100 may be bought from the company for £80). If convertibles are issued at a discount, the terms of conversion must ensure that the conversion shares are not also issued at a discount (see **4.9.4** and *Mosely* v *Koffyfontein Mines Ltd* [1904] 2 Ch 108).

5.3.8 INTERNATIONAL BONDS AND EUROBONDS

International bonds are securities issued by a borrower in a foreign country. They include foreign bonds, parallel bonds and Eurobonds. They are usually issued as bearer securities, but are sometimes registered securities. Some are convertible securities. The borrowers are large companies.

Foreign bonds, for example Yankee, Samurai and Bulldog bonds, are securities issued on a domestic capital market in the local currency by borrowers from abroad. Eurobonds are issued by foreign borrowers and are denominated either in a Eurocurrency, US dollars, Canadian dollars, Japanese yen or in euros. They are underwritten and sold by international syndicates of financial institutions. Interest can accrue either on a fixed-rate basis or at a floating rate.

5.4 Floating Charges

Specific charges were considered at **5.3.1**. A company is not restricted to giving fixed or specific charges, and can additionally give security by way of floating charge. A floating charge is a form of equitable charge on fluctuating assets. The distinction between the two types of security was described in the following way by Lord Macnaghten in *Illingworth* v *Houldsworth* [1904] AC 355, HL:

> A specific charge, I think, is one that without more fastens on ascertained and definite property or property capable of being ascertained and defined; a floating charge, on the other hand, is ambulatory and shifting in its nature, hovering over and so to speak floating with the property which it is intended to affect until some event occurs or some act is done which causes it to settle and fasten on the subject of the charge within its reach and grasp.

When the same case was before the Court of Appeal (sub nom. *Re Yorkshire Woolcombers Association Ltd* [1903] 2 Ch 284), Romer LJ described the usual characteristics of a floating charge in the following way:

> I certainly do not intend to attempt to give an exact definition of the term 'floating charge', nor am I prepared to say that there will not be a floating charge within the

meaning of the Act, which does not contain all of the three characteristics that I am about to mention, but I certainly think, that if a charge has the three characteristics that I am about to mention, it is a floating charge. (1.) If it is a charge on a class of assets of a company present and future; (2.) if that class is one which, in the ordinary course of the business of the company, would be changing from time to time; and (3.) if you find that by the charge it is contemplated that, until some future step is taken by or on behalf of those interested in the charge, the company may carry on its business in the ordinary way as far as concerns the particular class of assets I am dealing with.

Examples of floating charges include charges over a company's:

(a) Stock in trade from time to time.

(b) Book debts owing from its customers from time to time.

(c) Whole assets and undertaking for the time being.

Banks commonly take fixed charges and floating charges over the company's whole undertaking to secure overdrafts. It has been settled since the floating charge first emerged as a form of security that a charge 'on [the company's] undertaking' prima facie extends to all property which may become the property of the company as well as to the property at the date of the charge: see *Re Panama, New Zealand, and Australian Royal Mail Co.* (1870) LR 5 Ch App 318. This is so even if the property covered by the charge is not expressed in the debenture as being 'present and future' — this will be taken as read: *Re Croftbell Ltd* [1990] BCC 781.

A charge will be held to be a floating charge if it is floating in nature. Thus, in *Re Brightlife Ltd* [1987] Ch 200, Hoffmann J held that a charge over the company's 'book debts and other debts', although expressed to be a 'first specific charge', was a floating charge, because it related to fluctuating assets. However, it is possible for a charge over book debts to be a fixed charge in nature if appropriately drafted (*Siebe Gorman & Co. Ltd* v *Barclays Bank Ltd* [1979] 2 Lloyd's Rep 142). These decisions were reviewed in *Re New Bullas Trading Ltd* [1994] BCC 36, CA, where it was held that the debenture in question created a valid 'fixed charge' over a company's book debts, even though the terms of the debenture left the company free to deal with the book debts and their proceeds when collected, because the proceeds were to be paid into a designated account and dealt with in accordance with any directions of the debenture holder.

During the currency of a floating charge, the company can continue its business in the usual way. Assets from the categories charged may be bought and sold. Indeed, unless the company has entered into a negative pledge (see **5.7**), it has the power to enter into further mortgages or charges affecting the categories of assets subject to the floating charge. When a floating charge crystallises, it is converted into a fixed security attaching to all the company's assets in the categories charged at the date of crystallisation, and also any such assets which it acquires thereafter.

5.5 Crystallisation of Floating Charges

5.5.1 CRYSTALLISING EVENTS

At law, a floating charge will crystallise on the following events:

(a) On the appointment of a receiver, either by the court or by the lender under a power conferred by the debenture creating the floating charge.

(b) On the commencement of the winding up of the company.

(c) On the company ceasing to carry on business. This particular crystallising event was accepted by Nourse J in *Re Woodroffes (Musical Instruments) Ltd* [1986] Ch

366, and was treated as beyond argument at first instance by Chadwick J in *Re Real Meat Co. Ltd* [1996] BCC 254. It may be that the company ceasing business simply gives the lender grounds to appoint a receiver, and crystallisation takes place when the receiver is appointed.

Alternatively, the debenture itself may provide that certain events will cause the charge to crystallise. Such clauses fall into two categories:

(d) By intervention on the part of the lender, such as giving notice under an express power converting the charge into a fixed charge, as in *Re Brightlife Ltd* [1987] Ch 200.

(e) Automatic crystallisation, such as a term in the debenture providing for crystallisation on the company's assets falling below a specified level. Hoffmann J in *Re Brightlife Ltd* suggested that such a clause may be valid, but the matter is not yet settled.

5.5.2 EFFECTS OF CRYSTALLISATION

Under the new s. 410 of CA 1985, which was to be substituted when CA 1989, s. 100, was brought into force, regulations were to be made requiring notice to be given to the registrar of companies of the crystallisation of a floating charge. However, it is now clear that s. 100 is never going to be brought into force, so for the time being there is no need to notify the Companies Court Registrar.

A description of what happens on crystallisation by the appointment of a receiver was given by Mocatta J in *George Barker (Transport) Ltd* v *Eynon* [1973] 1 WLR 462:

> The appointment of a receiver by the debenture-holders does not end the legal life of the company; the company is so to speak anaesthetised, but the receiver may carry on business on its behalf. The legal persona of the company will continue to subsist until liquidation and the company in the case of the most successful receiverships may be restored to full conscious activity when the anaesthetic is no longer applied after the debts owing to the debenture-holders have been paid.

Of course, many receiverships are not so successful, and the company is soon put into liquidation.

5.6 Characteristics of Debentures

5.6.1 SPECIFIC PERFORMANCE

In *South African Territories Ltd* v *Wallington* [1898] AC 309 it was held that the rule that an intending borrower cannot obtain specific performance of the contract of loan (because a loan can be raised elsewhere) applied to issues of debentures. This was reversed in 1907 by a provision now in CA 1985, s. 195, that contracts to take up and pay for debentures may be enforced by specific performance.

5.6.2 CLOGS ON THE EQUITY OF REDEMPTION

Secured (as opposed to unsecured) debentures are types of mortgage, and so are subject to the rule that provisions that clog or fetter the right of redemption are void (*Samuel* v *Jarrah Timber & Wood Paving Corporation Ltd* [1904] AC 323).

It has been held under this rule that a bonus or premium payable on redemption (e.g., where a debenture with a nominal value of £100 is purchased at par but provides that on redemption the holder is entitled to the nominal value plus, say, £20) constitutes a clog (*Re Rainbow Syndicate Ltd* [1916] WN 178). However, this decision conflicts with CA 1985, s. 130(2), which permits a company to apply its share premium account to pay the premium payable on redemption of its debentures, and is probably wrong.

Debentures may be made irredeemable, or redeemable only on a remote contingency, and still be valid by virtue of CA 1985, s. 193, despite the usual rule that postponing the date of redemption of a mortgage for an excessive time is a clog on the equity of redemption.

5.7 Negative Pledges

A negative pledge (sometimes called a restrictive clause) is a term in a debenture or other loan security by which the company undertakes not to create later charges ranking in priority to or *pari passu* with the present security. If the present loan is unsecured, the pledge is not to charge the company's assets at all. The purpose of the pledge is to prevent the company from watering down the lenders' security, or, in the case of unsecured loans, to prevent the company from giving priority to later lenders. A negative pledge in an unsecured loan is often reinforced by a further term limiting the amount of further indebtedness that may be incurred by the company.

Although such terms have contractual effect between the company and the lender, and may be enforced against the company while it is a going concern, it is quite likely that any breach by the company will not come to light until after the company becomes insolvent. The question then is whether the negative pledge has any effect on the subsequent chargees.

If the pledge is contained in a secured debenture, it is an equitable restriction on the company's power to create later charges having priority to the first (*Rother Iron Works Ltd* v *Canterbury Precision Engineers Ltd* [1974] QB 1, CA per Russell LJ). It will therefore bind:

(a) a later chargee having notice of the pledge; and

(b) a later equitable chargee having no notice of the pledge if the equities between the first and second chargees are equal.

Conversely, a later legal mortgagee for value with no notice, and a later equitable chargee with no notice with a stronger equitable claim than the first chargee, would not be bound by such a pledge.

Where the pledge is contained in an unsecured loan, the lender has no interest in the company's assets other than the pledge, so the pledge will not constitute an equitable restriction on the company's power to create further charges, and will operate only contractually between the company and the original lender.

5.8 Avoidance of Floating Charges Created before Insolvency

Under the IA 1986, s. 245, certain floating charges created shortly before the onset of insolvency of the company are invalid. The 'onset of insolvency' is either:

(a) the date of presentation of a petition seeking an administration order; or

(b) the date of commencement of the winding up of the company (usually, the date of presentation of the winding-up petition).

If the floating charge is given to a person connected with the company (such as directors, their spouses, and employees), it is invalid if it is created within two years of the onset of insolvency. If given to anyone else, the period is one year. However, even if a floating charge is given to a person who is not connected with the company within the one-year period, the charge will only be invalidated if at the time the charge was given the company was unable to pay its debts or became unable to do so in consequence of the transaction.

A charge caught by IA 1986, s. 245 is only invalidated to the extent that value (in money paid, goods or services supplied, or discharge or reduction of debts of the company) is not given for it at the same time, as, or after, it is created (s. 245(2)). This latter provision largely destroys the utility of the section, as illustrated by *Re Yeovil Glove Co. Ltd* [1965] Ch 148, CA. The company gave its bank a floating charge to secure its previously unsecured overdraft of £68,000 less than a year before it went into liquidation. Before liquidation, the bank received £111,000 and paid out £110,000 on the company's accounts. Applying the rule in *Devaynes* v *Noble, Clayton's Case* (1816) 1 Mer 572 the court held that the £67,000 overdraft at the date winding up commenced was all new money received, so the charge was valid in full.

5.9 Registration of Charges

There are two duties on companies regarding registration of charges. First, if a register of debenture holders is kept by the company, it must be kept at its registered office, and copies of all charges it creates must be kept there too. Fines are prescribed in default.

Second, most charges created over the company's assets must be registered at Companies House. Default may result in the security becoming void for certain purposes. This section is concerned with this second form of registration and describes the new system of registration to be introduced by CA 1989, ss. 92 to 107. This system is not yet in force and it looks increasingly unlikely that it will ever be brought into force. However, it also seems likely that the old system of registration, which is to be found in the CA 1985, ss. 395–409, and which is still in force, will be replaced by some other system in the not too distant future.

5.9.1 CHARGES REQUIRING REGISTRATION

Under CA 1985, s. 396, the charges requiring registration are:

(a) Charges on land or any interest in land.

(b) Charges on goods or any interest in goods. 'Goods' means any tangible movable property other than money. However, a charge, such as a pledge, under which the chargee is entitled to possession either of the goods or a document of title to them is not registrable. Note that *Romalpa* clauses may or may not, depending on their terms, be registrable under this head. Almost everything turns on whether legal ownership of the goods vests in the purchasing company, in which case a clause retaining the creditor's equitable ownership in the goods will be registrable, or whether legal ownership is retained by the creditor, in which case it is not registrable. See, for example, *Aluminium Industrie Vaassen BV* v *Romalpa Aluminium Ltd* [1976] 1 WLR 676, CA; *Re Bond Worth Ltd* [1980] Ch 228 and *Borden (UK) Ltd* v *Scottish Timber Products Ltd* [1981] Ch 25, CA.

(c) Charges on intangible movable property in the following categories:

(i) goodwill,

(ii) intellectual property, i.e., patents, trade marks, registered designs, copyright and design right,

(iii) book debts, which are debts owing to the company arising out of its normal business activities,

(iv) uncalled share capital and calls made but not paid.

In addition, charges securing issues of debentures and floating charges on the whole or part of the company's property are always registrable regardless of the nature of the assets charged.

5.9.2 DUTY TO REGISTER

Particulars of registrable charges must be delivered to the registrar of companies in the prescribed form within 21 days after the charge is created. Primarily it is the company's duty to register such charges, but registration may be effected by any person interested in the charge (CA 1985, s. 398). It is commonly done by the chargee, who has most to lose. The particulars are filed by the registrar on a separate charges register for each company, showing the date of registration.

5.9.3 DATE OF CREATION

By CA 1985, s. 414(2), a registrable charge is taken as being created:

(a) in the case of a charge created by an instrument in writing, when the instrument is executed by the company or, if its execution by the company is conditional, upon the conditions being fulfilled, and

(b) in any other case, when an enforceable agreement is entered into by the company conferring a security interest intended to take effect forthwith or upon the company acquiring an interest in property subject to the charge.

5.9.4 PRESCRIBED PARTICULARS

The particulars of the charge that must be registered will be prescribed in regulations yet to be made (CA 1985, s. 415(1)). These are likely to include the date the charge was created (and the date an interest in the property charged was acquired, if appropriate), the amount secured, details of the property charged, and the names of the chargees. In addition, CA 1985, s. 415(2), provides that the prescribed particulars may include details of any negative pledge and whether the charge is a market charge.

If the charge secures an issue of debentures, the registered particulars must include the date on which any debentures of the issue were taken up, and the amount taken up (CA 1985, s. 408).

Further matters which may need to be registered at a later date are notices of appointment and ceasing to act as a receiver (CA 1985, s. 409) and crystallisation of floating charges (CA 1985, s. 410).

5.9.5 EFFECT OF FAILURE TO REGISTER

By CA 1985, s. 399(1), where a registrable charge is not registered within 21 days of its creation, it is void against:

(a) An administrator where a petition on which an administration order is made is presented after the creation of the charge (whether or not the 21-day registration period has passed).

(b) A liquidator where a petition on which a winding-up order is made is presented after the creation of the charge (again whether inside or outside the 21-day registration period).

(c) Any person acquiring for value an interest in or right over the property charged after the creation of the charge (again whether inside or outside the 21-day registration period).

Section 399 is subject to s. 400 (late delivery of particulars), and by s. 415(3) references to registered particulars at any time are to such particulars and further particulars of the charge as have at that time been duly delivered for registration. In the next two sections we will consider late delivery and further particulars.

5.9.6 LATE DELIVERY

Under CA 1985, s. 400, if particulars of a registrable charge are delivered but delivered late, the charge is only void under s. 399 against an administrator or liquidator where the relevant petition is presented before the delivery of the particulars, or against a purchaser acquiring a right or interest before the delivery of the particulars.

However, late delivery will not prevent a charge being void against an administrator or liquidator where the company is unable to pay its debts at the date the particulars are delivered if the relevant petition is presented within either:

(a) the next two years if the charge is a floating charge created in favour of a person connected with the company; or

(b) the next year if the charge is a floating charge in favour of a person who is not connected with the company; or

(c) the next six months if the charge is not a floating charge.

5.9.7 FURTHER PARTICULARS

Where a charge has already been registered, the registered particulars may be varied or supplemented by further particulars at any time (CA 1985, s. 401). This may be necessary to remedy defective particulars (ss. 402 and 415(3)) or because the original terms of the charge have been altered by agreement.

5.9.8 INCOMPLETE AND INACCURATE PARTICULARS

Where registered particulars are incomplete or inaccurate, the charge is void against administrators, liquidators and purchasers for value in the same circumstances as under CA 1985, s. 399 (see **5.9.5**) to the extent that rights which should have been disclosed are not disclosed by the registered particulars (CA 1985, s. 402).

Where rights given by a charge would be void under s. 402, the chargee may apply to the court for an order that the charge is effective. Where rights under the charge would otherwise be void against an administrator or liquidator, the court can only make an order if it is satisfied either that:

(a) the omission is not likely to have misled materially any unsecured creditor; or

(b) no person has become an unsecured creditor while the particulars were inaccurate.

Where rights under the charge would otherwise be void against a purchaser for value, an order can be made only if the court is satisfied the purchaser did not rely on the defective particulars when making the acquisition.

5.9.9 EFFECTS OF NON-REGISTRATION ON THE COMPANY

An unregistered, registrable charge is valid against the company that created it. The chargee may exercise a power to sell the charged assets and may do so free from any interest or right arising from the charge having become void under the registration provisions of the CA 1985. The proceeds of such a sale are held by the chargee on trust (see CA 1985, s. 406). Further, where a charge becomes void to any extent for want of registration, the whole sum secured by the charge becomes payable forthwith on demand (CA 1985, s. 407).

5.10 Priorities

The basic rules for determining the priorities (i.e., which creditor gets paid first) between charges appear to be as follows:

(a) The charge created first is paid first.

(b) A floating charge does not become fixed until crystallisation, so a later fixed charge will have priority if created before crystallisation of an earlier floating charge.

(c) The rule in (b) does not apply, and an earlier floating charge will retain priority over a later fixed (or other) charge, if the floating charge contains a duly registered negative pledge (see **5.7**).

(d) Debentures issued in a series may, by their terms, rank *pari passu.*

(e) An unregistered charge may be void under CA 1985, s. 399 (see **5.9.5**).

(f) An unregistered charge will only be void as against a subsequent charge if complete particulars of the second charge are either duly registered within 21 days after it is created, or before full particulars are delivered of the first charge (CA 1985, s. 404(1)).

(g) An unregistered charge is not void against a later charge if the later charge is expressly subject to the first (CA 1985, s. 405(1)).

(h) Where a receiver is appointed on behalf of the holders of debentures secured by a floating charge, the receiver must pay unsecured preferential debts in priority to the sums secured by the debentures (IA 1986, s. 40).

5.11 Administrative Receivers

Debentures invariably contain terms that if the company defaults in the payment of the principal or interest the lender may appoint a receiver. A receiver's function is to realise the assets charged for the benefit of the debenture holders. Very often, the terms of debentures allow the debenture holders to appoint a receiver and manager. Such a person has wider powers, with the intention that the possibility of preserving the company as a going concern be explored. Where the receiver is appointed by or on behalf of the holders of debentures secured by floating charge over the whole or substantially the whole of the company's undertaking, the receiver is an administrative receiver and has the additional powers and responsibilities set out in IA 1986, ss. 42 to 49.

Receivership is considered in further detail at **8.2**.

SIX

DECISION MAKING

6.1 Introduction

The members together own the company and therefore have the right to decide how it should be run. They must, however, act in accordance with the articles of association that have been adopted for the company. Shareholders' decisions have to be made in shareholders' meetings, and the normal rule is that motions are carried by simple majority. Initially this will be by a show of hands of those present, though there is usually provision for taking a poll under which the normal rule is that each share carries one vote.

In addition, every private company must have at least one director, and every public company must have at least two directors. The articles provide for their appointment, removal, powers and procedure at board meetings.

6.2 Delegation of Powers to Directors

It is invariably recognised that it is impracticable for the members to meet regularly for the purpose of making decisions on the day-to-day running of commercial companies. The invariable practice is therefore for the articles to provide for the delegation of most decision-making powers to the company's directors.

Thus reg. 70 in Table A provides that the business of the company shall be managed by the directors, who may exercise all the powers of the company, subject to provisions of the Act, the memorandum and articles and any direction given to them by special resolution. Thus very wide management powers are delegated to the directors who must exercise those powers as a board (i.e. collectively) unless they are empowered to sub-delegate (as they are by reg. 72 of Table A).

As a general rule, once members have delegated powers to directors, the members cannot simultaneously exercise those powers (see *Automatic Self-Cleansing Filter Syndicate Co. Ltd* v *Cunninghame* [1906] 2 Ch 34, and *Salmon* v *Quin & Axtens Ltd* [1909] 1 Ch 311). This principle is the subject of much debate and can cause difficulties, particularly when the directors' and members' views as to how the company should be managed and the business run differ. Note, however, that this wide management power delegated to the directors under Table A, reg. 70, is subject to:

(a) *Provisions of the Act.* CA 1985 specifically requires certain (constitutional) powers to be exercised by the members, e.g. alteration of articles (s. 9), of the objects clause of the memorandum (s. 4), share capital (s. 121), and voluntary liquidation of the company (IA 1986, s. 84). In addition, CA 1985, s. 303, empowers the members to remove directors by ordinary resolution and this power can be exercised by the members even if it has also been delegated to the board.

(b) *Provisions of the memorandum and articles.* The articles themselves may specifically give powers to the members. Under Table A members appoint directors (reg. 73) and declare dividends (reg. 102) (although if you read these you will see that these are very qualified powers).

(c) *Direction by special resolution (1985 Table A).* In the 1948 Table A the general delegation article is reg. 80, which reads 'subject to such regulations being not inconsistent with the aforesaid regulations or provisions as may be prescribed by the company in general meeting'. This was held not to be effective in empowering the members to instruct the directors as to the manner in which they should exercise delegated powers. It is not known what the effect is of the new 1985 provision but the general academic view seems to be that the new Table A, reg. 70, does clarify the position and will enable members, without withdrawing the powers from the directors, to give directions by special resolution as to how they should be used.

The directors must exercise their powers within the constitution (limits set in the memorandum and articles), the law (provisions of CA 1985) and for the benefit of the company as a whole. The exercise of their powers outside these limitations is an abuse of their power and unauthorised, although the members may ratify most acts which are not illegal. However, even where the directors are exercising their powers within the limits set but contrary to the view of the majority of the members, the members may exercise some control over the directors by removing one or more of them (ordinary resolution: CA 1985, s. 303), altering the articles and removing the power (special resolution: CA 1985, s. 9) or (under 1985 Table A) by direction by special resolution. However any such removal, alteration or direction will not invalidate any prior act and will operate only as to future actions.

6.3 Directors' Duties

Directors are in a powerful position in that they will run the company and control its assets. In addition, most articles delegate the power to directors to call and set the agenda for general meetings. They therefore owe various duties including a duty of good faith to the company. These duties are considered in more detail in **Chapter 7**.

6.4 Board Meetings

The division of powers within a company will be laid down in its articles, but it is usual for the power to manage the company's business to be conferred on the directors. The number of directors to be engaged by the company will usually be dealt with in the articles (at least two by Table A, reg. 64), but the articles cannot provide for less than one director for private companies or two directors for public companies (CA 1985, s. 282).

Where a company has more than one director, the principle is that the directors must act collectively as a board, and their collective will is decided at board meetings. The articles will govern the basic procedure relating to board meetings, but it is usual for the articles to allow the directors to 'regulate their proceedings as they think fit' (see Table A, reg. 88). The degree of formality encountered in practice varies widely. However, subject to reasonable departures, directors can normally expect any established practice in their company to continue until a change is agreed.

6.4.1 CALLING MEETINGS

There may be regular weekly or monthly board meetings, or the next meeting may be fixed at the end of business at each meeting. Table A, reg. 88, allows any director to call a meeting.

6.4.2 NOTICE

Subject to the practice in the company, generally directors are entitled to advance notice of meetings. A director objecting to short notice must object at the meeting, failing which the courts will not interfere (*Browne* v *La Trinidad* (1887) 37 ChD 1, CA). Usually there is no requirement that notice be given in writing, and Table A, reg. 88, provides that it is unnecessary to give notice to directors who are absent from the United Kingdom.

6.4.3 QUORUM

A quorum is the minimum number of voting members who must be present for a meeting to be competent to transact business. Table A, reg. 89, allows this to be fixed by the directors, failing which it shall be two. *Hood Sailmakers Ltd* v *Axford* [1997] 1 WLR 625 deals with the situation where one of two directors purports to transact business while the other director is out of the country. Articles of association of many companies provide that it is unnecessary to give notice of board meetings to directors who are abroad (see **6.4.2** and Table A, reg. 88), and fix the quorum at two (see reg. 89). It was held that the quorum requirement takes precedence, with the result that a director cannot evade its requirements simply by waiting until the other director leaves the country. In companies where the quorum is two, business transacted at 'board meetings' by one director while the other director is abroad is therefore invalid.

6.4.4 CHAIRMAN

Table A, reg. 91, allows the directors to appoint one of their number to be the chairman of the board and to preside at meetings.

6.4.5 CONFLICT OF INTEREST

CA 1985, s. 317(1), imposes a duty on directors to disclose any interest they may have in proposed contracts to the board of directors. The articles then usually provide that affected directors cannot vote on such contracts (e.g., Table A, reg. 94). This is discussed further at **7.4.1**.

6.4.6 VOTING

Subject to the articles, proposals are carried by a simply majority. In the event of a tie, the articles may give the chairman a second casting vote (Table A, reg. 88).

The interrelation of a number of these rules can be illustrated by *Barron* v *Potter* [1914] 1 Ch 895. The company's articles of association laid down that the quorum for board meetings was two. The company had two directors, Barron and Potter. They fell out, and Barron refused to attend any meetings with Potter. One day, Potter intercepted Barron as Barron alighted from a train at Paddington Station. While they were walking along the platform Potter said, 'I want to see you, please'. Barron replied, 'I have nothing to say to you'. Potter then said, 'I formally propose that we add the Reverend Charles Herbert, Mr William George Walter Barnard and Mr John Tolehurst Musgrave as additional directors to the board of the British Seagumite Co. Ltd [the company]. Do you agree or object?'. Barron replied, 'I object and I object to say anything to you at all'. Potter concluded, 'In my capacity as chairman I give my casting vote in their favour and declare them duly elected. That is all I want to say. I thank you. Good day.'

Warrington J pointed out that it is of course possible to hold a board meeting anywhere and under any circumstances, provided those present consent to the proceedings being regarded as a board meeting. On the facts Potter knew all along that Barron would not discuss the company's affairs with him. Accordingly, it was held that although Potter was present at the 'board meeting' at Paddington Station, Barron was not. The meeting was therefore inquorate, and the new directors were not validly appointed.

6.4.7 MINUTES

CA 1985, s. 382, requires the company to record minutes of all proceedings at board meetings. If signed by the chairman at that meeting or the next, the minutes are evidence of the proceedings. The company owes no duty to disclose minutes of its board meetings to its shareholders. In contrast, shareholders are entitled to inspect the minutes of general meetings: see **6.5.8**.

6.5 Shareholders' Meetings

6.5.1 DECISION-MAKING BY SHAREHOLDERS

Shareholders must act collectively and decisions of members are those taken by voting on resolutions at properly convened general meetings. For this reason every company must have an annual general meeting (AGM) at least once a year at which the annual accounts and reports will be considered, auditors appointed, any elections of directors made and any dividend declared (CA 1985, s. 366). All other meetings are extraordinary general meetings (EGM). Most decisions are made by ordinary resolution (simple majority of those who attend and vote) or special resolution (a 75% majority of those who attend and vote) for those more important constitutional decisions such as alteration of the articles or objects clause of the memorandum.

The CA 1985, ss. 366–83, set out requirements for the calling and conduct of such meetings. The articles may add to these requirements. The general rule is that decisions made at meetings which are not properly called and conducted are invalid. However this is subject to exceptions:

(a) The acquiescence/assent principle. If all members knew of and acquiesced in a decision, they and the company are bound. Although this principle was originally subject to the necessity of showing that they had all met, this would appear no longer to be the case (*Re Duomatic Ltd* [1969] 2 Ch 365).

(b) The articles may provide (as Table A does in reg. 53) that a written resolution signed by all members entitled to notice and vote is as valid and effective as if a resolution had been passed in general meeting.

(c) The CA 1989 recognises that the formality of the decision-making process, as set out in CA 1985, may not be appropriate for small private companies, and relaxes the rules on meetings for private companies. Subject to certain exceptions, anything which could be done by resolution may be done without a meeting by resolution in writing signed by all members entitled to attend and vote at meetings (CA 1985, s. 381A, as inserted by CA 1989, s. 113).

(d) In addition, other formalities are dispensed with for private companies. Section 379A, as inserted by CA 1989, s. 116, allows a private company by elective resolution (basically one agreed to by all members) to dispense with some of the requirements of CA 1985 including:

(i) the holding of an AGM every year (CA 1985, s. 366A, as inserted by CA 1989, s. 115(2));

(ii) dispensing with the annual appointment of auditors (i.e. the auditors will continue in office from year to year: CA 1985, s. 386 as inserted by CA 1989, s. 119);

(iii) dispensing with the need for the annual accounts, directors' and auditors' reports to be laid before the general meeting every year (CA 1985, s. 252 as inserted by CA 1989, s. 116).

6.5.2 TYPES OF SHAREHOLDERS' MEETINGS

There are three types of shareholders' meetings:

(a) Annual general meetings. These must be held every calendar year, and no more than 15 months apart. All members may attend, and the purpose of such meetings is to inform members of the company's activities and performance, debate issues, and pass resolutions binding on the members and the company. However, information and debate are often non-existent, and annual general meetings are frequently over in a matter of minutes. The usual matters that fall to be considered at the annual general meeting include consideration of the accounts, fixing the auditors' remuneration, election or re-election of directors, declaring dividends and approval of the minutes of the last meeting.

(b) Extraordinary general meetings. This is any general meeting (open to all members) other than an annual general meeting.

(c) Class meetings. These are meetings of individual classes of shareholders. Attendance must be restricted to members of the class, unless there is unanimous consent that others may attend. The purpose of such meetings is to approve variations in class rights, compromises and arrangements under CA 1985, s. 425, affecting the class etc.

6.5.3 TYPES OF RESOLUTION

The type of resolution required to transact any particular item of business depends on the subject matter of the business. Special or extraordinary resolutions are required under various provisions of the CA 1985. Nothing turns on the type of meeting. Elective resolutions are only available to private companies.

(a) Special resolutions. These require at least a 75 per cent majority. At least 21 days' notice of the resolution must be given to the members.

(b) Extraordinary resolutions. Again require a 75 per cent majority. At least 14 days' notice must be given, unless it is to be passed at an annual general meeting, where the period of notice is at least 21 days.

(c) Ordinary resolutions. These are passed by a simple majority. No period of notice of the resolution is required by the CA 1985.

(d) Elective resolutions. These must be agreed by all members entitled to attend and vote (and will be lost if anyone abstains or is absent). At least 21 days' notice must be given.

6.5.4 NOTICE

Primary responsibility for calling meetings rests with the directors. The length of notice required for calling meetings is governed by the CA 1985, s. 369, in the following terms:

(1) A provision of a company's articles is void in so far as it provides for the calling of a meeting of the company (other than an adjourned meeting) by a shorter notice than—

(a) in the case of the annual general meeting, 21 days' notice in writing; and

(b) in the case of a meeting other than an annual general meeting or a meeting for the passing of a special resolution—

(i) 7 days' notice in writing in the case of an unlimited company, and

(ii) otherwise, 14 days' notice in writing.

(2) Save in so far as the articles of a company make other provision in that behalf (not being a provision avoided by subsection (1)), a meeting of the company (other than an adjourned meeting) may be called—

(a) in the case of the annual general meeting, by 21 days' notice in writing, and
(b) in the case of a meeting other than an annual general meeting or a meeting for the passing of a special resolution—
(i) by 7 days' notice in writing in the case of an unlimited company, and
(ii) otherwise, 14 days' notice in writing.
(3) Notwithstanding that a meeting is called by shorter notice than that specified in subsection (2) or in the company's articles (as the case may be), it is deemed to have been duly called if it is so agreed—
(a) in the case of a meeting called as the annual general meeting, by all the members entitled to attend and vote at it; and
(b) otherwise, by the requisite majority.
(4) The requisite majority for this purpose is a majority in number of the members having a right to attend and vote at the meeting, being a majority—
(a) together holding not less than 95 per cent in nominal value of the shares giving a right to attend and vote at the meeting, or
(b) in the case of a company not having a share capital, together representing not less than 95 per cent of the total voting rights at that meeting of all the members.

The effect of the section is that written notice must be given to every member of the company:

(a) at least 21 days in advance if it is an annual general meeting or if the meeting is called to pass any special resolutions; or

(b) at least 14 days in advance in other cases.

The above periods of notice may be waived by unanimous consent in the case of annual general meetings, or by a 95 per cent majority in other cases.

If the Act requires special notice of a resolution, the period of notice is 28 days (CA 1985, s. 379).

At common law the notice of a general meeting must give a fair, candid and reasonable explanation of the general nature of the business to be transacted (*Kaye* v *Croydon Tramways Co.* [1898] 1 Ch 358, CA). However, it is the directors who draw up the notice, and in practice they are able to exercise considerable control over the agenda of the meeting.

6.5.5 REQUISITIONING

It may be that the directors of the company are manipulating the agenda for their own purposes. In such a case, members representing 5 per cent of the voting rights (or 100 members each of whom has paid up at least £100) may requisition that all members be given notice of any resolution which may properly be moved at the next annual general meeting, and that members be circulated with a statement not exceeding 1,000 words on such resolution (CA 1985, s. 376).

Alternatively, it sometimes happens that shareholders are unhappy with the management of the company and wish to challenge the present directors, but due to the urgency of the situation, would be prejudiced if they had to wait for the next annual general meeting. It is therefore provided in CA 1985, s. 368, that members holding at least 10 per cent of the paid-up capital of the company may requisition an extraordinary general meeting. Section 368 provides as follows:

(1) The directors of a company shall, on a members' requisition, forthwith proceed duly to convene an extraordinary general meeting of the company.
This applies notwithstanding anything in the company's articles.
(2) A members' requisition is a requisition of—
(a) members of the company holding at the date of the deposit of the requisition not less than one-tenth of such of the paid-up capital of the company as at that date carries the right of voting at general meetings of the company; or

(b) in the case of a company not having a share capital, members of it representing not less than one-tenth of the total voting rights of all the members having at the date of deposit of the requisition a right to vote at general meetings.

(3) The requisition must state the objects of the meeting and must be signed by the requisitionists and deposited at the registered office of the company, and may consist of several documents in like form each signed by one or more requisitionists.

(4) If the directors do not within 21 days from the date of the deposit of the requisition proceed duly to convene a meeting, the requisitionists, or any of them representing more than one half of the total voting rights of all of them, may themselves convene a meeting, but any meeting so convened shall not be held after the expiration of 3 months from that date.

(5) A meeting convened under this section by requisitionists shall be convened in the same manner, as nearly as possible, as that in which meetings are to be convened by directors.

(6) Any reasonable expenses incurred by the requisitionists by reason of the failure of the directors duly to convene a meeting shall be repaid to the requisitionists by the company, and any sum so repaid shall be retained by the company out of any sums due or to become due from the company by way of fees or other remuneration in respect of their services to such of the directors as were in default.

(7) In the case of a meeting at which a resolution is to be proposed as a special resolution, the directors are deemed not to have duly convened the meeting if they do not give the notice required for special resolutions by section 378(2).

(8) The directors are deemed not to have duly convened a meeting if they convene a meeting for a date more than 28 days after the date of the notice convening the meeting.

6.5.6 PROXIES

A proxy is a person appointed by a member to attend a meeting in place of the member. The word is also used to describe the document making the appointment.

The governing section is CA 1985, s. 372, which provides:

(1) Any member of a company entitled to attend and vote at a meeting of it is entitled to appoint another person (whether a member or not) as his proxy to attend and vote instead of him; and in the case of a private company a proxy appointed to attend and vote instead of a member has also the same right as the member to speak at the meeting.

(2) But, unless the articles otherwise provide—

(a) subsection (1) does not apply in the case of a company not having a share capital; and

(b) a member of a private company is not entitled to appoint more than one proxy to attend on the same occasion; and

(c) a proxy is not entitled to vote except on a poll.

(3) In the case of a company having a share capital, in every notice calling a meeting of the company there shall appear with reasonable prominence a statement that a member entitled to attend and vote is entitled to appoint a proxy or, where that is allowed, one or more proxies to attend and vote instead of him, and that a proxy need not also be a member.

(4) If default is made in complying with subsection (3) as respects any meeting, every officer of the company who is in default is liable to a fine.

(5) A provision contained in a company's articles is void in so far as it would have the effect of requiring the instrument appointing a proxy, or any other document necessary to show the validity of, or otherwise relating to, the appointment of a proxy, to be received by the company or any other person more than 48 hours before a meeting or adjourned meeting in order that the appointment may be effective.

(6) If for the purpose of any meeting of a company invitations to appoint as proxy a person or one of a number of persons specified in the invitations are issued at the company's expense to some only of the members entitled to be sent a notice of the meeting and to vote at it by proxy, then every officer of the company who knowingly and wilfully authorises or permits their issue in that manner is liable to a fine.

However, an officer is not so liable by reason only of the issue to a member at his request in writing of a form of appointment naming the proxy, or of a list of persons willing to act as proxy, if the form or list is available on request in writing to every member entitled to vote at the meeting by proxy.

(7) This section applies to meetings of any class of members of a company as it applies to general meetings of the company.

All notices calling meetings must contain a prominent notice stating that members may appoint proxies. Proxy forms are often incorporated into notices calling meetings. A member may give a proxy complete discretion over how to use the member's votes, or may give specific instructions on individual resolutions. Usually the company's articles will restrict proxies to voting on a poll, but proxies may join in a demand for a poll.

Usually, proxy forms are required by the articles to be received by the company in advance of the meeting. If this period of advance notice were particularly long, few members could avail themselves of the procedure. Accordingly, articles requiring proxy forms to be lodged more than 48 hours in advance of the meeting are void.

6.5.7 VOTING

In the first instance, votes are usually taken on a show of hands. Each member attending in person has one vote, regardless of the number of shares each holds. This can produce a distorted picture, and a poll may be demanded. On a poll, subject to the articles, each share carries one vote.

The articles will usually prescribe how a poll may be demanded. Table A allows, *inter alia,* the chairman of the meeting or at least two members to demand a poll. Different articles may make different provision, but cannot deny a poll if demanded by at least five members or members representing at least 10 per cent of the voting rights in the company (CA 1985, s. 373).

In the event of a tie, the articles may (as in Table A, reg. 50) give the chairman an additional, casting vote.

Under Table A, reg. 47, on a show of hands, the chairman's declaration that a resolution has been carried, carried by a particular majority, or lost, when entered in the minutes, is conclusive proof of the fact. By reg. 49 on a poll the chairman is given power to appoint scrutineers and to fix a time and place for declaring the result.

6.5.8 MINUTES

Books containing minutes of proceedings at general meetings must be kept, and copies made available to members (CA 1985, ss. 382 and 383).

6.5.9 PRIVATE COMPANIES

A private company may, by elective resolution (see **6.5.3**) dispense with holding annual general meetings. The election may be revoked by ordinary resolution (see CA 1985, ss. 366A and 379A).

A private company may also pass written resolutions without holding a meeting, provided the resolution is signed by all the members who would be entitled to vote (CA 1985, s. 381A). A public company can achieve a similar result by adopting a regulation on the lines of Table A, reg. 53.

6.6 Deadlock

It happens from time to time that companies are unable to hold effective meetings. This may occur, for example, where a company's articles of association require meetings (whether of the directors or shareholders) to have a quorum of at least two persons; the company has only two directors and shareholders; and one of them refuses to attend meetings. The same thing may happen through the death or disappearance of some of the original members. The problem should not arise where, through differing rules on quorums or differing membership, it is possible to have effective board or shareholders' meetings, as further shares may be issued or directors appointed as appropriate.

Where a company is truly unable to hold effective meetings, an application may be made to the court under the CA 1985, s. 371. This section provides:

> *(1) If for any reason it is impracticable to call a meeting of a company in any manner in which meetings of that company may be called, or to conduct the meeting in manner prescribed by the articles or this Act, the court may, either of its own motion or on the application—*
>
> *(a) of any director of the company, or*
>
> *(b) of any member of the company who would be entitled to vote at the meeting, order a meeting to be called, held and conducted in any manner the court thinks fit.*
>
> *(2) Where such an order is made, the court may give such ancillary or consequential directions as it thinks expedient; and these may include a direction that one member of the company present in person or by proxy be deemed to constitute a meeting.*
>
> *(3) A meeting called, held and conducted in accordance with an order under subsection (1) is deemed for all purposes a meeting of the company duly called, held and conducted.*

This section catches situations like that in *Barron* v *Potter* [1914] 1 Ch 895, discussed at **6.4.6** above. The section empowers the court to order a company meeting for the purpose of passing resolutions, e.g. to appoint new directors, and to direct that if the applicant alone attends, the meeting shall nevertheless be deemed to constitute a 'meeting'.

In *Re Sticky Fingers Restaurant Ltd* [1991] BCC 754, the company had two directors who also held all its issued shares (66 and 34 each). The minority shareholder was complaining of unfair prejudice (for which, see **Chapter 13**) and had issued a petition against the majority shareholder. The majority shareholder wanted to appoint extra directors, but the minority shareholder, who feared he would lose his directorship, refused to attend meetings, which were ineffective through lack of a quorum. It takes some time for unfair prejudice petitions to be dealt with, so the court made an order under the CA 1985, s. 371 on the application of the majority shareholder, adding provisos that any new directors appointed would first undertake pending the resolution of the petition:

(a) not to vote to dismiss the minority shareholder from his directorship; and

(b) not to vote for any alteration in the constitution or capital of the company.

In *Harman* v *BML Group Ltd* [1994] 1 WLR 893, on the other hand, the Court of Appeal refused to make an order under s. 371 in a deadlocked company. An unfair prejudice petition was pending. The court accepted that that did not preclude the making of an order under s. 371, but decided its existence was a relevant factor to be taken into account. Dillon LJ said it was not the court's function to require cross-undertakings from the parties to ensure the company's business was conducted along sensible lines. That was a matter for the company's advisers. However, the most important factor was that the effect of the proposed s. 371 order was to override the objecting shareholder's class rights which enabled him to exercise a right of veto, which was held to be an improper use of s. 371.

For similar reasons the application under s. 371 was refused in *Ross* v *Telford* [1998] 1 BCLC 82, CA. Mr Ross, who was one of two 50 per cent shareholders in a company called Linkside, wanted to hold a meeting to ratify proceedings brought by Linkside against a bank. The second shareholder was another limited liability company, PLB, whose shares were held equally by Mr Ross and Mrs Telford. In effect, therefore, Mr

Ross held 75 per cent of the shares in Linkside. However, Mr Ross and Mrs Telford had previously been married to each other, and in ancillary relief proceedings they had been awarded equal beneficial interests in Linkside. Linkside's articles provided for a quorum of two, and in the absence of someone to represent PLB it was impossible to have effective meetings. It was held that s. 371 is a procedural section, and is not designed to shift the balance of power between equal shareholders, who must be taken to have agreed that either of them could block decisions by non-attendance. Nourse LJ said that in these circumstances there is no jurisdiction to make an order under s. 371, alternatively, the court would exercise its discretion against making an order. It is difficult to say whether this decision will apply to another common situation where a company has two shareholders with unequal numbers of shares. It could be said that they too must be taken to have agreed that even the minority shareholder could block future decision-making simply by non-attendance. On the other hand, this assumption may be taken as displaced by the fact that one of the shareholders has by agreement been given a majority holding.

6.7 Members' Action against Directors

If the members wish to take action against the directors they must resolve to do so in the name of the company at a general meeting (either AGM or EGM). However, most articles will delegate the power to call meetings and set the agenda to the directors. The CA 1985 therefore gives members the statutory right to require the directors to call an EGM (s. 368) or to put a resolution to an AGM (s. 376) (see **6.5.5**).

However, if a minority of shareholders wish to take action against the directors, even if they have the requisite shareholding to require an EGM to be called or a resolution put to an AGM, they must still have sufficient votes to carry the resolution (simple majority for ordinary resolution; 75% majority for special resolution). Further, the members may ratify, by majority vote, most breaches of duty. However, they may wish to sue the director(s) for breach. Thus if the majority vote against the requisitionists, the general rule is that no further action is possible. (For shareholder protection see **Chapters 11** to **13**.)

6.8 Appointment and Removal of Directors

Shareholders' primary function in the management of their companies is in hiring and firing the directors. This is buttressed by CA 1985, s. 303:

> *(1) A company may by ordinary resolution remove a director before the expiration of his period of office, notwithstanding anything in its articles or in any agreement between it and him.*
>
> *(2) Special notice is required of a resolution to remove a director under this section or to appoint somebody instead of a director so removed at the meeting at which he is removed. . . .*
>
> *(5) This section is not to be taken as depriving a person removed under it of compensation or damages payable to him in respect of the termination of his appointment as director or of any appointment terminating with that as director, or as derogating from any power to remove a director which may exist apart from this section.*

Special notice of the resolution is required by s. 303(2), which means that notice of the intention to move it must be given to the company at least 28 days before the meeting (CA 1985, s. 379(1)).

Where notice is given of a proposed resolution for removal under s. 303(2), the director must be informed (s. 304(1)) and given an opportunity to protest. Section 304(1), (2) provide:

(1) On receipt of notice of an intended resolution to remove a director under section 303, the company shall forthwith send a copy of the notice to the director concerned; and he (whether or not a member of the company) is entitled to be heard on the resolution at the meeting.

(2) Where notice is given of an intended resolution to remove a director under that section, and the director concerned makes with respect to it representations in writing to the company (not exceeding a reasonable length) and requests their notification to members of the company, the company shall, unless the representations are received by it too late for it to do so—

(a) in any notice of the resolution given to members of the company state the fact of the representations having been made; and

(b) send a copy of the representations to every member of the company to whom notice of the meeting is sent (whether before or after receipt of the representations by the company).

There is no need to circularise defamatory representations. Instead, s. 304(4) provides that an application can be made to the court for an order declaring that there is no need to send the representations out.

6.9 Exercise 2

RE: AT YOUR SERVICE LIMITED

INSTRUCTIONS TO COUNSEL

Counsel is instructed on behalf of Miss Catherine Anne Barton, of 6 University Mews, Cambridge, CB4 8RT, a director of and shareholder in the above-named company. The company was incorporated on 14th September 1984. Its capital consists of 100 fully paid-up £1 ordinary shares. 60 are held by Miss Barton, and 40 are held by Miss Amanda Louise Simpson, who is also the second director and company secretary. Since its incorporation the company has carried on the business run by Miss Barton and Miss Simpson as a recruitment agency. This business was set up as a joint venture, and, until July 1999 the two women were the only people employed by the company.

The company trades from its registered office at 53 College Road, Cambridge, CB1 4LN, and its clients are drawn from the area around Cambridge. In the spring of this year matters turned sour between the two women over questions of how the business should be run. In July Miss Simpson orally informed our client that she would be leaving at the end of the week and would be starting her own business in Lincoln. Since that time Miss Simpson has severed all links with the company, and has not visited its premises or communicated with our client in any way. It is understood that Miss Simpson now devotes herself full-time to her new business in Lincoln.

It has been quite impossible for Miss Barton to run the business single-handed, and she has taken on a Miss Deborah Welsh of 12 Parkside Road, Cambridge, CB4 3LR to perform the duties previously undertaken by Miss Simpson. Ideally, it is desired that Miss Simpson should be replaced as a director by Miss Welsh. However, subject to Counsel's advice, on a practical level this cannot be done. The company does have registered articles, but they are silent on the question of meetings etc. Under Table A of the 1948 Act two people are required to form a valid meeting (both of directors and shareholders), and as Miss Simpson will have nothing to do with the company at present meetings to elect new directors cannot be held. Relevant extracts from Table A are enclosed.

Counsel is therefore asked to advise on any appropriate steps to be taken and to draft any necessary documents.

Counsel is instructed to advise and draft documents.

Relevant regulations from Table A (Companies Act 1948)

General Meetings

49. The directors may, whenever they think fit, convene an extraordinary general meeting, and extraordinary general meetings shall also be convened on such requisition, or, in default, may be convened by such requisitionists, as provided by Section 132 of the Act. If at any time there are not within the United Kingdom sufficient directors capable of acting to form a quorum, any director or any two members of the company may convene an extraordinary general meeting in the same manner as nearly as possible as that in which meetings may be convened by the directors.

Notice of General Meetings

50. An annual general meeting and a meeting called for the passing of a special resolution shall be called by twenty-one days' notice in writing at the least, and a meeting of the company other than an annual general meeting or a meeting for the passing of a special resolution shall be called by fourteen days' notice in writing at the least. The notice shall be exclusive of the day on which it is served or deemed to be served and of the day for which it is given, and shall specify the place, the day and the hour of meeting and, in case of special business, the general nature of that business, and shall be given, in manner hereinafter mentioned or in such other manner, if any, as may be prescribed by the company in general meeting, to such persons as are, under the regulations of the company, entitled to receive such notices from the company;

Provided that a meeting of the company shall, notwithstanding that it is called by shorter notice than that specified in this regulation, be deemed to have been duly called if it is so agreed—

(a) in the case of a meeting called as the annual general meeting, by all the members entitled to attend and vote thereat; and
(b) in the case of any other meeting, by a majority in number of the members having a right to attend and vote at the meeting, being a majority together holding not less than 95 per cent in nominal value of the shares giving that right.

Proceedings at General Meetings

53. No business shall be transacted at any general meeting unless a quorum of members is present at the time when the meeting proceeds to business; save as herein otherwise provided two members present in person or by proxy shall be a quorum.

68. The instrument appointing a proxy shall be in writing under the hand of the appointer or of his attorney duly authorised in writing, or, if the appointer is a corporation, either under seal, or under the hand of an officer or attorney duly authorised. A proxy need not be a member of the company.

69. The instrument appointing a proxy and the power of attorney or other authority, if any, under which it is signed or a notarially certified copy of that power or authority shall be deposited at the registered office of the company or at such other place within the United Kingdom as is specified for that purpose in the notice convening the meeting, not less than 48 hours before the time for holding the meeting or adjourned meeting, at which the person named in the instrument proposes to vote, or, in the case of a poll, not less than 24 hours before the time appointed for the taking of the poll, and in default the instrument of proxy shall not be treated as valid.

Proceedings of Directors

98. The directors may meet together for the despatch of business, adjourn, and otherwise regulate their meetings, as they think fit. Questions arising at any meeting shall be decided by a majority of votes. In case of an equality of votes, the chairman shall have a second or casting vote. A director may, and the secretary on the requisition of a director shall, at any time summon a meeting of the directors. It shall not be necessary to give notice of a meeting of directors to any director for the time being absent from the United Kingdom.

99. The quorum necessary for the transaction of the business of the directors may be fixed by the directors, and unless so fixed shall be two.

SEVEN

DIRECTORS

7.1 Introduction

7.1.1 DEFINITION

Every private company must have at least one director and every public company at least two (CA 1985, s. 282). Directors are usually in a powerful position as wide management powers are generally delegated to them by the articles. This division of power between members and directors was discussed at **6.2**. This chapter will cover the appointment of directors in outline, their position and duties to the company, action which can be taken if they are in breach of their duties, and disqualification under the Company Directors Disqualification Act 1986.

7.1.2 WHO IS A DIRECTOR?

There is no comprehensive definition of a director. CA 1985, s. 741(1), states that it 'includes any person occupying the position of director, by whatever name called'. The test is therefore one of function not title, and the terms 'manager', 'governor' etc. may sometimes be used. On the other hand the fact that an employee is called the marketing director will not make that person a director in law. The directors of a company will be those people who take part in board meetings of the company. In addition the Companies Act 1985 applies certain provisions to any person not actually appointed as a director but who is a 'shadow director'. This is defined in CA 1985, s. 741(2), as 'a person in accordance with whose directions or instructions the directors of the company are accustomed to act'. However, a person is not deemed to be a shadow director by reason only that the directors act on advice given by him in a professional capacity. It is not clear exactly who may be caught by the 'shadow director' provision. It would appear from the decision in *Re Unisys Group Ltd (No. 2)* [1994] BCC 166 to require a 'regular course of conduct' by the board or governing majority of it in accordance with such directions. In *Re a Company (No. 005009 of 1987)* [1989] BCLC 13 it was said that it was arguable that where a company was managed in accordance with a bank's instructions to avoid the appointment of an administrative receiver by the bank, the bank was acting as a shadow director.

7.1.3 APPOINTMENT

The documents delivered to the registrar of companies on incorporation must include particulars of first directors and their signed consent to act (CA 1985, s. 10). These people will be named in the articles or appointed by the subscribers. Subsequent appointment is regulated by the articles, which usually follow Table A. This provides that at each AGM the third who have been in the office longest retire but are eligible for re-election (regs 73 and 74). A managing director does not retire by rotation (reg. 84). The board have power to appoint new directors to fill a vacancy or as additional directors but such directors retire at the next AGM (although they are also eligible for re-election (reg. 79)). Small private companies' articles may provide that the directors remain in office indefinitely.

Generally anyone (including a company), can be a director, and a director need not be a member of the company unless the articles contain a share qualification clause (now rare). A person over 70 years of age cannot be a director of a public company unless the articles specifically allow it or special notice under CA 1985, s. 379, of the director's age was given before the meeting which appointed him or her (CA 1985, s. 293).

7.1.4 STATUS OF DIRECTORS

A director is an officer of the company (CA 1985, s. 744) and may also be an employee, e.g., if he or she also acts as managing director. As an officer the director may be paid director's fees (in Table A, reg. 82, these are set by the company by ordinary resolution). As an employee, a director will have a contract of service like any other employee. The articles usually provide (Table A, reg. 84) that the appointment as employee and the terms of the service contract are fixed by the board. Although the director concerned will not count in the quorum nor be eligible to vote on his or her own service contract (see **7.4.1**) additional protection is given to prevent abuse by the board by CA 1985, s. 319. This provides that a company cannot include a term in the contract whereby the director's employment is or may be continued for a period of more than five years during which it cannot be terminated by notice by the company unless the contract is first approved by ordinary resolution in general meeting. A copy of the proposed agreement must be available for 15 days before the meeting and at the meeting. Failure to obtain the required agreement results in the service contract being deemed to contain a term enabling the company to terminate on reasonable notice. (Note CA 1985, s. 319, also applies to contracts for services of directors.) The company must also keep a copy of the contracts of service of directors at its registered office or other appropriate place (CA 1985, s. 318).

7.2 Directors as Agents of the Company

The company cannot act on its own; it must act through the agency of humans. Employees will be agents for the company. In addition, the directors who act on the company's behalf will do so as agents of the company and the company will be bound by acts for which the agent has actual or apparent authority.

Actual authority was defined in *Freeman & Lockyer* v *Buckhurst Park Properties (Mangal) Ltd* [1964] 2 QB 48 as 'a legal relationship between principal and agent created by a consensual agreement to which they alone are parties'. Such actual authority may be express or implied:

(a) Express, if given by express words e.g. when a board of directors authorises a director to contract on behalf of the company.

(b) Implied, from the conduct of the parties e.g. when a board appoints a managing director the implication is that he or she may do all things which fall within the scope of that office, see *Hely-Hutchinson* v *Brayhead Ltd* [1968] 1 QB 549.

Apparent authority is the authority which is perceived by others based on a representation of such authority by someone who has actual authority and which is relied on, see again *Freeman* (above). Generally there must be no limitation in the memorandum or articles forbidding such delegation but even if there is, s. 35A would operate in favour of the third party (see below). A managing director will have fairly extensive apparent authority. However, the scope of the apparent authority of a single director (who is not the managing director) is probably fairly limited. The principal role of a director is to attend board meetings and vote on resolutions (i.e. be part of the decision-making process). The exact scope of such a director's authority to act as agent of the company is open to question. One view is that even an executive director is not invested with any apparent authority to act on the company's behalf (see *George Whitechurch Ltd* v *Cavanagh* [1902] AC 117). This may have changed with time and the position may now be that while a non-executive director will have no apparent authority to bind the company, an executive director will have apparent authority to transact business on behalf of the company within a specific area; e.g. the apparent authority of a finance director would be restricted to matters of finance.

CA 1985, s. 35A, as inserted by CA 1989, s. 108 (in force from 4 February 1991) provides:

> *(1) In favour of a person dealing with a company in good faith, the power of the board of directors to bind the company, or authorise others to do so, shall be deemed to be free of any limitations under the company's constitution.*
> *(2) For this purpose—*
> *(a) a person 'deals with' a company if he is party to any transaction or other act to which the company is a party;*
> *(b) a person shall not be regarded as acting in bad faith by reason only of his knowing that an act is beyond the powers of the directors under the company's constitution; and*
> *(c) a person shall be presumed to have acted in good faith unless the contrary is proved.*
> *(3) . . .*
> *(4) Subsection (1) does not affect any right of a member of the company to bring proceedings to restrain the doing of an act which is beyond the powers of the directors; but no such proceedings shall lie in respect of an act to be done in fulfilment of a legal obligation arising from a previous act of the company.*
> *(5) Nor does that subsection affect any liability incurred by the directors, or any other person, by reason of the directors exceeding their powers.*
> *(6) . . . [deals with charities]. . . ; and section 322A below (invalidity of certain transactions to which directors or their associates are parties) has effect notwithstanding this section.*

CA 1985, s. 35B, as inserted by CA 1989, s. 108, provides that a party to a transaction with a company is not bound to enquire as to whether it is permitted by the company's memorandum, or as to any limitation on the powers of the board of directors to bind the company or authorise others to do so.

Note that both ss. 35A and 35B use the word 'directors' (i.e. plural) and thus may not protect an outsider where a single director acts on behalf of the company without actual or apparent authority.

Finally, one should be aware of CA 1985, s. 285, which provides:

> *The acts of a director or manager are valid notwithstanding any defect that may afterwards be discovered in his appointment or qualification.*

This will not validate acts of a director where there was no appointment at all (as opposed to a defective one) — *Morris* v *Kanssen* [1946] AC 459.

It is important to note that agency is not confined to directors. A company secretary has apparent authority to bind the company to contracts relating to the administrative affairs of the company: *Panorama Developments (Guildford) Ltd* v *Fidelis Furnishing Fabrics Ltd* [1971] 2 QB 711.

7.3 Directors' Duties: General

7.3.1 TO WHOM OWED

Directors in practice control the company, and its success or failure largely depends on them. They are fiduciaries and owe duties of good faith. There are potentially a number of individuals or bodies to whom the directors might owe duties — the company, the members, the employees, the creditors. However, the general rule is that the directors owe their duties to the company as a whole. This has traditionally been used to mean the shareholders as a collective body including present and future shareholders. CA 1985, s. 309, provides that the matters to which the directors are to have regard include the interests of the company's employees in general, as well as the interest of its members. However, it continues by stating that the duty is owed to the company and the company alone and is enforceable in the same way as any other fiduciary duty owed to a company by its directors. The traditional view is that directors owe no general duty to individual members (*Percival* v *Wright* [1902] 2 Ch 421) although there may be circumstances which do give rise to such a duty, e.g., where they are authorised to act as agents for particular shareholders (*Allen* v *Hyatt* (1914) 30 TLR 444). There are a number of cases on the duty of directors to shareholders, largely dealing with advising on takeover bids (see *Gething* v *Kilner* [1972] 1 WLR 337; *Heron International Ltd* v *Lord Grade* [1983] BCLC 244; *Dawson International plc* v *Coats Patons plc* (1989) 5 BCC 405). The role of employees in companies is beginning to be recognised (CA 1985, s. 309) and will, with European influence, become greater but no duty is owed to individual employees. The law has as yet not recognised any duty owed by directors to creditors (*Multinational Gas & Petrochemical Co.* v *Multinational Gas & Petrochemical Services Ltd* [1983] Ch 258). However, recent decisions show that creditors' interests are relevant particularly in cases of insolvency (see *Lonrho Ltd* v *Shell Petroleum Co. Ltd* [1980] 1 WLR 627; *Winkworth* v *Edward Baron Development Co. Ltd* [1986] 1 WLR 1512 and *Brady* v *Brady* [1989] AC 755). Note also IA 1986, s. 214 (wrongful trading) and CDDA 1986 (see **7.7.3**).

7.3.2 ACT BONA FIDE IN INTERESTS OF COMPANY AS A WHOLE

Directors must act bona fide in the interests of the company as a whole. The test is subjective, i.e., provided they act lawfully and bona fide in what they consider to be the interests of the company and not for a collateral purpose the court will not interfere. The lack of any reasonable ground for being a benefit to the company may be sufficient for the court to interfere and find lack of good faith (*Shuttleworth* v *Cox Brothers & Co. (Maidenhead) Ltd* [1927] 2 KB 9). This is an area on which there is a vast amount of case law.

7.3.3 EXERCISE POWERS FOR PROPER PURPOSE

Directors must exercise their powers for proper purposes. The directors must decide how to exercise their powers but may only do so for the purposes for which the powers were given. Thus they must exercise their powers to achieve the objects of the company as stated in the memorandum of association (see *Rolled Steel Products (Holdings) Ltd* v *British Steel Corporation* [1982] Ch 478). Many of the cases on the improper use of powers are on the issue of shares, in particular where directors issue shares to prevent a takeover bid which might oust them from power. The traditional view has been that shares are issued to raise capital and any other purpose is a collateral purpose. Where the power may be exercised for a variety of reasons it is the substantial or dominant purpose which is important (*Howard Smith Ltd* v *Ampol Petroleum Ltd* [1974] AC 821). Where a power is used for a collateral or improper purpose the directors are acting in an unauthorised manner and the company may not be bound. Note, however, the general agency rules and CA 1985, s. 35A, by which the company may be bound (see **7.2**). Even where the company is bound, however, the directors will have acted in breach of their duty to the company and will be liable to it. The company may, however, generally ratify the directors' actions (*Bamford* v *Bamford* [1970] Ch 212). Such ratification will not be effective if there is a fraud on the minority (see **11.5.3.4**) or possibly where the breach of duty prejudices the interest of creditors when the company is insolvent (*West Mercia Safetywear Ltd* v *Dodd* (1987) 4 BCC 30).

7.4 Conflict of Interest

Directors must not put themselves in a position where their personal interests conflict with their duty to the company. This 'no conflict of interest' rule manifests itself in a number of sub-rules.

7.4.1 CONTRACTS WITH THE COMPANY

Where a director enters into a contract with the company, it is voidable by the company even where it was made on fair terms after full disclosure (*Aberdeen Railway Co.* v

Blaikie Brothers (1854) 1 Macq 461). However, the right to rescind may be lost by delay, affirmation or the intervention of third-party interests. In addition the members may ratify the contract after full disclosure, such ratification being by ordinary resolution in general meeting, at which the director concerned may vote as a member (*North-West Transportation Co. Ltd* v *Beatty* (1887) 12 App Cas 589).

The strict rule may be relaxed by the articles. Table A, reg. 85, allows a director to have a service contract with the company and Table A, reg. 86, allows a director who has disclosed the nature and extent of any material interest to be a party or otherwise interested in transactions generally with the company and to retain any benefit derived. General notice may be given, e.g., where a director is a partner in a firm which deals with the company on a regular basis. The director concerned may not be counted in the quorum nor vote on the transaction except in very limited circumstances (see regs 94 and 95). CA 1985, s. 317, imposes a statutory duty on directors in any event to declare the nature of any interest at the first meeting at which the contract is proposed or when the director's interest first arose (if later). Again general notice will suffice. (However, disclosure must be to the board and not a committee of the board: *Guinness plc* v *Saunders* [1988] BCLC 43.) Failure to comply with this section renders the director liable to a fine.

7.4.2 SUBSTANTIAL PROPERTY TRANSACTIONS

CA 1985, s. 320, provides that, subject to certain exceptions, a company shall not enter into an arrangement whereby a director of the company or its holding company or a person connected with such director, acquires or is to acquire one or more non-cash assets of the requisite value from the company or the company acquires or is to acquire such non-cash asset(s) from a director or connected person unless the arrangement is first approved by a resolution of the company in general meeting (and of the holding company where relevant). A non-cash asset is of the requisite value if at the time the arrangement is entered into its value is not less than £2,000 and exceeds the lesser of £100,000 or 10 per cent of the company's net assets in the last annual accounts. Connected persons are defined in CA 1985, s. 346, to include spouses, children, companies where the directors control 20 per cent of the votes or more, partners etc.

The exceptions in CA 1985, s. 321, principally permit intragroup transactions, distributions on winding up and to directors in their capacity as members.

If the resolution is not obtained the transaction is voidable by the company unless restitution is no longer possible, the company has been indemnified for loss or damage suffered, rights acquired bona fide for value without actual notice of the contravention would be affected, or the arrangement is within a reasonable period affirmed by the company in general meeting. In addition the director or connected person and any director who authorised the arrangement is liable to account for any gain or indemnify the company for any loss or damage (CA 1985, s. 322). For a case on the measure of the indemnity, see *Re Duckwari plc (No. 3)* (1999) 1 BCLC 168.

7.4.3 LOANS, QUASI-LOANS AND CREDIT TRANSACTIONS

All companies are prohibited from making a loan, entering into a guarantee or providing security for a loan to a director of the company or its holding company (CA 1985, s. 330). The section contains further prohibitions on relevant companies (public companies or private companies which are part of a group containing a public company). They are prohibited from:

(a) Making a loan or guaranteeing or providing security for a loan to a connected person (defined as for substantial property transactions, **7.4.2**).

(b) Making a quasi-loan (e.g., agreeing to pay the director's credit card on condition that the director will later repay the company) or guaranteeing or providing security for a quasi-loan to a director or connected person.

(c) Entering into a credit transaction (e.g., hire-purchase or conditional sale) or guaranteeing or providing security for a credit transaction to a director or connected person.

The exceptions to the above prohibitions are:

(a) A loan to a director not exceeding £5,000 (s. 334).

(b) Loans to directors to enable them to perform their duties provided they have prior approval in general meeting or are made on condition that if no approval is given they are repaid within six months of the next AGM (the maximum for relevant companies under this exception is £20,000) (s. 337).

(c) Loans and quasi-loans by moneylending companies, provided the loan was made in the ordinary course of business and not on more favourable terms than to customers (maximum of £100,000 for non-bank companies). House purchase loans may be on more favourable terms if these are also given to employees (s. 338).

(d) Small short-term quasi-loans to directors (maximum £5,000 for two months) (s. 332).

(e) Credit transactions for £10,000 or less or made in the ordinary course of business and not on more favourable terms than to customers (s. 335).

If a company contravenes the prohibitions in CA 1985, s. 330, the arrangement is voidable by the company unless restitution is no longer possible, the company has been indemnified for any loss suffered or rights acquired by a bona fide purchaser for value without notice would be affected. The company cannot ratify the transaction. In addition the director or connected person and any director who authorised the transaction is liable to account for any gain or indemnify the company for any loss or damage (CA 1985, s. 341). In addition, in the case of a relevant company, the company, the directors who authorised the transaction and any person who procured it knowing or reasonably believing it to contravene the provisions are guilty of an offence (CA 1985, s. 342). (Note that all loans, quasi-loans or credit transactions with directors must be disclosed in the company's annual accounts.)

7.4.4 PROFITS OBTAINED FROM POSITION AS DIRECTOR

Directors as fiduciaries are not allowed to profit from their position and will hold any such profit on trust for the company. They will be so liable where they actively divert opportunities away from the company to themselves (*Cook* v *Deeks* [1916] 1 AC 554 — contract so diverted) or even where they have acted honestly and openly and the benefit is not diverted from the company (*Regal (Hastings) Ltd* v *Gulliver* [1967] 2 AC 134 — directors made a profit on shares which the company was not in a position to take up and they were held liable to account to the company even though they had acted bona fide throughout). The actual limits on the duty to account are not clear, particularly where a former director pursues opportunities after leaving the company or the company (through the board) decides not to pursue the opportunity (see *Industrial Development Consultants Ltd* v *Cooley* [1972] 1 WLR 443 and *Island Export Finance Ltd* v *Umunna* [1986] BCLC 460).

However, the company may ratify the transaction and permit the director to retain the profit by unanimous consent of all the members or possibly by ordinary resolution in general meeting. In *Regal (Hastings) Ltd* v *Gulliver* it was stated that the directors could have protected themselves by obtaining a resolution in general meeting. However, in *Cook* v *Deeks* such attempted ratification was held to be ineffective. The standard explanation to reconcile these two cases is that in *Cook* v *Deeks* the directors were diverting opportunities away from the company and not acting bona fide whereas in *Regal (Hastings) Ltd* v *Gulliver* they were not diverting assets and were acting bona fide. This has been said to be the difference between ratifiable and non-ratifiable breaches.

Where the breaches are ratifiable it would appear that the directors may exercise their votes as members (see *North-West Transportation Co. Ltd* v *Beatty* (1887) 12 App Cas 589). The articles may also permit the directors to retain such profits as does reg. 85 of Table A.

7.4.5 INTERESTS IN SHARES OR DEBENTURES

7.4.5.1 Common law

Directors are in the best position to acquire information which may be used unfairly in dealing in the company's securities, At common law it is a breach of the director's duty to use such information and any profit acquired will be held on trust for the company (*Regal (Hastings) Ltd* v *Gulliver* [1967] 2 AC 134, see **7.4.4**). However, directors owe no such duty to individual shareholders and will not be liable to account to them if they buy shares from them without disclosing, e.g., a potential takeover bid which will increase their value (*Percival* v *Wright* [1902] 2 Ch 421) although they may be liable if they are acting as agents for the shareholders (*Allen* v *Hyatt* (1914) 30 TLR 444).

7.4.5.2 Insider dealing

CA 1985, ss. 323–329, provide that it is an offence for a director (or spouse or child) to deal in options in the company's securities if they are listed.

Under the Criminal Justice Act 1993, s. 52, an individual with 'insider' information who deals with shares, debentures and other price-affected company securities on a regulated market (such as the London Stock Exchange) is guilty of an offence punishable by a fine and/or imprisonment for up to seven years. There are also offences where 'insiders' encourage others to deal with price-affected securities or disclose 'inside' information to others otherwise than in the proper performance of their duties. 'Inside' information must relate to particular securities rather than securities in general. It must not have been made public and must be likely to have a significant effect on the price of the securities in question (CJA 1993, s. 56). To be an 'insider' a person must know that the relevant information is 'inside' information and that it comes from an inside source, i.e. that it was obtained directly or indirectly from a director, employee or shareholder in the company, or through a person having access to the information by virtue of that person's employment, office or profession (CJA 1993, s. 57).

A number of defences are set out in CJA 1993, s. 53. These include the defendant not expecting to make a profit on account of the information used being price-sensitive, and reasonable belief that others taking part in the deal would not be prejudiced due to wide disclosure of the information. The CJA 1993 merely renders the person guilty of an offence. It does not make the transaction void or unenforceable.

7.5 Duty of Care and Skill

7.5.1 COMMON LAW

Case law has established a fairly low standard of care and skill below which directors may be liable. The leading case of *Re City Equitable Fire Insurance Co. Ltd* [1925] Ch 407 set out the three criteria by which they are judged:

(a) A director need not exhibit in the performance of his or her duties a greater degree of skill than may reasonably be expected from a person of his or her knowledge and experience. Directors are not liable for mere errors of judgment. However, an employed director has the implied duty to exercise reasonable care and skill. Where the director is a professional the standard will be of a reasonably competent member of that profession.

(b) A director is not bound to give continuous attention to the affairs of the company. A director's duties are of an intermittent nature to be performed at periodic board meetings and at meetings of any committee of the board upon which he or she happens to be placed. A director is not bound to attend all meetings although he or she ought to attend whenever, in the circumstances, he or she is reasonably able to do so.

(c) In respect of all duties that, having regard to the exigencies of business and the articles of association, may properly be left to some other official, a director is, in the absence of grounds for suspicion, justified in trusting that official to perform such duties honestly.

The standard of care has been subjective with the result that a director with little skill was judged by a standard which would reasonably be expected of a person with that level of knowledge or experience. However, it is likely that this standard will increase and become more objective as a result of:

(a) The increasing professional standards required of accountants, lawyers etc.

(b) The role played by executive (as opposed to non-executive) directors.

(c) IA 1986, s. 214 (wrongful trading; see **7.5.2**), which imposes a combined objective and subjective test in determining the knowledge, skill and experience reasonably to be expected of the director and the steps which ought to have been taken to minimise loss to creditors.

7.5.2 WRONGFUL TRADING

A rather higher standard of care is required from directors under the IA 1986, s. 214, which applies to companies which have gone into insolvent liquidation. Under this provision a director will be liable to contribute to the company's assets if at some time before the commencement of the liquidation he or she knew or ought to have concluded that there was no reasonable prospect that the company would avoid going into insolvent liquidation, but the court will not make an order if satisfied that the director took every step with a view to minimising loss to creditors which ought to have been taken. The standard in judging the facts which the director ought to have known, the conclusions reached and steps taken is that of a reasonably diligent person having the knowledge, skill, and experience of that director and that which might reasonably be expected of a person carrying out the same functions as the director. Thus the test is both objective and subjective.

7.6 Consequences of Breach of Duty

Where a director is in breach of a duty to the company, there are a number of possible actions.

7.6.1 REMOVAL AS AN OFFICER AND DISMISSAL AS AN EMPLOYEE

A director may be removed from office by the board where the articles so provide. Table A, reg. 81, provides that a director shall vacate office if absent without permission of the directors from meetings of directors for more than six consecutive months and the board so resolves. CA 1985, s. 303, provides that a company may by ordinary resolution remove a director before the expiration of his or her period of office, notwithstanding anything in its articles or any agreement between the company and the director. Special notice (28 days to the company: CA 1985, s. 379) is required of such a resolution and the director must be sent notice of the resolution and has the right to have representations circulated to the members and to attend and speak at the meeting (CA 1985, s. 304). See **6.8**.

Members who wish to have such a resolution put to a meeting must have the shareholding necessary to requisition an EGM, see **6.5.5**.

Where a director is retiring by rotation (e.g., under Table A, reg. 76), the directors may recommend someone else be elected in place of the retiring director. If members wish to propose someone other than the retiring director then, under Table A, reg. 76, notice must be given to the company not less than 14 nor more than 35 days before the meeting. In addition notice must be given to members not less than eight nor more than 28 days before the meeting at which any director other than a retiring director is recommended for appointment.

Where a director is removed from office any contract of service, e.g., as managing director, is terminated (Table A, reg. 84). The director may therefore have a claim for wrongful or unfair dismissal unless the terms of the service contract are observed and/or the behaviour warrants summary dismissal.

7.6.2 PROCEEDINGS AGAINST THE DIRECTOR

An action may be brought to obtain an injunction to restrain an actual or threatened breach of duty or claim damages for breach of duty or an account of profits received in breach of duty. The action will be brought by the company which means that a resolution to institute proceedings must be passed either at a board meeting or in a general meeting.

7.6.3 RELIEF FROM LIABILITY

The director may be relieved from liability by the company or the court:

(a) The company may approve what the directors have done or intend to do by a resolution to that effect or resolve not to sue for breach. Although directors may generally use their votes as shareholders in general meetings, there are limits to this use in such circumstances (see *Cook* v *Deeks* [1916] 1 AC 554 and *Daniels* v *Daniels* [1978] Ch 406, and fraud on the minority **11.5.3.4**).

(b) By CA 1985, s. 310, any provision in a company's articles or any contract of employment or otherwise for exempting any officer or indemnifying any officer against any liability in respect of any negligence, default, breach of duty or breach of trust in relation to the company is void. However, this does not prevent a company from insuring any officer against such liability or from giving an indemnity against liability for costs in a successful defence against such proceedings.

(c) CA 1985, s. 727, empowers the court in any proceedings for negligence, default, breach of duty or breach of trust against an officer of a company to grant relief in whole or in part from such liability on such terms as it thinks fit. Such relief may be granted where it appears to the court that the officer has acted honestly and reasonably and, having regard to all the circumstances, ought fairly to be excused, but is not available where directors are liable for wrongful trading under IA 1986, s. 214 (*Re Produce Marketing Consortium Ltd* [1989] 1 WLR 745).

7.7 Liability for Mismanagement of the Company

Past attempts to get at errant directors, who traded companies into insolvent liquidation and then set up other companies which went on trading, have not been successful. The rationale behind the Company Directors Disqualification Act 1986, and many of the provisions in the Insolvency Act 1986, is to render such directors liable for their actions and disqualify them from running other companies.

7.7.1 INSOLVENCY ACT 1986, SS. 213, 214A

These sections provide that directors can be made to contribute to the company's assets. See s. 213 (fraudulent trading) and s. 214 (wrongful trading). For further detail see **8.5.4.2**.

7.7.2 INSOLVENCY ACT 1986, S. 216

This section provides that where a company has gone into insolvent liquidation, directors and shadow directors are prohibited from using the company's name, or a similar name which might suggest an association with the company, for five years. A person who breaches this provision commits an offence and will be personally liable for the debts of the new business trading under the prohibited name.

7.7.3 COMPANY DIRECTORS DISQUALIFICATION ACT 1986

This Act empowers the court to disqualify a person from being a director, liquidator, administrator, receiver or manager or in any way, directly or indirectly, be concerned or take part in the promotion, formation or management of a company for the period specified in the order. The court *may* make an order where a person:

(a) Is convicted of an indictable offence in connection with a company (s. 2 — maximum 15 years).

(b) Is in persistent default of the filing requirements under the companies legislation (ss. 3 and 5 — maximum five years).

(c) On the winding up of a company, appears to be guilty of fraudulent trading under CA 1985, s. 458, or of any fraud or breach of duty (s. 4 — maximum 15 years).

(d) Is found to be unfit by the court after a DTI investigation (s. 4 — maximum 15 years).

(e) Is ordered to contribute to the company's assets on liquidation under IA 1986, ss. 213 or 214 (fraudulent or wrongful trading) (s. 10 — maximum 15 years).

The above provisions apply to directors and shadow directors (see **7.1.2**).

The court *must* make an order if satisfied that a person was a director of an insolvent company (i.e., it went into liquidation when unable to pay its debts, an administrative receiver is appointed or an administration order is made) and his or her conduct makes him/her unfit to be concerned in the management of a company (s. 6 — minimum two years, maximum 15 years). Schedule 1 contains matters which the court shall have regard to in determining whether the conduct makes the person unfit. These include breach of duty, misapplication or retention of company property, responsibility for defrauding creditors, or insolvency. *Re Sevenoaks Stationers (Retail) Ltd* [1991] Ch 164 was the first case to go to the Court of Appeal. The court set out guidelines for the length of the order under s. 6: 10 to 15 years for cases of utmost severity (e.g., where a director has been disqualified before), six to 10 years for middle-ranking cases and two to five years for lesser cases. In addition it stressed that the proper procedure must be followed in bringing cases, in particular, notice must be given to the director of the allegations made. It endorsed the approach that a disqualification order could be made where a director was not found to be dishonest but was incompetent or negligent to a 'very marked degree'. A variety of cases had indicated that the use of money owed to the Crown was more culpable than failure to pay commercial debts. The court stressed that failure to pay Crown debts does not automatically justify disqualification, and that the courts should not adopt some of the hard-and-fast tests suggested in earlier cases.

A person who acts in contravention of a disqualification order commits an offence and is personally liable for the debts of the company while so acting (ss. 13 and 15). It is also an offence to act as a director etc. while an undischarged bankrupt and personal liability is also incurred while so acting (ss. 11 and 15).

A disqualified director can apply for permission to act (ss. 1 and 17). Such applications are made either by issuing an application notice in existing disqualification proceedings, or by issuing a Part 8 claim form (see Directors Disqualification Proceedings PD, para. 20).

EIGHT

INSOLVENCY

8.1 Introduction

A significant proportion of the work undertaken by company law practitioners relates to corporate insolvency. As could be predicted, the amount of insolvency work increases in times of economic recession. 'Insolvency' as an expression has a number of different meanings in the law relating to corporate collapse. In broad terms a company may be said to be insolvent when it finds itself in the position of being unable to pay its debts as they fall due. However, this may describe a temporary, trivial cash flow difficulty, and it may describe the situation where a company has incurred massive debts and is left with negligible assets and no hope of repaying what it owes.

The law relating to company insolvency seeks to achieve a number of objectives:

(a) to provide means by which companies in temporary financial difficulties can trade out of those difficulties without being killed off by overzealous creditors, while protecting the interests of the general body of creditors while this is happening;

(b) to provide means by which companies that cannot be saved are taken off the register and thereby cease trading;

(c) to ensure that the assets of insolvent companies are distributed in a fair and orderly manner (without an unseemly scramble to grab whatever can be salvaged from the wreckage);

(d) to provide means by which the causes of a company's collapse can be investigated, and by which any failure of those in control of the company to act properly can be investigated and if necessary penalised; and

(e) to ensure that those charged with the responsibility for getting in the assets of insolvent companies and making distributions to creditors do so honestly and are accountable.

Insolvency proceedings are governed by the Insolvency Act 1986 (IA 1986) and rules made thereunder. These are principally the Insolvency Rules 1986 (IR 1986). In addition the Company Directors Disqualification Act 1986 is important as it provides for penalties on directors who have run their companies into insolvency in disregard of the interests of the creditors of their companies.

A creditor faced with a company that has not paid its debts has a number of options:

(a) If creditor has been able to obtain security for the indebtedness from the company, it may seek to enforce its security. This is done typically either by selling the assets comprising the security, or by appointing a receiver.

(b) To apply to the court for an administration order. This is an order under which an administrator is appointed by the court to formulate and put into operation a recovery plan, which is aimed at enabling the company to pay its debts.

(c) Seek a voluntary arrangement, i.e. an agreement with creditors as to how debts will be paid.

(d) Wind up or liquidate the company, which will ultimately dissolve it.

8.2 Receivership, IA 1986, ss. 28–49, and IR 1986, Part 3

Receivership is one of the principal ways in which a chargeholder may enforce his charge. The debenture will usually give debentureholders the power to appoint a receiver. However, if it does not, the court has power to appoint a receiver on the application of the debentureholders in certain circumstances including default in payment of the debt.

The principal effects of the appointment of a receiver are:

(a) directors' powers over the charged assets are suspended;

(b) floating charges crystallise;

(c) notice of the appointment must be given to the Registrar of Companies and put on all documents (s. 39; giving notice to outsiders that the company is in financial difficulty).

The principal duty of the receiver is to take control of the assets subject to the charge and pay off the debentureholders having due regard to the rights of others under IA 1986. Thus the order of priority is:

(a) Fixed chargeholders (who may realise the assets subject to their charge).

(b) Preferential creditors (who will be paid out of money subject to floating charges if there are insufficient other funds to pay them). These creditors are set out in sch. 6 and include PAYE income tax for the previous 12 months, VAT for the previous six months, National Insurance contributions (12 months), occupational and State pension scheme contributions, employees' pay (four months or £800 per employee) and holiday pay.

(c) Floating chargeholders.

(d) Ordinary unsecured creditors.

To enable the duty to be carried out, the receiver is given certain powers in the debenture, e.g. to sell the assets subject to the charge. However, if appointed under a floating charge over the whole or substantially the whole of the company's undertaking, the receiver is called an administrative receiver (s. 29) and will have all the powers set out in the debenture plus those in IA 1986, ss. 42, 43 and sch. 1, so far as consistent with the debenture. These powers are very wide and include the power to carry on the business of the company (sch. 1, para. 4). This power is particularly important where the physical assets of the company are not of much value and there is a possibility of trading the company out of financial difficulty or 'hiving down' (by creating a new company, selling the viable parts of the business to the new company in exchange for shares in the new company and then selling the shares in the new company to a willing buyer; the new company thereby having the assets but not the liabilities of the old company). Either of these two alternatives may mean more money for the debentureholders.

The receiver is not concerned with ordinary unsecured creditors as they rank below any secured creditor. However, an administrative receiver now has a duty (s. 47) to obtain a statement of affairs from officers of the company as to the assets, liabilities and creditors and prepare a report as to why he or she was appointed, the amount due to debentureholders and the amount likely to be available for other creditors. This report must be sent to the Registrar of Companies and all unsecured creditors. A meeting must be called of all unsecured creditors (s. 48) at which the report will be presented, and a committee of creditors may be appointed which may then, from time to time, require information from the administrative receiver as to steps being taken. Thus the unsecured creditors should be kept informed and may, in light of this information, decide to take steps themselves, e.g. petition for the liquidation of the company or an administrative order.

8.3 Administration Orders, IA 1986, ss. 8–27, and IR 1986, Part 2

This is a provision inspired by the success of receivers and managers (now called administrative receivers) prior to the IA 1986 in turning round or hiving down companies. It is a procedure whereby a court-appointed administrator has much the same (and in fact greater) powers as an administrative receiver. The procedure is as follows:

(a) A petition is presented to the court by, *inter alia*, the creditor(s) (secured or unsecured) and served on the company and those debentureholders entitled to appoint an administrative receiver (s. 9).

(b) On issue of the petition there is a freeze on the company in that there may be no:

  (i) order made or resolution passed to wind up the company;

  (ii) security enforced, hire purchase goods (which includes goods under conditional sale and retention of title agreements) repossessed, or legal proceedings taken against the company without leave of the court (s. 10). (However, an administrative receiver may be appointed and a petition to wind up the company may be presented.)

(c) The court will determine whether or not an order should be made. The application must be dismissed unless it is satisfied that the debentureholders who may appoint or have appointed an administrative receiver consent to it being made. The court may make an order if satisfied that the company is, or is likely to become unable to pay its debts and the order is likely to achieve one of the purposes set out in s. 8 of the Act, e.g., the survival of the company or a more advantageous realisation of the company's assets than on liquidation.

(d) If the court is so satisfied, an order is made with the effect that an administrator is appointed, any administrative receiver in post automatically vacates office and any petition to wind up the company is dismissed. In addition the ban on enforcement of security, repossession of hire purchase goods and proceedings against the company continues, subject to leave of the administrator or the court. In addition all documents must state that the company is being managed by an administrator.

(e) The administrator must obtain a statement of affairs setting out the assets, liabilities and creditors of the company, prepare proposals for achieving the purpose set out in the order (s. 23) and present these to a meeting of creditors (s. 24).

(f) If the creditors approve the proposals, the administrator carries them out.

The administrator has the same wide powers as the administrative receiver, which are set out in IA 1986, sch. 1, plus additional powers, not available to administrative receivers, to remove any director and appoint a replacement (s. 14(2)), to sell property subject to a floating charge (s. 15(1)) and, with permission of the court, to sell property subject to a fixed charge or held on hire purchase (s. 15(2)). The proceeds of any such sale must be used to pay the persons with an interest in the property. Once the purpose of the order has been achieved, the administrator applies to the court for the order to be discharged.

8.4 Voluntary Arrangements, IA 1986, ss. 1–7, and IR 1986, Part 1

This is a new provision not previously available to companies to enable them to make binding agreements with creditors. It has not been much used as it is a fairly complicated procedure involving a series of court hearings, does not bind secured or preferential creditors without their consent and contains no provisions for a moratorium while the proposals for the arrangement are being drawn up and considered (unlike administration orders which have become popular, and voluntary arrangements for insolvent individuals in ss. 252–4).

8.5 Liquidation, IA 1986, Parts IV and VI, and IR 1986, Part 4

This is the ultimate sanction against a company which fails to pay debts as it will dissolve the company. Liquidation can be voluntary (i.e. the company resolves to liquidate) or compulsory (the court orders that it be liquidated). Either way the effect is the same; a liquidator is appointed to realise the assets and pay off the debts. Once this task has been completed, a return is made to the Registrar of Companies and the company is dissolved and removed from the register of companies (IA 1986, s. 205).

8.5.1 VOLUNTARY LIQUIDATION, IA 1986, SS. 84–116, AND IR 1986, PART 4

This commences by a resolution of members in general meeting and will be a members' or creditors' liquidation. If the directors swear a statutory declaration of solvency (i.e. that the company will be able to pay its debts in full within a specified period not exceeding 12 months (s. 89)) it will be a members' voluntary liquidation in which the creditors play no part. The liquidator is appointed by the members and reports to them.

If the directors are not prepared to swear a statutory declaration, it will be a creditors' voluntary liquidation in which the creditors will play a role. A meeting of creditors will be called within 14 days of the resolution being passed and they will appoint a liquidator (if members nominated a different person the creditors' nominee will act). The liquidator will report to a liquidation committee which is composed of representatives of members and creditors, a maximum of five of each.

If the directors make a statutory declaration without reasonable grounds for their opinion that the company will be able to pay its debts, they commit an offence, and if the company does not pay its debts within the stated period, they are presumed to have had no reasonable grounds for their opinion (s. 89). Hence the incentive for the directors to ensure that the declaration is accurate.

8.5.2 COMPULSORY LIQUIDATION, IA 1986, SS. 117–162, AND IR 1986, PART 4

This is commenced by the presentation of a petition to the court by the company (rare), the directors, any creditor(s) (most frequent) or member(s) (s. 124). To obtain an order, one of the grounds set out in s. 122 must be proved, which includes the ground that the company is unable to pay its debts. By s. 123 a company is deemed to be unable to pay its debts if:

(a) a statutory demand for a debt exceeding £750 has been served on the company and not paid, secured or compounded within three weeks;

(b) execution of a judgment debt is unsatisfied;

(c) the court is satisfied that the company is unable to pay its debts as they fall due.

Compulsory liquidation is considered in greater detail in **Chapter 9**, and guidance on presenting winding-up petitions in court is given in **Chapter 10**.

8.5.3 THE EFFECT OF LIQUIDATION, IA 1986, SS. 175–219, 230–246, AND IR 1986, PART 4

The effects of the making of an order or passing of a resolution to wind up a company are largely the same. A liquidator is appointed, the company must cease business except as necessary to wind up, all floating charges crystallise, the directors' powers cease and are assumed by the liquidator and all invoices, letters etc. must show that the company is being wound up. The liquidator takes control of the assets, realises them and pays off the debts in the order of priority under IA 1986, which is basically:

(a) fixed chargeholders (who may realise the assets subject to their charge);

(b) preferential creditors;

(c) floating chargeholders;

(d) unsecured creditors;

(e) payments due to members (e.g. unpaid declared dividends);

(f) return of capital to members; and

(g) distribution of any surplus to members in accordance with their rights.

8.5.4 SWELLING THE COMPANY'S ASSETS

IA 1986 contains provisions to enable the liquidator to swell the assets available to pay the debts of the company by invalidating certain transactions of the company (also available to administrators) or rendering people liable to contribute to the assets.

8.5.4.1 Invalid transactions

Section 245 provides that a floating charge is invalid, except in so far as consideration is given for it, if given within a specified period before the onset of insolvency (defined as the commencement of liquidation or presentation of petition for an administration order). The period depends on whether the charge was given to a connected person (defined in ss. 249 and 435 to include directors, their relatives and companies under their control), in which case it is two years; or unconnected persons, in which case it is one year. In addition, if the charge was given to an unconnected person it must be shown that at the time the charge was granted the company was unable to pay its debts or became so as a result of the charge.

IA 1986, s. 238, empowers the court to set aside any transaction at an undervalue (i.e. where the company makes a gift or receives consideration significantly less than that provided by the company), unless it was made in good faith on reasonable belief that it would benefit the company. The transaction may be set aside if it was made within two years of the onset of insolvency provided that at the time of the transaction the company was unable to pay its debts or became unable to do so as a result of the transaction (presumed if the transaction was with a connected person).

IA 1986, s. 239, empowers the court to set aside preferences, i.e. any transaction whereby the company puts a creditor in a better position in the event of the company's insolvency than he would otherwise have been, provided the company was influenced by a desire to prefer the creditor (this is presumed if the preference was given to a connected person) and the preference was given within six months of insolvency (if to an unconnected person) or two years (if to a connected person).

Under IA 1986, ss. 423–5, a transaction at an undervalue may be set aside if it can be shown that the purpose of the transaction was to put assets beyond the reach of creditors, or to prejudice creditors' interests in some other way. A transaction is at an undervalue if:

(a) it is by way of gift, or otherwise made in return for no consideration;

(b) the transaction is entered into in contemplation of marriage; or

(c) the consideration is significantly less than the value of the consideration provided by the company.

There is no time limit for setting aside such transactions. The principal difficulty is in proving the prohibited purpose of the transaction.

8.5.4.2 Personal liability

The liquidator may obtain a court order that certain persons contribute to the company's assets to assist in paying the company's debts.

IA 1986, s. 212, if on the winding up of a company it appears that an officer or person concerned in the management, promotion or formation of the company has misapplied and retained or become accountable for company property and been guilty of any misfeasance or breach of duty to the company, the court may compel him or her to repay, restore or account for the property or pay compensation for the breach.

IA 1986, s. 213 (fraudulent trading) where on the winding up of a company, it appears to the court that the company has been carried on with intent to defraud creditors, it may declare any persons knowingly parties to it liable to contribute to the company's assets. This provision was taken from an existing provision in CA 1985 which had little success because of the difficulty in proving the necessary intent.

IA 1986, s. 214 (wrongful trading) if on the insolvent liquidation of a company, the court finds that before commencement a director knew, or ought to have concluded, that there was no reasonable prospect that the company could avoid insolvent liquidation, the court may order that director to contribute to the company's assets. However, the court will not make an order if it is satisfied that the director had taken every step he or she ought to have to minimise loss to creditors. The standard by which a director is to be judged under s. 214 contains both objective and subjective elements of knowledge, skill and experience. In *Re Produce Marketing Consortium Ltd* [1989] 1 WLR 745, the first case on this provision, it was held that, when judging the director, regard should be had to the functions of the director and the nature of the company's business, and the standards should be those of a person fulfilling that function with reasonable diligence. The director is to be treated as possessing information which was capable of being ascertained had the company fulfilled its statutory duties and which the director ought to have ascertained. The directors were found liable and ordered to contribute £75,000. (See now also *Re DKG Contractors Ltd* [1990] BCC 903.)

Note that s. 213 applies to any person party to the fraudulent trading, and s. 214 applies only to directors, although shadow directors (those on whose instructions the board is accustomed to act) are included.

NINE

COMPULSORY WINDING UP

9.1 Introduction

Liquidation (or winding up) is the process whereby a company's business, assets and liabilities are terminated, realised and distributed, after which the company is dissolved and ceases to exist. Liquidations fall into two categories: voluntary and compulsory. Voluntary liquidations fall into two sub-categories: members' voluntary liquidations and creditors' voluntary liquidations. A members' voluntary liquidation is initiated by a solvent company's shareholders, the directors making a declaration of solvency (that after full inquiry they are of the opinion that the company will be able to pay its debts in full within a specified period not exceeding 12 months). A creditors' voluntary liquidation is also initiated by the shareholders, but the directors have not made a declaration of the company's solvency. The liquidator will usually be appointed by the company's unsecured creditors (as opposed to the shareholders in a members' voluntary liquidation).

A compulsory liquidation, on the other hand, is commenced by a petition being presented to the court, usually by an unpaid creditor. Petitions may also be presented by the company, its directors, and contributories (which broadly means those persons, such as holders of partly paid shares, who are liable to contribute to the assets of the company in the event of it being wound up: IA 1986, s. 79). Compulsory winding up is a form of hostile litigation, generally resorted to by unpaid creditors as a means of recovering unpaid debts, with the threat of dissolution if the company does not pay.

Provisional liquidators may be appointed by the court at any time between the presentation of a winding-up petition and the disposal of the petition. Their function is to maintain the status quo pending the determination of the petition.

9.2 Superseding Voluntary Winding up with Compulsory Winding up

In *Re Gordon & Breach Science Publishers Ltd* [1995] BCC 261 the company was in voluntary liquidation. It was alleged that the controllers of the company had arranged to pay certain favoured creditors at the expense of the rest. Companies associated with the debtor company claimed they were owed substantial sums, and voted, it was alleged, to have a liquidator appointed in the voluntary liquidation who would view matters in a way favourable to the debtor company. It was held that even though the voluntary liquidation was well advanced, a substantial independent creditor was entitled to an order for the compulsory liquidation of the company, because such a creditor is entitled to have an independent investigation of the company's affairs.

9.3 Grounds for Compulsory Winding up

The grounds on which a company may be compulsorily wound up are set out in IA 1986, s. 122(1) as follows:

A company may be wound up by the court if—
(a) the company has by special resolution resolved that the company be wound up by the court,
(b) being a public company which was registered as such on its original incorporation, the company has not been issued with a certificate under section 117 of the Companies Act (public company share capital requirements) and more than a year has expired since it was so registered,
(c) it is an old public company, within the meaning of the Consequential Provisions Act,
(d) the company does not commence its business within a year from its incorporation or suspends its business for a whole year,
(e) except in the case of a private company limited by shares or by guarantee, the number of members is reduced below 2,
(f) the company is unable to pay its debts,
(g) the court is of the opinion that it is just and equitable that the company should be wound up.

Further, by IA 1986, s. 124A, the Secretary of State may present petitions to wind up companies in certain circumstances where it is in the public interest for this to be done.

Ground (g), that it is just and equitable that the company be wound up, is often met in the context of giving relief to disgruntled minority shareholders, and will be considered in more detail in **Chapter 12**. The ground most commonly relied on is ground (f), that the company is unable to pay its debts. Four statutory presumptions of inability to pay debts are contained in IA 1986, s. 123(1), (2), namely where:

(a) The company owes a debt exceeding £750 and the creditor has left a statutory demand for it at the company's registered office, and the company neglects to pay or to secure or compound for it to the creditor's satisfaction within 21 days. Statutory demands are governed by IR 1986, rr. 4.2 and 4.4 to 4.6. A prescribed form must be used. It states the amount of the debt and interest, and how it was incurred, and warns that if payment or an acceptable proposal for payment is not made within 21 days after it is received, winding-up proceedings may be instituted.

As just stated, the statutory demand must be 'left' at the company's registered office. After some doubt, it now appears to be the case that it is sufficient if the demand is posted to the registered office: see *Re a Company (No. 008790 of 1990)* [1992] BCC 11, disapproving *Re a Company* [1985] BCLC 37. However, there are no presumptions as to the fact and date of service if the Post Office is used, so delivery has to be proved or admitted.

A winding-up petition can be validly based on a statutory demand claiming the wrong amount, provided the statutory demand is sufficiently clear and provided there is still an indisputable debt above the statutory minimum of £750: *Re Tweeds Garages Ltd* [1962] Ch 406. An obligation to pay the costs of an action was regarded as being a 'debt' for these purposes even before taxation in *Tottenham Hotspur plc* v *Edennote plc* [1994] BCC 681.

(b) Judgment has been entered against the company, and execution on that judgment has been returned unsatisfied in whole or in part.

(c) It is proved to the satisfaction of the court that the company is unable to pay its debts as they fall due. The circumstances surrounding the non-payment of a debt may justify the inference that the company is unable to pay its debts as they fall due. A series of dishonoured cheques may be good evidence to justify this inference. Further, the mere failure to pay a debt is of itself evidence of inability to pay where the debt is due, an invoice has been sent, and the company has not advanced reasons for non-payment: *Re Taylor's Industrial Flooring Ltd* [1990] BCC 44, CA. Consequently, it is not always necessary to serve a statutory demand before issuing a winding-up petition based on non-payment of a debt. However, care must be taken before petitioning on this basis. If it later transpires there was a genuine dispute over the petition debt, not only will the petition be dismissed, but indemnity-basis costs and even wasted-costs orders may be imposed (see *Re a Company (No. 006798 of 1995)* [1996] 1 WLR 491).

(d) It is proved to the satisfaction of the court that the value of the company's assets is less than its liabilities, taking into account its contingent and prospective liabilities.

9.4 *Locus Standi*

The following persons can present a winding-up petition (see IA 1986, s. 124):

(a) the company;

(b) its directors;

(c) a creditor;

(d) a contingent or prospective creditor;

(e) a contributory (i.e. shareholder), subject to complying with IA 1986, s. 124(2);

(f) various officials, e.g. the Secretary of State for Trade and Industry, the Attorney-General, official receivers; and

(g) administrators and administrative receivers.

Section 124(2) is to the effect that to be entitled to petition as a contributory a shareholder must have held the shares for at least six out of the 18 months before presenting the petition, or must have been the original allottee of the shares, or they must have devolved on the petitioner through the death of a previous owner. Further, the courts have decided that the petitioner must have a financial interest in the winding up of the company. This will be satisfied either if the shares are partly paid (fairly rare in modern times) or if there is likely to be a surplus available for distribution to shareholders on a winding up of the company. The holder of fully paid shares in an insolvent company has no sufficient financial interest: *Re Rica Gold Washing Co.* (1879) 11 ChD 36. The fact the petitioner holds a small proportion of the issued shares is not a bar to presenting a petition if the company is likely to be solvent (see *Bryanston Finance Ltd* v *de Vries (No. 2)* [1976] Ch 63).

9.5 Procedure on the Petition

9.5.1 THE PETITION

The level of detail required to be set out in the petition depends on the nature of the case. For example, petitions presented by contingent creditors (which are relatively unusual) must contain material from which the court can infer the company is unable to pay its debts. General allegations in petitions presented by contingent creditors merely stating the grounds in the statute will be struck out as abuses of process: *Securum Finance Ltd* v *Camswell Ltd* [1994] BCC 434. On the other hand, petitions based on non-payment after service of a statutory demand, the failure to satisfy a judgment debt, or non-payment of invoices, give little more than the basic details required by the prescribed form of petition. All petitions must follow IR 1986, sch. 4, Form 4.2.

The precedent in **Figure 9.1** is an example of a winding-up petition based on a statutory demand. As mentioned in **2.1**, generally the High Courts and county courts have concurrent jurisdiction, so the petitioner can choose which court to proceed in. In addition to preparing the petition, the petitioner or someone concerned with or having knowledge of the matters giving rise to the petition must swear an affidavit or make a witness statement in Form 4.3 verifying the petition. The petitioner pays the £150 court fee for issuing the petition and deposits the sum of £500 to cover the official receiver's fees. The petition and verifying affidavit or witness statement are filed in court, and the court allocates a case number to the petition and fixes a hearing date, which is endorsed on the petition. This is usually several weeks in advance, to provide sufficient time for service and advertisement.

Figure 9.1 Winding-up petition based on service of statutory demand

IN THE HIGH COURT OF JUSTICE — No. 1329 of 2000

CHANCERY DIVISION

COMPANIES COURT

IN THE MATTER of Woodcroft Kitchen Company Limited

AND IN THE MATTER of the Insolvency Act 1986

To Her Majesty's High Court of Justice

The petition of Rosewall Electricals Limited of 17 Commercial Road, Enfield, EN1 6DZ

1. Woodcroft Kitchen Company Limited (hereinafter called 'the Company') was incorporated on the 20th day of May 1991 under the Companies Act 1985 as a company limited by shares.

2. The registered office of the Company is at 39 London Road, Potters Bar, Hertfordshire.

3. The nominal capital of the Company is £1,000 divided into 1,000 shares of £1 each. The amount of the capital paid up or credited as paid up is £200.

4. The principal objects for which the Company was established are to carry on business as retailers of kitchen furnishings and appliances and other objects stated in the memorandum of association of the Company.

5. The Company is indebted to the Petitioner in the sum of £3,642.43 in respect of 19 XM–20 washing machines sold and delivered by the Petitioner to the Company on 26th of October 1999.

6. On 29th of January 2000 the Petitioner served on the Company by leaving it at the Company's registered office a demand under its hand requiring the Company to pay the said sum, which demand was in the prescribed form.

7. Over 3 weeks have now elapsed since the Petitioner served the said demand, but the Company has neglected to pay or satisfy the said sum or any part thereof or to make any offer to the Petitioner to secure or compound the same.

8. In the circumstances it is just and equitable that the Company should be wound up.

The Petitioner therefore prays as follows:

(1) that Woodcroft Kitchen Company Limited may be wound up by the Court under the provisions of the Insolvency Act 1986 or
(2) that such other order may be made as the court thinks fit.

Note: It is intended to serve this petition on Woodcroft Kitchen Company Limited.

ENDORSEMENT

This petition having been presented to the court on the 23rd of February 2000 will be heard at the Royal Courts of Justice, Strand, London WC2A 2LL on:

Date 26th of April 2000

Time 10.30 hours
(or as soon thereafter as the petition can be heard)

The solicitor to the petitioner is:
Messrs Thomas and Williams, of 28 Commercial Road, Enfield EN1 6DZ.
Telephone: 0181-609290.
Reference JBT.

9.5.2 SERVICE

Service of the petition and verifying affidavit or witness statement is the responsibility of the petitioner (IPPD, para. 1.3), and must generally be effected at the company's registered office: IR 1986, r. 4.8(2). Permissible methods of service are set out in r. 4.8(3), which provides:

> *Service of the petition at the registered office may be effected in any of the following ways—*
> *(a) it may be handed to a person who there and then acknowledges himself to be, or to the best of the server's knowledge, information and belief is, a director or other officer, or employee, of the company; or*
> *(b) it may be handed to a person who there and then acknowledges himself to be authorised to accept service of documents on the company's behalf; or*
> *(c) in the absence of any such person as is mentioned in sub-paragraph (a) or (b), it may be deposited at or about the registered office in such a way that it is likely to come to the notice of a person attending at the office.*

If service by any of the above methods is not practicable, the petitioner may instead either:

(a) effect service at the company's last known principal place of business, under IR 1986, r. 4.8(4); or

(b) apply without notice by affidavit or witness statement for an order for substituted service under IR 1986, r. 4.8(6), (7).

Service of the petition is proved by affidavit or witness statement. There are two alternative prescribed forms (Forms 4.4 and 4.5). The affidavit or witness statement must specify the method of service used, and exhibit the petition and any order for substituted service: IR 1986, r. 4.9.

9.5.3 ADVERTISEMENT

Winding up of a company obviously affects not only the company itself, but also its members and creditors. Shareholders and existing creditors may have their own views on whether the company should be wound up, and may wish to support or oppose the petitition. Persons who may do business with the company in the future will be affected by IA 1986, s. 127 (for which, see **9.7**), which will, subject to the court validating the transaction, avoid any disposal of the company's property after the presentation of the petition if a winding-up order is eventually made. All of these people need to be notified of the petition, and this is done by advertising it in the *London Gazette.*

By virtue of IR 1986, r. 4.11(2)(b) the advertisement must appear not less than seven business days after service of the petition on the company and not less than seven business days before the hearing of the petition. Business days are all days apart from

Saturdays, Sundays and bank holidays. These periods are to give the company sufficient time to pay or to seek an injunction (for which, see **9.6**) before the appearance of the potentially damaging advertisement, and to give other affected persons (shareholders and creditors) time to appear at the hearing.

In *Re Signland Ltd* [1982] 2 All ER 609, Slade J said:

> . . . the principal reasons why the rules have directed that advertisement shall take place not less than seven clear days after service on the company are (1) to give a company served with a winding-up petition the opportunity to discharge the debt in question, if it is undisputed, before advertisement takes place, with all the necessarily potentially damaging consequences to the company, and (2) to enable the company, if it wishes to dispute the debt, to apply to the court to restrain advertisement.

Restraining advertisement is considered at **9.6**.

In this context there is some doubt as to whether 'advertisement' includes notifying a person of the existence of a petition by letter, or whether it is restricted to the formal advertisment in the *Gazette*: see *Re a Company (No. 00687 of 1991)* [1991] BCC 210 and contrast *SN Group plc* v *Barclays Bank plc* [1993] BCC 506. In *Re Bill Hennessey Associates Ltd* [1992] BCC 386, the petitioner sent a copy of the petition to the company's bank on the day it was issued. The account was in credit, and, as is the usual policy with most banks once they know of a winding-up petition, the bank immediately froze the account. The effect was to stop the company being able to conduct its business. To mark its disapproval of the premature advertisement the court dismissed the petition. Technically, such a dismissal is based either on an abuse of the IR 1986 or on the court's inherent jurisdiction. A similar sequence of events occurred in *Re a Company (No. 001127 of 1992)* [1992] BCC 477, where, in addition to striking out the petition, Mummery J granted an injunction restraining the presentation of a further petition based on the debt founding the original petition. An injunction is probably unnecessary, as any subsequent petition based on the original debt would almost certainly be an abuse of the court's process: see *Janov* v *Morris* [1981] 1 WLR 1389 and the ***Civil Litigation Manual*, 28.3.8**. In *SN Group plc* v *Barclays Bank plc* [1993] BCC 506, the creditor, as in the cases discussed above, notified the company's bank of the presentation of the petition before the expiry of the seven-day period laid down in r. 4.11. Jonathan Parker J's view was that there had been no 'advertisement' within the meaning of r. 4.11 as the rule is restricted to advertisements in the *Gazette*. If he was wrong on that, His Lordship distinguished the *Re Bill Hennessey Associates* line of cases on the grounds that in the case in front of him the debt was undisputed, the company was insolvent, and there was no evidence of a deliberate attempt to put undue pressure on the company. Although the decision in *SN Group plc* can be criticised, it is broadly in line with the reluctance to impose draconian penalties on parties who failed to comply with the rules of court and court orders exemplified in cases like *Mortgage Corporation Ltd* v *Sandoes* [1997] PNLR 263. However, since the introduction of the CPR in April 1999, a tougher attitude is now taken when parties do not comply with the rules of court.

Restraining advertisement in public interest petitions was considered in *Re a Company (No. 007923 of 1994)* [1995] BCC 634.

There is a prescribed form of advertisement, Form 4.6. Its contents are laid down by IR 1986, r. 4.11(4) as follows:

> *The advertisement of the petition must state—*
> *(a) the name of the company and the address of its registered office, or—*
> *(i) in the case of an unregistered company, the address of its principal place of business;*
> *(ii) in the case of an overseas company, the address at which service of the petition was effected;*
> *(b) the name and address of the petitioner;*

(c) where the petitioner is the company itself, the address of its registered office or, in the case of an unregistered company, of its principal place of business;
(d) the date on which the petition was presented;
(e) the venue fixed for the hearing of the petition;
(f) the name and address of the petitioner's solicitor (if any); and
(g) that any person intending to appear at the hearing (whether to support or oppose the petition) must give notice of his intention in accordance with Rule 4.16.

9.5.4 CERTIFICATE OF COMPLIANCE

A certificate in Form 4.7 must be filed (in High Court petitions) by 4.30 p.m. on the Friday before the hearing showing the dates of presentation, service, advertisement and hearing (IPPD, para. 3.1). For county court petitions, the certificate must be filed five days before the hearing. A copy of the advertisement must be filed with the certificate.

9.5.5 DISPUTE BY THE COMPANY

Winding up is not a suitable procedure for trying a disputed debt. If the company genuinely disputes the debt on which a petition is founded, it may:

(a) apply to strike out the petition; or

(b) apply for an injunction to restrain the petition (see **9.6**); or

(c) file an affidavit or witness statement in opposition no less than seven days before the hearing under IR 1986, r. 4.18 and argue that a winding-up order should not be made.

Defended petitions are referred to the judge and are considered in the Companies Court on Mondays.

An example of a genuinely disputed claim was *Re a Company (No. 00751 of 1992), ex parte Avocet Aviation Ltd* [1992] BCLC 869. The company entered into an agreement with the creditor under which the creditor agreed to supply an aircraft undercarriage for £34,400. This sum was paid, but the creditor raised a second invoice for £44,109 for additional work done, relying on terms in its standard terms and conditions allowing it to make such a charge. The company immediately wrote back denying it had agreed to pay the supplementary charge, and denying it had knowledge of the standard terms or that they had been agreed. There was no previous course of dealing between the parties, and there was conflicting evidence of trade usage. Without serving a statutory demand, the creditor petitioned for the winding-up of the company. This was held to be a case where there was a substantial dispute, so the petition was an abuse of process. In this case, and in the earlier case of *Re a Company (No. 0012209 of 1991)* [1992] 1 WLR 351, it was also ordered that the creditor should pay the company's costs on the indemnity basis.

An unsuccessful petitioner may also find itself in further difficulty. If it is held that there was no rational basis for genuinely believing there was a proper basis for presenting the petition, that there were no reasonable grounds in law for presenting it, and that presentation of the petition was actuated by malice or improper motive, the company may bring separate proceedings claiming damages for the tort of malicious presentation of the petition (see *Partizan Ltd* v *O.J. Kilkenny & Co. Ltd* [1998] 1 BCLC 157).

9.5.6 SUPPORTING AND OPPOSING CREDITORS

Any creditors or shareholders who wish to support or oppose the making of a winding-up order may appear at the hearing provided they first serve notice of their intention to appear on the petitioner's solicitors by 4 p.m. on the day before the hearing. The notice is in Form 4.9, and states whether the intention is to support or oppose the petition. A creditor giving notice must state the amount and nature of its debt. If notice is not given, a creditor can only appear if leave is granted to do so out of time.

On the day before the hearing the petitioner compiles a list in Form 4.10 of supporting and opposing creditors and contributories, which is provided for the court on the day of the hearing.

The court's practice is to allow the rationally supportable view of the majority of independent creditors to prevail. However, it is always possible for the majority view to be displaced in the circumstances of any individual case.

9.5.7 THE HEARING

Disputed petitions are given special appointments. The bulk of undisputed petitions in the High Court are heard by the Companies Court Registrar in open court on Wednesdays. Under IA 1986, s. 125(1) the court has power to dismiss the petition, adjourn the hearing conditionally or unconditionally, make any interim order, or any other order it thinks fit. Hearings are usually very short. Guidance on the presentation of winding-up petitions can be found in **Chapter 10**.

9.5.8 SUBSTITUTION

Sometimes a petitioner does not see a petition through to obtaining a winding-up order. When this happens, another creditor may consider taking over the proceedings by asking for a substitution order. This is dealt with by IR 1986, r. 4.19, which provides:

> *(1) This Rule applies where a person petitions and is subsequently found not entitled to do so, or where the petitioner—*
> *(a) fails to advertise his petition within the time prescribed by the Rules or such extended time as the court may allow, or*
> *(b) consents to withdraw his petition, or to allow it to be dismissed, consents to an adjournment, or fails to appear in support of his petition when it is called on in court on the day originally fixed for the hearing, or on a day to which it is adjourned, or*
> *(c) appears, but does not apply for an order in the terms of the prayer of his petition.*
> *(2) The court may, on such terms as it thinks just, substitute as petitioner any creditor or contributory who in its opinion would have a right to present a petition, and who is desirous of prosecuting it.*
> *(3) An order of the court under this Rule may, where a petitioner fails to advertise his petition within the time prescribed by these Rules, or consents to withdraw his petition, be made at any time.*

Where the court allows the substitution of a supporting creditor, the practice is to adjourn the petition to allow time for the petition to be amended to name the new petitioner and give details of the new petition debt, and for re-advertisement. Further notices from supporting and opposing creditors must, of course, be sent to the substituted creditor's solicitor,

9.5.9 APPEALS AND RESCISSION

An appeal from a decision to wind up a company made by the Companies Court Registrar or a county court with winding-up jurisdiction lies to a single judge of the High Court. Such an appeal must be brought within 28 days. A further appeal may be brought to the Court of Appeal, but only with permission. See IR 1986, r. 7.47(2). An appeal in a disputed petition case from the decision of the judge lies to the Court of Appeal.

Further, every court having jurisdiction to wind up companies may review, rescind or vary any order it makes: IR 1986, r. 7.47(1). An application to rescind must be made within seven days of the original order: r. 7.47(4). Such an application will only be entertained if it is made by a creditor or a contributory, or by the company jointly with a creditor or contributory: *Re Mid East Trading Ltd* [1997] 3 All ER 481. The application must be supported by an affidavit of assets and liabilities. If the winding-up order was made unopposed owing to some administrative error, such as some misunderstanding in briefing counsel, the application, if made promptly, may be dealt with on a statement by counsel of the circumstances. Otherwise the application will have to be further supported by an affidavit setting out the circumstances.

On hearing an application to rescind a winding-up order the court may give leave for creditors who did not appear when the original order was made to be heard: *Re Dollar Land (Feltham) Ltd* [1995] BCC 740. The jurisdiction to rescind is exercised with great caution. Generally, a winding-up order will only be rescinded if the original petition debt has been or will be paid, if there is evidence the company is solvent in a general sense, and if the official receiver is satisfied there is nothing requiring investigation and his costs can be paid. However, as made clear in *Re Dollar Land*, these are not invariable requirements.

9.6 Restraining Winding-up Proceedings

Injunctions restraining the prosecution of proceedings are recognised by the courts as being an extreme measure, but, given the commercial damage that usually results from the advertisement of winding-up petitions, it is also recognised that in suitable cases such injunctions can be granted. In fact, as mentioned at **9.5.5**, a company that finds itself the subject of unmeritorious winding-up proceedings can either apply to strike out or apply for an injunction if it wishes to stop further steps from being taken. Striking out can only be done after a petition has been presented, whereas it is possible to apply for an injunction on a *quia timet* basis. Otherwise, the results of the two options are similar, and it has been held that the principles to be applied are the same: *Re a Company (No. 003079 of 1990)* [1991] BCC 683.

9.6.1 PROCEDURE

Applications for *quia timet* injunctions are made by issuing an originating application in Form 7.1 (IPPD, para. 8.1). After presentation of a petition, an ordinary application in those proceedings is made for an interim injunction. Being injunctions, they must be heard by a judge, see IPPD, para. 9.1(2).

9.6.2 GENERAL PRINCIPLES

The jurisdiction to grant interim injunctions to restrain winding-up proceedings and the advertisement of the same derives from the court's inherent jurisdiction to prevent an abuse of its process. It is settled that the jurisdiction to grant such injunctions, whether *quia timet* or after presentation of the petition, is to be exercised with great caution, and only if there are clear and persuasive grounds. This situation is not governed by the principles in *American Cyanamid Co.* v *Ethicon Ltd* [1975] AC 396, HL (for which, see the ***Civil Litigation Manual*, 14.3**). Instead, an injunction will only be granted if there is prima facie evidence that a petition will be an abuse of process: *Bryanston Finance* v *de Vries (No.2)* [1976] 1 Ch 63, CA.

9.6.3 DISPUTED DEBTS

It has been said that a winding-up petition is not to be used as machinery for trying a common law action: *Re Imperial Guardian Life Assurance Society* (1869) LR 9 Eq 447 at p. 450, per Sir William James V-C. Accordingly, where the petition debt is disputed by the company on not insubstantial grounds, the petition will be regarded as an abuse of process and an injunction may be granted. A further justification for this position is that if the debt is genuinely disputed the petitioner cannot be described as a 'creditor' and has no *locus standi* in the Companies Court, see *Mann* v *Goldstein* [1968] 1 WLR 1091, Ungoed-Thomas J.

What amounts to a genuine dispute as to liability on an alleged debt can give rise to difficult factual issues. Whether a dispute is 'substantial' turns on the quality of the evidence, not its quantity (*Re Claybridge Shipping Co. SA* [1997] 1 BCLC 572, CA, where the evidence on the application extended to nine thick volumes of affidavits and exhibits). In this case a bank's petition was based on an alleged overdraft of about $30 million. The company alleged that the account had been manipulated by one of its directors acting in concert with one of the bank's employees in breach of what the company alleged was an altered mandate for operating the account. No mention of the defence had been given in a number of previous freezing injunction hearings; there was no documentary evidence to prove the new form of mandate contended for by the company; an accountancy expert had demonstrated that $15 million was, on any analysis, owing on the account; and the company was unable to demonstrate how it could contend that the account was not overdrawn. Despite the complexities, it was held that the debt was not disputed on substantial grounds. An agreement between the company and the petitioner that an accepted debt may be paid by instalments is unenforceable for want of consideration moving from the petitioner, so will not constitute a substantial dispute warranting an injunction; see *Re Selectmove Ltd* [1994] BCC 349, CA. In *Re a Company (No. 003079 of 1990)* [1991] BCC 683, Ferris J held that an injunction can be granted despite the possibility that another creditor may seek to be substituted as the petitioner at the hearing.

9.6.4 CONTINGENT DEBTS

As indicated at **9.4**, a winding-up petition can be presented by a contingent creditor. The problem faced by a contingent creditor is finding a ground on which to petition, such as proving the company cannot pay its debts as they fall due. What a contingent creditor cannot do is to petition on the basis of an unsatisfied statutory demand. As a contingent debt will only become due, if at all, in the future, it is premature to serve a statutory demand before the contingency occurs. If a contingent creditor nevertheless serves a statutory demand, the company should be entitled to an injunction limited to restraining the respondent from petitioning on the statutory demand: *Stonegate Securities Ltd* v *Gregory* [1980] 1 Ch 576, CA.

9.6.5 CROSS-CLAIMS

It has been established for some time that an undisputed counterclaim amounting to a set-off in a sum exceeding the petition debt provides good grounds for granting an injunction. Conversely, where despite the existence of a counterclaim there is an undisputed balance owing to the petitioner exceeding the winding-up threshold, the petition will not be restrained: *Re Pendigo Ltd* [1996] BCC 608. Where there is a disputed counterclaim exceeding the petition debt, until recently there was a great deal of confusion as to whether it would be right to grant an injunction. Cases like *Re FSA Business Software Ltd* [1990] BCLC 825 at first instance were to the effect that the discretion to grant an injunction should be refused where the cross-claim did not have the status of being a setoff. The law has been clarified by *Re Bayoil SA* [1999] 1 All ER 374, CA, where it was held that an injunction could be granted (or a petition dismissed) where the company could point to a genuine and serious cross-claim against the petitioning creditor which it had not reasonably been able to litigate. Ward LJ pointed out that even if these elements were satisfied the judge still has a judicial discretion whether to grant the injunction (or dismiss the petition) and there may be special circumstances justifying the petition being allowed to proceed. In *Re Bayoil SA* the Petitioner sought to show special circumstances, in that the petition debt was based on a final and unappealable award, security had been given for the company's counterclaim, the company was of doubtful solvency, and there was no real evidence that the petition debt could be paid. With the exception of the security, these points were regarded as being common in most cross-claim cases, and the addition of the security did not convert the case into a special one. The petition was dismissed.

In *Re a Company (No. 006685 of 1996)* [1997] 1 BCLC 639 the petition was based on £80,000 in advertising fees said to be due under an oral contract for providing two-page inserts in a television guide. The company said in its affidavit that the agreement was for payment of £5,000 per issue, not the £10,000 per issue charged by the creditor. It was also alleged by the company that the agreement was for the adverts to be stapled into the guide, whereas the creditor only provided inserts, which it was said were significantly less effective as a marketing tool. Accordingly, the company claimed it had a substantial counterclaim for breach of contract exceeding the amount actually due. The court reaffirmed the principle that an injunction would only be granted if there was a genuine dispute based on substantial grounds. That was not the case here, as the allegations made by the company were not referred to in contemporaneous correspondence, and the creditor's invoices for £10,000 per issue were not objected to at the time. The injunction was refused.

If the cross-claim is a set-off, but does not exceed the amount of the petition debt, it is arguable that an injunction could still be granted if the balance is less than £750, the threshold for petitioning on a statutory demand.

9.6.6 JUST AND EQUITABLE PETITIONS

Injunctions may be granted where the evidence establishes that the grounds alleged in the petition are bound to fail, for then the petition would be an abuse of process: *Charles Forte Investments Ltd* v *Amanda* [1964] 1 Ch 240, CA.

9.6.7 EXCEPTIONAL CASES

Dismissing petitions where the respondent company can show a substantial dispute may in certain circumstances cause undue difficulty to the petitioning creditor. In *Re Claybridge Shipping Co. SA* [1997] 1 BCLC 572 Lord Denning MR pointed out the ease with which, under modern conditions, assets can be removed from the jurisdiction. There may also be significant or insurmountable difficulties in bringing ordinary proceedings against foreign companies, particularly those which might be amenable to freezing injunctions. In order to prevent foreign companies that trade in this country from frustrating their creditors in this way when things start going wrong, the courts will depart from the general rule that a disputed debt cannot form the basis of a creditor's petition. The former Master of the Rolls also said that a similar and more relaxed approach would be appropriate where the respondent company is English, but where the circumstances show there is a significant danger of its assets being put out of the reach of its creditors. In other words, there may be circumstances where winding up can be used in a similar way to freezing injunctions. The *Claybridge Shipping* approach has been applied in more recent cases in the interests of justice where a petitioner is likely to be left without an effective remedy if the petition is struck out (see, for example, *Alipour* v *Ary* [1997] 1 WLR 534, CA).

9.6.8 INTERRELATION WITH SUMMARY JUDGMENT

Re Welsh Brick Industries Ltd [1946] 2 All ER 197 is an interesting case. A creditor brought an ordinary action to recover a debt, and sought summary judgment. Unconditional leave to defend was granted. Not being prepared to wait for trial, the creditor petitioned to wind up the company on the ground it was unable to pay its debts. The company sought an injunction to restrain the petition. It was held by the Court of Appeal that the order on the summary judgment application did not establish there was a genuine dispute, and the winding-up court was entitled to consider the whole of the evidence. Although the order granting unconditional leave to defend would be taken into account, Lord Greene MR said the grounds justifying such an order could fall far short of a substantial ground of defence.

9.7 Avoidance of Dispositions after Winding Up

9.7.1 THE STATUTE

IA 1986, s. 127, provides:

In a winding up by the court, any disposition of the company's property, and any transfer of shares, or alteration in the status of the company's members, made after the commencement of the winding up is, unless the court otherwise orders, void.

The section only applies in respect of compulsory liquidations by the court and has no application in relation to voluntary liquidations. By IA 1986, s. 129(2), a compulsory winding up is deemed to commence at the time of the presentation of the winding-up petition. The actual winding-up order, if made at all, will not be made until some weeks after the presentation of the petition. During that period, any disposals of the company's property are avoided by s. 127, unless they are validated by the court. Some time is bound to elapse between presentation of the petition and service on the company. It is inevitable that persons dealing with the company will not become aware of the petition until some time later.

Persons may well have traded in good faith with the company while unaware of the winding-up petition, but the effect of s. 127 is to avoid the consideration given by the company. Once they have notice of the petition, third parties are likely to be unwilling to trade with the company. It is to offset these difficulties that the court is given power by the section to validate such dispositions of the company's property.

9.7.2 THE POLICY OF THE SECTION

In *Re Civil Service & General Store Ltd* (1887) 57 LJ Ch 119, Chitty J said the purpose of the then current section was to ensure that the company's unsecured creditors at the date of presentation of the petition were paid *pari passu*. In *Re Wiltshire Iron Co., ex parte Pearson* (1868) LR 3 Ch App 443 Lord Cairns LJ said: 'This is a wholesome and necessary provision, to prevent, during the period which must elapse before a petition can be heard, the improper alienation and dissipation of the property of a company *in extremis*'.

9.7.3 PROPERTY

IA 1986, s. 127, avoids dispositions of the company's 'property'. In *Re Hirth* [1899] 1 QB 612, Rigby LJ said that 'the property of the company' in relation to a winding up is the property which ultimately turns out to be the property of the company when the time comes for the division of the company's assets. Thus if there is a dispute about the ownership of property which the company purports to dispose of after the presentation of a petition, the disposal will only be avoided if it is eventually determined that ownership of the property was vested in the company. Alternatively, on a sale of goods by the company, the disposition may be made at the time the contract was entered into (and which may be before the commencement of the winding up) rather than the later time when the goods are delivered by the company. See *Re Wiltshire Iron Co., ex parte Pearson* (1868) LR 3 Ch App 443.

9.7.4 WHAT AMOUNTS TO A DISPOSITION?

IA 1986, s. 127, avoids 'dispositions' of the company's property.

Payments into and out of the company's bank accounts, if overdrawn, are dispositions. Payments out are obviously dispositions. Where the account is overdrawn, the bank is a creditor of the company. A payment in (whether in cash or by a third party's cheque) will, in the ordinary course of banking business, be credited by reducing the overdraft by the amount paid in. That reduction is a disposition made by the bank on the company's behalf, discharging *pro tanto* the company's liability on its overdraft. See *Re Gray's Inn Construction Co. Ltd* [1980] 1 WLR 711 per Buckley LJ.

Buckley LJ in *Re Gray's Inn Construction Co. Ltd* said that the position regarding payments into and out of bank accounts in credit was not materially different from that described in the preceding paragraph. The relevant account in *Re Gray's Inn* was overdrawn, so this comment was obviously *obiter*. The point arose directly in *Re Barn Crown Ltd* [1994] BCC 381 at first instance. The bank conceded that payments out were dispositions, and the liquidator conceded that the grounds for seeking repayment of the payments out would have to be formally reduced to writing (other than in mere restitution) and adjudicated upon. Regarding the payments into the bank account, it was held that while the account was in credit there was no disposition of the company's property within the meaning of s. 127, and the declaration sought by the liquidator was dismissed.

In *Re J. Leslie Engineers Co. Ltd* [1976] 1 WLR 292, Oliver J said: 'It seems to me to be wholly immaterial, so long as one is dealing with the company's property, whether the purported disposition is made by the company or by a third party, or whether it is made directly or indirectly'. In this case a director of the company drew two cheques, one for £250 the other for £800, on the company's bank account after the presentation of the winding-up petition. The £250 cheque was payable 'to cash', and the cash obtained from it was used to buy money orders from the Post Office payable in favour of one of the company's creditors. This was held to be an indirect disposition of the company's property. The £800 cheque was drawn in favour of the director himself, and was paid into a joint account in the names of the director and his wife. Twelve days earlier the director had drawn a different cheque for £800 in favour of one of the company's creditors. The earlier £800 cheque was honoured after the company's £800 cheque was paid into the director's joint account. Although there was a disposition of the company's property when its cheque was paid into the director's joint account, once it had been paid in and mixed with other moneys in the account it ceased to be identifiable as the company's property. There being no evidence that it was a collusive payment, there was no disposition of the company's property when the cheque from the director's joint account was paid to the creditor.

9.7.5 CONSEQUENCE OF AVOIDANCE

By its terms, IA 1986, s. 127, merely avoids dispositions. It says nothing about recovery of the property disposed of. Invalidation and recovery are two distinct matters, and recovery is not regulated by the statute, but by the general law. Further, simply because a disposition is 'void' does not mean that it never took place. Generally, however, unless a disposition caught by the section is validated by the court, the liquidator will be able to recover the property, for example, as money had and received.

9.7.6 THE NATURE OF THE VALIDATING POWER

In *Re Steane's (Bournemouth) Ltd* [1950] 1 All ER 21, in a passage approved by the Court of Appeal in *Re Clifton Place Garage Ltd* [1970] Ch 477, Vaisey J said:

> The legislature, by omitting to indicate any particular principles which should govern the exercise of the discretion vested in the court, must be deemed to have left it entirely at large, and controlled only by the general principles which apply to every kind of judicial discretion.

In exercising that discretion:

> . . . each case must be dealt with on its own facts and particular circumstances (special regard being had to the question of the good faith and honest intention of the persons concerned), . . . the court is free to act according to the judge's opinion of what would be just and fair in each case.

There is an inherent reluctance to make validating orders because they derogate from the principle of *pari passu* distribution of the company's assets. That reluctance may be overcome if there is evidence that there is no serious risk to creditors because the company is solvent, or where there is evidence that the company is likely to improve the position of its creditors by trading at a profit during the period before the hearing of the winding-up petition. However, the court always does its best to ensure the interests of the company's unsecured creditors are not prejudiced.

Applications to validate post-presentation dispositions fall into three categories:

(a) Applications intended to keep the company in business. The underlying thought may be that the petition will come to nothing, or it may be an intention to sell the business as a going concern. This is discussed at **9.7.7**.

(b) Applications to validate some specific transaction. These are considered at **9.7.8**.

(c) Applications to validate transactions involved in the operation of a bank account, discussed at **9.7.9**.

In each case the burden of proof is on the party seeking an order validating the disposition: *Re Webb Electrical Ltd* (1988) 4 BCC 230.

9.7.7 SALVAGE CASES

In a frequently cited passage, Lord Cairns LJ in *Re Wiltshire Iron Co., ex parte Pearson* (1868) LR 3 Ch App 443 said:

> . . . where a company actually trading, which it is the interest of everyone to preserve, and ultimately to sell, as a going concern, is made the object of a winding-up petition, which may fail or may succeed, if it were to be supposed that transactions in the ordinary course of its current trade, bona fide entered into and completed, would be avoided, and would not, in the discretion given to the court, be maintained, the result would be that the presentation of a petition, groundless or well-founded, would, *ipso facto*, paralyse the trade of the company, and great injury, without any counterbalance of advantage, would be done to those interested in the assets of the company.

The general approach was considered by Buckley LJ in *Re Gray's Inn Construction Co. Ltd* [1980] 1 WLR 711. The desirability of the company being enabled to carry on its business is often speculative. It usually depends on whether a sale of the business as a going concern will probably be more beneficial than a break-up realisation of the company's assets. The court must carry out a balancing exercise weighing the likely benefits and dangers of the company continuing in business against the benefits and losses which may be the consequence of an immediate cessation of business.

In striking this balance the court acts on general common-sense lines. It will not demand a massive investigation into the consequences if the company is closed down: see Staughton LJ in *Re S.A. & D. Wright Ltd* [1992] BCC 503.

The above principles were applied in *Re Park Ward & Co. Ltd* [1926] Ch 828. With full notice of the presentation of a winding-up petition, and in order to provide funds for the payment of the company's workmen to enable the company to be sold as a going concern, a Mr Rowley advanced the company the sum of £1,200 secured by a debenture. The transaction was clearly for the benefit of the company, and was validated under the section.

9.7.8 SPECIFIC TRANSACTIONS

In applications to validate specific transactions the guiding principle is that the court seeks to preserve the value of the company's assets for the benefit of its creditors and contributories, while not unduly hampering the company in carrying out transactions which may be beneficial: *Re A.I. Levy (Holdings) Ltd* [1964] Ch 19.

A sale of an asset at its full market value after presentation of a petition involves no dissipation of the company's assets, and therefore cannot harm the company's creditors. Consequently, there is usually no reason why the court should not exercise its discretion to validate it. Even more so if the transaction preserves assets which would otherwise be lost (as in *Re Park Ward & Co. Ltd* [1926] Ch 828), or where the value of the company's assets is increased by the transaction. See *Re Gray's Inn Construction Co. Ltd* [1980] 1 WLR 711 and *Re Sugar Properties (Derisley Wood) Ltd* (1987) 3 BCC 88. Sometimes the benefit obtained by the company from a transaction will be susceptible of positive proof. However, there may be a dispute as to what is the true 'market value' of an asset. Also, if the application relates to the completion of a partially completed contract the question of prejudice to unsecured creditors may be more uncertain.

According to Staughton LJ in *Re S.A. & D. Wright Ltd* [1992] BCC 503, a judge is entitled to conclude that a transaction is at least *apt* to benefit the company's unsecured creditors and to validate the transaction even if there is no evidence to prove it will in fact do so. Contrast this with *Re Mountforest Ltd* [1993] BCC 565, where a s. 127 order was refused. The company was in business running nursing homes. It was convicted of an offence connected with that business and under legislation introduced in 1990 was precluded from continuing running the homes. About the same time an unfair prejudice petition under the Companies Act 1985, s. 459 was presented. In those circumstances it was obvious that its business had to be sold. An application was made under s. 127 seeking advance validation of a sale of the business to a company called Unicare plc. All the shares in Unicare were held by the majority shareholders in Mountforest, and both companies had three directors in common. Harman J held that although the court may validate a self-dealing transaction, it would not do so unless those proposing the transaction gave full and detailed particulars of the transaction. If full particulars are given, the court will also consider whether an intelligent and honest man could reasonably decide that the proposed transaction is necessary or expedient in the interest of the company.

9.7.9 BANK ACCOUNTS

An application to validate the operation of a bank account is a specific and common example of applications designed to allow the company to continue trading, as discussed at **9.7.7**. The principal considerations for the court are whether or not the company is solvent in the sense of being able to pay its bills as they fall due, with current assets exceeding current liabilities, and whether the order is likely to prejudice the company's unsecured creditors.

Most banks always check the *Gazette* to see if any of their customers are subject to winding-up petitions. A bank concerned about the effect of IA 1986, s. 127 will simply freeze a customer's accounts once it hears of the petition. A slightly more sophisticated (and slightly more risky) method of self-help available to banks is to take the following steps:

(a) Freeze the company's accounts and insist that all subsequent dealings be conducted on a separate account.

(b) Require personal assurances from the directors that no payments from the new ccount will be made in discharge of preliquidation debts.

(c) Insist that all new payments be in the ordinary course of the company's business.

In *Re Gray's Inn Construction Co. Ltd* [1980] 1 WLR 711, instead of doing the above the bank allowed the company to continue using its existing account, without seeking a validation order. A total of £24,000 was paid out of the account after presentation of the petition. Although all of this was potentially void under s. 127, the Court of Appeal refused to penalise the bank further than was necessary to restore the fund of assets available for distribution in the liquidation. The total post-liquidation trading loss was found to be £5,000, so payments out totalling £19,000 were validated.

Either the company or its bank may apply for a validation order before the petition is heard. A standard form of s. 127 order is shown at **Figure 9.2**. Paragraph (1) validates payments into or out of the company's accounts if they are 'in the ordinary course of the business of the company'. Although the company will know whether it is complying with this clause, it will be very expensive for banks to ensure it is complied with. The proviso to the order, which is in the form drafted by Mrs Jane Giret of Counsel and approved in *Re a Company (No. 00687 of 1991)* [1991] BCC 210, removes this difficulty.

Figure 9.2 Standard form of s. 127 order

IN THE HIGH COURT OF JUSTICE No. 1329 of 2000

CHANCERY DIVISION

COMPANIES COURT

IN THE MATTER of Woodcroft Kitchen Company Limited

AND IN THE MATTER of the Insolvency Act 1986

UPON THE APPLICATION of Woodcroft Kitchen Company Limited
AND UPON HEARING counsel for the Applicant and counsel for the Petitioner named in the petition to wind up the company presented to the court on the 28th of February 2000.

AND UPON READING the evidence.

ORDER that notwithstanding the presentation of the said petition

(1) payments made into or out of the bank accounts of the company in the ordinary course of the business of the company and
(2) dispositions of the property of the company made in the ordinary course of its business for proper value

between the date of presentation of the petition and the date of judgment on the petition or further order in the meantime shall not be void by virtue of the provisions of section 127 of the Insolvency Act 1986 in the event of an order for the winding up of the company being made on the said petition.

Provided that Regional Bank plc shall be under no obligation to verify for itself whether any transaction through the company's bank accounts is in the ordinary course of the company's business or that it represents full market value for the relevant transaction.

DATED the 15th of March 2000

9.7.10 ADVANCE VALIDATION

It is a very common exercise of the discretion under s. 127 for payments in the ordinary course of business to be sanctioned in advance of the making of the winding-up order. It is particularly important to seek advance validation when a proposed transaction is unusual, such as the sale of a business tenancy. Sometimes the courts take into account a failure to seek advance validation in considering whether to validate a disposition at a later stage.

9.7.11 NOTICE OF THE PETITION

As mentioned at **9.7.1**, time will certainly elapse between the presentation of a petition and persons dealing with the company receiving notice of it. Oliver J in *Re J. Leslie Engineers Co. Ltd* [1976] 1 WLR 292 regarded the absence of actual notice to the recipient of the company's property as being a very powerful factor in the exercise of the court's discretion, but not in itself conclusive.

A bona fide transaction in the ordinary course of the company's business at a time when the parties are unaware of the petition will, however, normally by validated (*Re Neath Harbour Smelting & Rolling Works* (1887) 56 LT 727).

9.7.12 ATTEMPTS TO PREFER

If the disposition is construed as an attempt to prefer a pre-presentation creditor, it will not be validated, even if the recipient was unaware of the petition and the company's intention to prefer (*Re J. Leslie Engineers Co. Ltd* [1976] 1 WLR 292). Contrast the situation where it is in the interests of the creditors generally that the company's business should be carried on and this could only be achieved by paying for unpaid goods already supplied to the company when the petition was presented. In such a case the court might think fit to exercise its discretion to validate the payment (*Re Gray's Inn Construction Co. Ltd* [1980] 1 WLR 711 per Buckley LJ).

9.7.13 RECEIVERS

A similar approach to that adopted in *Re Gray's Inn Construction Co. Ltd* [1980] 1 WLR 711 is taken when a receiver carries on the company's business after presentation of a winding-up petition (see *Re Clifton Place Garage Ltd* [1970] Ch 477).

9.7.14 SOLVENT COMPANIES

A winding-up petition may be presented by a contributory (e.g., a shareholder), and in such cases the company is likely to be solvent. In such cases:

(a) Payments in the ordinary course of the company's business will almost certainly be validated.

(b) Other transactions will also be validated if:

(i) the directors consider that the transaction is within their powers and is necessary or expedient in the interests of the company; and

(ii) their reasons for this opinion are such that an intelligent and honest person could reasonably hold.

See *Re Burton & Deakin Ltd* [1977] 1 All ER 631.

9.7.15 CONTRIBUTORY'S PETITION

In *Practice Direction (Companies Court: Contributory's Petition)* [1990] 1 WLR 490 it is stated that the prayer in a contributory's petition must state whether the petitioner consents to a s. 127 order in the standard form. If the petitioner objects, or would consent to a modification of the standard form, a short statement of the reasons must be included in the affidavit in support of the petition.

9.7.16 SHARE TRANSACTIONS

Share transactions are specifically referred to in IA 1986, s. 127. Different considerations apply than in respect of trading dispositions. Strong reasons are required before the court will exercise its discretion. In *Re Onward Building Society* [1891] 2 QB 463, Kay LJ said: '. . . before the court gives leave to register such a transfer, it ought to see that to do so would be of some benefit to the company or those interested in its assets, and . . . it would not so exercise its discretion unless for very strong reasons.'

9.7.17 PROCEDURE

Urgent applications under IA 1986, s. 127 before the hearing of the winding-up petition are made to the judge. Applications after a winding-up order has been made are heard by the Registrar.

9.7.18 COSTS

As always, costs are in the discretion of the court. However, if the application for validation is in respect of a transaction for the benefit of the company, the order will not be seen as simply an indulgence. Thus, in *Re Park Ward & Co. Ltd* [1926] Ch 828 the debenture holder was entitled to add the costs of the application to the security.

9.8 Subsequent Steps in the Liquidation

9.8.1 ON MAKING THE ORDER

If a winding-up order is made, the court then notifies the official receiver (who becomes the liquidator of the company) and draws up the order. The official receiver serves a copy of the order on the company and on the registrar of companies. He also advertises it in the *Gazette* and another newspaper.

9.8.2 EARLY DISSOLUTION

If the official receiver considers:

(a) that the realisable assets of the company are insufficient to cover the expenses of the winding up; and

(b) that the affairs of the company do not require investigation,

he may apply to the registrar of companies for the early dissolution of the company. The official receiver first gives 28 days' notice to the company's creditors and contributories, then gives notice to the registrar. Dissolution takes effect three months later.

9.8.3 LIQUIDATION

The official receiver will normally summon meetings of creditors and contributors, who choose a liquidator. The liquidator's main task is to take custody or control of all the company's property and things in action. Officers and employees of the company are required to give the liquidator information about the company's business and affairs. Various powers available to the liquidator are set out in IA 1986, sch. 4. These include powers to make compromises with creditors, to hold meetings of creditors, and even to carry on the company's business (provided this is necessary for the beneficial winding up of the company, e.g. to sell it as a going concern).

When all the assets have been realised, the funds are applied to pay:

(a) the costs of the liquidation;

(b) preferential debts (some taxes, VAT, four months' pay for employees);

(c) unsecured creditors;

(d) shareholders.

Members within each category rank *pari passu*. If there are insufficient funds to pay a category, the liquidator pays a dividend.

When the winding up is complete, the liquidator prepares a report, which is placed before a final meeting of creditors. The creditors receive the report and, if it is in order, release the liquidator. The liquidator then notifies the court and files his return with the registrar of companies. Three months later the company is dissolved.

9.8.4 DISSOLUTION

On dissolution, the company's corporate existence ends. This is subject to an application being made to declare the dissolution void under CA 1985, s. 651.

Figure 9.3 Usual order for the compulsory winding up of a company

IN THE HIGH COURT OF JUSTICE — No. 1329 of 2000

CHANCERY DIVISION

COMPANIES COURT

Mr Registrar Jenkins

Wednesday the 26th day of April 2000

IN THE MATTER of Woodcroft Kitchen Company Limited

AND IN THE MATTER of the Insolvency Act 1986

UPON THE PETITION of a creditor of the company presented to this court on 23rd day of February 2000.

AND UPON HEARING counsel for the Petitioner and no one appearing for and on behalf of the said Respondent company.

AND UPON READING the evidence.

IT IS ORDERED that Woodcroft Kitchen Company Limited be wound up by this court under the provisions of the Insolvency Act 1986.

AND IT IS ORDERED that the costs of Rosewall Electricals Limited of the said petition be paid out of the assets of the company.

DATED the 26th day of April 2000.

NOTE

One of the official receivers attached to the court is by virtue of this order liquidator of the company.

TEN

ADVOCACY IN COMPANIES COURT PROCEEDINGS

10.1 Introduction

This chapter will consider how to prepare for and how to present winding-up petitions before the Companies Court Registrar and applications before the judges of the Chancery Division.

High Court winding-up petitions proceeding in London are heard in one of the main court rooms in the Royal Courts of Justice on Wednesdays. Large numbers of petitions, about 40 every half hour, are heard throughout the morning and sometimes into the afternoon. Each petition is allocated, in effect, less than a minute of court time. All the papers will have been considered in advance both by the court and the parties. Opposed petitions are dealt with separately, so the Wednesday lists are intended for unopposed petitions. Essentially, the task of the Companies Court Registrar is to either make the winding-up order, stand it over if the formalities have not been completed, or to dismiss the petition (if the creditor does not attend, or has been paid, or if the Registrar takes the view the petition is not being proceeded with). Counsel's task is to assist with this process, and to present the key factors to the court in an efficient and accurate manner.

Judge's applications are made in open court. If the proceedings are in the High Court in London, the matter will be heard in one of the main court rooms in the Royal Courts of Justice, but in this case commonly in the Thomas More Building. Companies Court applications are heard on Mondays, but general Chancery Division applications can be listed for any day of the week.

10.2 Winding-up Petitions

10.2.1 BACKGROUND

A petition for the compulsory winding up of a company incorporated by registration under the Companies Acts may be presented by the company, or its directors, or by any creditor or creditors (including any contingent or prospective creditor or creditors), or by a contributory (i.e., shareholder) or contributories, various officials (e.g., Secretary of State for Trade and Industry and the Attorney-General), administrators and administrative receivers, or by all or any of those parties, separately or together (Insolvency Act 1986, s. 124(1)). The one met most frequently in practice is a creditor's petition on the ground that the company is unable to pay its debts. An inexperienced advocate should beware of believing that such petitions present no difficulties simply because they are very numerous and usually undisputed. Before appearing on the hearing of such a petition, the advocate should study carefully the relevant provisions of the Insolvency Act 1986 and the Insolvency Rules 1986 (SI No. 1925). References to forms, by number, are references to the forms prescribed by the IR 1986. The IR 1986 prescribe the form which a petition should take (see sch. 4, Form 4. 2 and **Figure 9.1**).

Generally the High Court and county courts have concurrent jurisdiction and a petitioner may choose in which court to proceed. The procedure laid down by the IR 1986 is described at **9.5**.

10.2.2 THE COURT

Winding-up petitions are listed for hearing before the Registrar of the Companies Court sitting in open court on Wednesday mornings at 10.30 a.m. Petitions are listed in 30 minute batches, so that a number of matters will be found in the list marked 'not before 11.00' and so on. The registrar is addressed as 'Sir'; counsel and solicitors must appear in robes.

10.2.3 DISPUTED PETITIONS

While petitions may be presented by a variety of parties mentioned above, the most common category of petitioners are creditors. Some creditors may be described as 'trade' creditors (meaning that their debts have been incurred in the course of the company's business). Others may be 'judgment' creditors where the company has failed to satisfy a judgment order made against it. If the company disputes the *locus standi* of the petitioner as a creditor, on the ground that the debt upon which a petition is to be or has been presented is disputed, the company may apply for an injunction restraining presentation in court or advertisement of the petition (which occurs after the petition has been served on the company). Such application will be made to the judge taking the Companies Court business. If the company fails to take such preventive steps, it may still dispute the petitioner's entitlement to a winding-up order on the ground that the debt is disputed by giving notice to the solicitors for the petitioner. Because of the danger of spurious disputes being used to defeat creditors, the Companies Court judges have recently introduced a practice of requiring the company in doubtful cases to make a payment into court of (or otherwise securing the amount of) the debt, pending an application for summary judgment by the petitioner.

10.2.4 BEFORE THE HEARING

The following is a checklist of the matters which must have been attended to by the instructing solicitors before the hearing. Counsel should ensure that he or she has copies of these documents in preparing the file for the hearing and that any defects which are found in them, e.g., inconsistent dates or sums owed, erroneous title of company in the advertisement etc. are discussed with the solicitor before the hearing. If there has been non-compliance with the rules, remedial action will be required, as indicated after each point.

10.2.4.1 Petition and verifying affidavit or witness statement

Counsel should have a copy of both of these documents.

10.2.4.2 Affidavit or witness statement of service

Service must be proved by affidavit or witness statement in the form set out in Form 4.4 or 4.5. The text of the affidavit should state the date on which the petition was served. It is a strict requirement that it must also specify the method of service used. Service of the petition and verifying affidavit must generally be effected at the company's registered office: IR 1986, r. 4.8(2). Permissible methods of service are set out in r. 4.8(3), for which, see **9.5.2**:

The affidavit or witness statement of service should exhibit the petition and any order for substituted service: r. 4.9. It is important to double-check that these requirements have been satisfied, as defects in service and proving service are among the most common problems encountered in winding-up petitions.

10.2.4.3 Remedies

If the affidavit or witness statement is defective the court will have to be asked for an adjournment of the petition either:

(a) to reswear the affidavit, if the petition was properly served but the affidavit does not correctly state the facts or has failed to specify the manner of service; or

(b) to effect reservice, if the petition has not been properly served.

If the company appears on the hearing, it may seek dismissal of the petition on the ground that it has been advertised after a defective service. If the company has been properly served and appears, a defect in the affidavit will cease to be relevant.

10.2.4.4 Advertisement

Unless the court directs otherwise, each petition must be advertised once in the *Gazette* and contain certain required information as set out in r. 4.11. There is a prescribed form of advertisement, Form 4.6.

A copy of the advertisement should be included in the brief for counsel for the petitioner. Unless it is the company's own petition, the advertisement must have appeared not less than seven business days after service of the petition, nor less than seven business days (which do not include Saturdays, Sundays or bank holidays) before the hearing date (see r. 4.11(2)(b)). This is a most important requirement, as it enables the company to prevent the highly damaging consequences of advertisement by applying for an injunction if the petitioner's debt is disputed. It is also designed to ensure that the class remedy of winding up by the court is made available to all creditors, and is not used as a means of putting pressure on the company to pay the petitioner's debt. Failure to comply with the rule, without good reason, may lead to the summary dismissal of the petition on the return date (see IPPD, para. 2.1). Counsel should ensure that the advertisement complied with r. 4.11, that the time requirements have been met, and that there are no typographical errors in the advertisement.

10.2.4.5 Remedies

If the advertisement rules have not been complied with, the court may dismiss the petition. In the case of premature publication, if the publication is a day early, e.g., because of an innocent failure to count a bank holiday, the court may waive the defect. Counsel should point out the premature advertisement, state the reason shortly, and ask that the defect be waived. There is always a serious risk that the petition will be dismissed on this ground.

If a court orders that a petition be re-served due to defective service, counsel should ask whether a second advertisement will also be required. If this is required, counsel may request that the required time periods be abated although this is at the discretion of the court.

If the court, in its discretion, grants an adjournment after a failure to advertise, this will be on the condition that the petition is advertised in due time for the adjourned hearing. No further adjournment for the purpose of advertisement will normally be granted (IPPD, para. 2.1).

10.2.4.6 Certificate of compliance

Under IR 1986, r. 4.14, the petitioner or its solicitor must, at least five days before the hearing of the petition, file with the court a certificate of due compliance showing the dates of presentation, service, advertisement and hearing (Form 4.7), together with a copy of the advertisement. By IPPD, para. 3.1, in High Court cases, the certificate must be filed not later than 4.30 p.m. on the Friday before the hearing. Applications to file the certificate any later will only be allowed 'if some good reason is shown for the delay'. The present practice is for the court office to refuse to accept a certificate brought to the court after the Friday deadline. The registrar will normally mention this matter as soon as the petition is called on.

10.2.4.7 Remedy

If counsel has a certificate which has been filed out of time and has no instructions as to the explanation, counsel may ask that the court take the matter second time around for instructions to be obtained. On giving an explanation counsel can request that the defect be waived. However, counsel should be aware that, particularly in London, the court is likely to refuse to allow the matter to be taken second time around, and will simply stand over (adjourn) the application for, e.g., 14 days to allow for a re-filing within the time requirements. In these cases, counsel should ask for the petition to be stood over for 14 days for filing of the certificate of compliance.

10.2.4.8 List of appearances

Every person, including creditors or the company itself, intending to appear on the hearing to support or oppose the making of a winding-up order must give notice to the solicitors for the petitioner not later than 16.00 hours (4 p.m.) on the business day before the hearing (IR 1986, r. 4.16). If the company intends to oppose the petition, its affidavit must be filed in court not less than seven days before the hearing (IR 1986, r. 4.18). It is the duty of the petitioner's solicitors to prepare a list of the persons who have given such notice (Form 4.10, known formally as the 'list of appearances', informally in court as 'the list', and colloquially from its colour as 'the blue form'). The list must be handed in **before the hearing** (IR 1986, r. 4.17(3)). If it is not handed in, the registrar will usually simply say when the petition is called on, 'There is no list', and decline to proceed further.

10.2.4.9 Remedy

The only help for this is to make sure that the solicitors' representative is seen well before the time for which the petition is listed, and told to hand in the list when the current half-hour's petitions are over. If the list has not been handed in, ask the registrar to 'take this matter second time round'.

10.2.4.10 Substitution

If the original petition is not proceeded with (because the petitioner withdraws), or is not advertised, or in other similar circumstances (see IR 1986, r. 4.19(1)), the court may, on such terms as it thinks just, substitute as petitioner any creditor or contributory who in the court's opinion would have a right to present a petition, and who is desirous of prosecuting it. The 'new' petitioner asks for a substitution order (see **10.4.1**, 'The Hearing', Counsel C below).

10.3 Noting the Back Sheet

It is helpful to compile the relevant information and the dates on which the required steps were taken for use as a quick guide during the hearing to avoid having to search through a file during the presentation. One example would be as follows:

Re: [name of company]
Trade creditor's petition based on a statutory demand in the sum of £______
List: [enter any creditors, contributories, or others supporting/opposing the petition and the nature of their interest]
Co: [note whether the company will make an appearance]

Relevant dates:

Presented:	[e.g., 28/3/2000]
Verified:	[29/3/2000]
Served:	[3/4/2000]
Affidavit:	[4/4/2000]
Advert:	[19/4/2000]
Cert. Comp:	[26/4/2000]

UCO (Asking for the usual compulsory order.)

10.4 The Hearing

10.4.1 EXAMPLES

The following applications may be heard in unopposed petition situations:

(1)	Associate:	'Petition number 546, Tyro Advisers Limited.'
	Counsel A (for Petitioner):	'This is a trade creditor's petition based on a statutory demand for the sum of £3,459 odd. The company is not represented, and the list is clear (or 'negative'). I ask for the usual compulsory order.'
	Registrar:	'Usual compulsory order.'
(2)	Associate:	'Petition number 547, D-I-Y Services Limited.'
	Counsel B:	'This is a petition based on a statutory demand for unpaid solicitors' fees.'
	Registrar:	'This petition was advertised only five business days after service, and r. 4.11 has not been complied with.'
	Counsel B:	'Sir, I am instructed that my instructing solicitors unfortunately overlooked the fact that seven business days must elapse between service and advertisement, and therefore did not omit from their calculation of the time two weekends and a bank holiday. In those circumstances, I ask that the defect be waived.'
	Registrar:	'No. These errors are capable of causing severe damage to a company which may wish to dispute the debt. There has been no effort in this case by the solicitors to cure the error, or to communicate with the court office in lieu of complying with r. 4.11. In the circumstances I propose to dismiss the petition.'
	Counsel C:	'I appear for Suppliers Limited, a supporting creditor which has not given notice to the petitioner's solicitors prior to this hearing. My client has a trade debt amounting to £78,968 odd, and my application is for permission to be added to the list out of time and for an order substituting my client as petitioner.'
	Registrar:	'I will give you permission to be added to the list out of time on the usual terms. I will also make an order substituting Miss C's client as the petitioner, and adjourn the matter for 28 days for amendment of the petition, re-service and re-advertisement.'

10.4.2 NOTES ON THE HEARING

(a) It is usual to describe the basis of the petition and to show what is alleged to prove the inability of the company to pay its debts (in this case failure to comply with a statutory demand, but other evidence may also be adduced).

(b) The court is told whether the company is represented: occasionally, the registrar will permit directors of the company to address the court to seek an adjournment, but strictly, a company can only appear by counsel or a solicitor.

(c) The court should be informed whether there are any supporting or opposing creditors or contributories on the list of appearances, and if so, how many of each and whether any of them have in fact appeared at the hearing. If there are none, the court is told that the list is clear or 'negative'.

(d) The usual compulsory order is set out in Form 4.11. (See **Figure 9.3**.)

(e) The 'usual terms' on which a creditor is added to the list of appearances out of time are that the applicant's solicitor undertakes not to seek any costs of giving notice or of the application to be added to the list in the event of a compulsory winding up being made. (A substituted petitioner will normally obtain an order for the subsequent costs of amendment, re-service, re-advertisement, and hearing.)

10.4.3 OPPOSED PETITIONS

If it becomes apparent that the petition is opposed the registrar will adjourn the matter for hearing before the judge of the Companies Court for that term (who sits to take companies business on Mondays).

10.4.4 ADJOURNMENTS

If an order is made, the winding up commences with the presentation of the petition (s. 129(2) of the Act). Section 127 avoids dispositions of property of a company made after the commencement of the winding up, unless the court has otherwise ordered. For this reason, the court will not permit a petition to remain outstanding for more than a few months (except in the case of petitions by contributories, where a winding up is sought, the company is solvent, and the judge has made appropriate orders under s. 127). Even if the petitioner and the company have agreed that the company should have time to attempt to pay the petition debt, the court may refuse an adjournment if the petition has been current for a long period, and require the petitioner to seek a winding-up order or will dismiss the petition. Adjournments may also be necessary in disputed petitions in order to allow the company to prepare its evidence and for the petitioner to respond. If the need for the adjournment can be attributed to the fault of the company, stringent orders as to the costs of the adjournment may be imposed (*Re a Company (No. 005448 of 1996)* [1998] 1 BCLC 98).

10.5 Function of Judge's Applications

Judge's applications in the Chancery Division usually seek interim relief, although orders may be made which dispose finally of some question in issue in the proceedings (e.g., rectification of the register of members). Although any interim application in the Chancery Division might in theory be made to a judge, paragraph 7.2 of the Chancery Guide says that only applications which need to be heard by a judge (such as those for injunctions and committal proceedings) should be made to a judge. Procedural applications, such as for directions, should be made to a Master unless there is some special reason for making it to a judge. Otherwise the application may be dismissed with costs. A special reason for applying to a judge may exist, for example, where the Applicant wants to apply to strike out and the Respondent has already issued an application seeking an injunction.

10.6 Procedural Aspects

Unless an application is to be made without notice, or the court gives permission to the contrary, the notice of application must be served at least three clear days before the day named in the application notice for the hearing (CPR, r. 23.7(1)(b)). Where permission has been given to serve short notice, that fact must be stated in the notice. A judge of the Chancery Division sits to hear applications on every weekday (except the last day) of each sitting, and applications are listed for hearing by that judge at 10.30 a.m. The Chancery Listing Office is responsible for the listing of judge's applications. An application will only be listed if two copies of the claim form and the application notice (with a fee, currently £50.00) are lodged with the Clerk of the Lists, Chancery Listing Office, Room W15, Thomas More Building, Royal Courts of Justice, before 12 noon on the day before the hearing date or on the preceding Friday if the date given for the hearing is a Monday (CDPD 5).

If an application without notice is required urgently, the Clerk to the Applications Judge should be notified by telephone. If the Applications Judge is unable to hear it promptly, it may be heard by any judge who is available, though the request must first be made to the Clerk. If it is desired to have the application listed, two copies of the order sought should be lodged as well as an application notice (CDPD 5).

Applications are generally heard in open court and the procedure to be followed can be found in CDPD 3. Where it may be unjust for the application to be heard in public, the judge may exercise a discretion to sit otherwise than in open court; see CPR, r. 39.2.

Practitioners should be aware of the *Chancery Guide*, which consolidates information on practice in the Chancery Division including new and significant changes. The appendices to the *Chancery Guide* contain guidelines on the preparation of bundles, content of skeleton arguments and relevant addresses, room numbers, telephone and fax numbers. It also contains a model for the Judge's Application Information Form, which has to be completed with details of counsel and solicitors, and must be filed at the Chancery Listing Office.

Bundles of documents for use in court will generally be required for all applications where more than 25 pages are involved (see the *Chancery Guide*, para. 8.19). The usual rules on preparing bundles apply (see ***Civil Litigation Manual*, 33.7**). Also, the general rule is that skeleton arguments should be prepared for all judge's applications (*Chancery Guide*, para. 8.31). The exceptions are where the application does not warrant a skeleton, or is so urgent that preparing a skeleton is impracticable. For substantial matters, skeletons should be lodged two clear days before the hearing (para. 8.32), and for applications without notice the skeleton should be lodged with the papers (para. 8.33).

10.7 Conduct of Judge's Applications

10.7.1 GENERAL

Counsel briefed on a judge's application must robe and the application will be heard in open court. Where the circumstances of a case require a 'short notice' period, permission may be obtained on an application without notice, usually made after the midday adjournment.

The usual practice for normal applications is that the judge will ascertain at the sitting of the court which of the listed applications will be 'effective', that is, disputed, and if so, what counsel's estimate of length is, or 'ineffective', that is, disposed of by agreement. It is a matter of courtesy both to the court and to other counsel and litigants:

(a) to be present in court when the judge takes his seat;

(b) to be ready to say whether the application is 'effective' or 'ineffective';

(c) to have carefully considered the estimate of length (if the application is to be effective) and to have agreed that estimate with one's opponent;

(d) not to waste the time of the court when the judge is going through the list 'first time round' by explaining the substance of the application instead of simply indicating whether the application is effective or ineffective.

Although the judge has a discretion as to the order of hearing applications, he or she will normally deal with ineffective applications first, e.g., matters which are to be adjourned or have been settled. All other listed, unlisted and applications without notice will be heard in the order determined by the judge. Applications affecting the liberty of a subject (e.g., for release from committal to prison for contempt, or for habeas corpus) are always accorded priority.

Counsel with effective applications may be asked to wait, in case another judge becomes free to hear their application. The Applications Judge may transfer such of the day's applications as deemed appropriate, irrespective of priority. Counsel should not leave the precincts of the court unless released by the judge until a particular time. Counsel should also ensure that the court staff can easily locate them if a judge becomes free. Any application which at the end of the day is part heard (i.e., unfinished) will normally head the listed applications for the next court day.

10.7.2 TIME ESTIMATES

Time estimates are critical. Counsel are only permitted to make applications which are estimated to last less than two hours. If the application is estimated to last longer, it must be stood over (i.e., be adjourned) to come on as an 'application by order' (that is, on a specially fixed appointment, arranged by the solicitors or the clerks to counsel with the Clerk of the Lists). Counsel will be required to lodge with the Clerk a signed certificate stating the estimated length. An indication may be given that an application by order is to be treated as urgent. If it is apparent that the application will be likely to last more than two hours, the only proper course is to inform the court that it is ineffective, and 'second time round' to inform the judge, 'This application is likely to occupy the court for two days, and I therefore ask your Lordship to stand it over as an application by order. Subject to your Lordship's approval, the defendant is to give certain undertakings in the meantime'.

10.7.3 UNLISTED APPLICATIONS AND EMERGENCY APPLICATIONS

Frequently, counsel is instructed to move the court urgently without notice, so that the application has not been listed. It also happens that the instructing solicitors forget to lodge the papers for an application on notice in accordance with the directions mentioned above. Counsel may in these circumstances ask the judge to hear an application although unlisted. The judge's clerk should be notified (usually through counsel's clerk) as early in the day as possible, that an application is to be made, and two copies of the claim form (showing the title of the action), a completed Application Information Form and the draft of the order to be sought should be made available. If the proceedings have not yet been issued, every effort should be made to issue the originating process before the application is made. If this is not practical, the party making the application gives an undertaking to the court to issue the process forthwith. The usual practice is to rise in counsel's place after the judge has worked through the list for the first time, and to say, 'I have an unlisted application in the action of Smith and Jones [giving the number]'. Such an application will only rarely be ineffective, and counsel should go on to indicate the time estimate. Unless the application affects the liberty of the subject or is of exceptional urgency and importance, listed applications will be given priority.

10.7.4 INEFFECTIVE APPLICATIONS

An application can only genuinely be described as 'ineffective' if there is *no point of disagreement between the parties which requires the decision of the judge.* Counsel must ensure that all such points have been dealt with, and not attempt to be heard first under the guise of an ineffective application. The degree of information which the judge will require to have on the substance of an application depends on the nature of the order which the court is to be asked to make. It is usual to indicate in very general terms the nature of the action (e.g., 'This is an application for an injunction to restrain the defendant from dealing with certain land which is alleged to be subject to an option agreement'). Counsel will then usually inform the judge orally of the terms of the order which the judge is invited to make. If the order involves undertakings to the court or submission to an order (other than a purely procedural order) by one of the parties, the judge is likely to wish to know the exact terms of the undertakings. It is therefore not merely a formality to say 'The parties have agreed *subject to your Lordship's approval* that the application should stand over for 14 days on the defendant's undertaking not to dispose of the land known as [describing it]': the terms of the undertaking or an order in the same terms are subject to the approval of the judge.

If a party who is to consent to an order or give undertakings is neither present nor represented (either by counsel or a solicitor on the record), an order will only be made on production of a 'letter of consent' signed by or on behalf of the solicitors on the record for the party (see CDPD 3). An acknowledgment of service by the respondent to an application is required and time is often wasted in court because the solicitors offering written consent (to avoid the cost of an attendance) have failed to return the acknowledgment. Counsel for the claimant should always check in these circumstances whether the solicitors giving the consent are on the record. If they are not, the judge will sometimes make an order in the terms agreed, but direct that the order is not to be drawn up until the solicitors are on the record. It usually assists in obtaining that result if counsel has ascertained before the hearing that the solicitors are not yet on the record, and has explained that fact to the court.

10.7.5 EFFECTIVE APPLICATIONS

The order in which effective, i.e., disputed, listed applications are dealt with is in the discretion of the judge. Counsel will normally offer their colleagues the courtesy of allowing shorter applications to be made first. Naturally, this must not be abused by underestimating the time which an application will take. The procedure will then follow this outline:

(a) Counsel making the application will open by giving a short account of the facts giving rise to the application.

(b) Counsel then reads the evidence in support of the application.

(c) The opposing counsel will read (in the appropriate order) the evidence served by the other side.

(d) Counsel for the applicant then makes his or her submissions on the evidence as presented.

(e) Counsel for the respondent makes his or her submissions.

(f) Counsel for the applicant is entitled to reply on the submissions of the opposing party.

It will be noticed that the evidence is read aloud in court. When applications are made effectively for the first time, there has naturally been no opportunity for the judge to read any witness statements or affidavits, as these will not have been filed before the application is made. If the application has been stood over as an application by order, it is good practice to advise the instructing solicitors to prepare a paginated bundle of the evidence on the application and to lodge it in advance of the hearing. It may then be possible to follow the Commercial Court practice of hearing argument in open court only on those aspects of the evidence which are disputed. When making time estimates, therefore, counsel should bear in mind the probability that the evidence on an application will have to be read *in extenso* in court.

10.7.6 AGREED ADJOURNMENTS

If all parties agree, an application can be adjourned for not more than 14 days by delivering (or sending by fax) the written consent of counsel or solicitors to the Clerk of the Lists no later than 4.30 p.m. on the day before the listed hearing. A litigant in person who is a party must attend before the Clerk as well as sign a consent. Not more than three successive adjournments may be made and no adjournments are to be made to the last two application days of any sitting. Undertakings previously given to the court may be continued unchanged over the duration of any adjournment. If an existing undertaking is to be varied or a new undertaking given, the adjournment must be dealt with by the judge.

An application may be adjourned to be heard as an application by order without attendance before the judge where the parties are agreed that the application will take two hours or more. Written consent of all parties' solicitors or counsel must be delivered to the Clerk by 4.00 p.m. on the day before the hearing. See CDPD 3.

10.7.7 DRAFTING OF ORDERS

10.7.7.1 Orders made by masters

Interim orders will be drawn up by the court (CDPD 8).

10.7.7.2 Orders made by judges

Unless the court directs or permits a party to draw it up, the court will draw up the order and send it out without reference to the parties. An unusually complicated order may require that an initial draft be sent to the parties.

10.7.7.3 Tomlin order

Where the action is to be stayed on agreed terms to be scheduled to the order, the minutes should contain a specially drafted clause. See CDPD 8.

10.7.8 USE OF INFORMATION TECHNOLOGY

No standard practice for the use of information technology in Chancery cases has yet been prescribed although this is likely to change over the next few years. In any case where the solicitors for one or more parties take the view that some form of IT will assist the presentation or management of a case, the solicitor should obtain, at an early stage, directions from the judge who is to try the case. Where no nomination of a specific judge has yet been made, solicitors who wish to use any form of IT should invite the Vice-Chancellor (by request to his or her clerk) to nominate a judge to hear the case including all interim matters.

When skeleton arguments or chronologies exist in electronic form, inquiries should be made of the judge (via his or her clerk) as to whether the provision of these documents on disk as well as in hard copy would be welcome. Any disk supplied to a judge should be new and newly formatted to minimise the risk of transferring a computer virus.

Where a party is entitled to a copy of a document which has been prepared by another party for use in court in electronic form, he or she may require that it also be provided to him or her in electronic form.

ELEVEN

SHAREHOLDER PROTECTION

11.1 Introduction

Control of the company rests with the members voting in general meeting or the directors to the extent that powers have been delegated to them. Members will have such control over the directors as the articles and statute give them, in particular they have the right to remove the directors or alter the articles and withdraw their powers (see **6.2**).

Members' decisions are usually by ordinary resolution (simple majority) of those who attend and vote at general meetings. All members will be bound by the resolutions properly passed at general meetings. In smaller private companies the directors may also be the majority shareholders with the result that minority shareholders have virtually no control over the company's activities.

Clearly where a shareholder objects to the manner in which a company is being conducted the most logical thing to do is to sell the shares and invest elsewhere. However, this is not always possible, as in small private companies there may be restrictions on the ability of shareholders to sell contained in the articles or in a practical sense in that no one will buy them. In addition, the mismanagement may be such that the aggrieved shareholder wishes to do something about it because the value of the shares has been affected or purely as a matter of principle. However, it is usually the case that shareholders who are aggrieved will simply sell their shares.

This chapter will consider a number of miscellaneous methods of affording some protection to a company's shareholders, and will then concentrate on the rule in *Foss* v *Harbottle*. Two very important statutory measures for protecting minority shareholders, namely, just and equitable winding up and petitions for relief against unfair prejudice, will be considered in **Chapters 12** and **13** respectively.

11.2 Breach of Articles

If a member is dissatisfied with his or her treatment by the company, an action may be brought against the company if the treatment amounts to an abuse of individual rights given by the articles (e.g. the right to a notice of meetings, or to vote): CA 1985, s. 14; *Salmon* v *Quin & Axtens Ltd* [1909] AC 442. Such an action may be a personal action to protect a personal right only or it may be a representative action to protect all those whose rights have been denied (e.g. for all shareholders not paid their dividend). Such an action would be governed by RSC O. 15, r. 12(1) (as preserved in the CPR, sch. 1), and can only be brought if all parties have the same interest in the proceedings (see *Prudential Assurance Co. Ltd* v *Newman Industries Ltd* [1981] Ch 229).

11.3 Statutory Protection in Running of a Company

Statute gives some protection to the minority in the general running of the company by:

(a) Requiring a greater majority (e.g., special resolution) to pass resolutions to effect major changes in the company's constitution — e.g., alter objects (CA 1985, s. 4), articles (s. 9), name (s. 28) or reduce capital (s. 135).

(b) Providing that some things cannot be done without the consent of all members — e.g., a member's liability cannot be increased without that member's written consent (CA 1985, s. 16).

(c) Empowering members to require meetings to be called and/or information to be circulated to members (important as directors generally have the power to call meetings, set agendas and circulate information) (see **6.7**).

(d) Giving members the right to object to the court in some cases even though a resolution has been passed with the requisite majority — e.g., alteration of class rights (CA 1985, s. 127), financial assistance and purchase of own shares out of capital in a private company (CA 1985, s. 157 and s. 176).

11.4 DTI Investigation

Under CA 1985, s. 431, the DTI may investigate the affairs of a company on the application of 200 shareholders or the holders of one-tenth of the share capital. Under CA 1985, s. 432, the DTI may investigate the affairs of a company where the department considers that they have been conducted, *inter alia*, in a manner unfairly prejudicial to some of its members, or proper information has not been given to its members. Inspectors are appointed with extensive powers to investigate and on receipt of their report the DTI may take a variety of actions including instituting civil proceedings on behalf of the company, petitioning for an order under CA 1985, s. 459, or for liquidation under IA 1986, s. 122(1)(g).

11.5 The Rule in *Foss* v *Harbottle*

11.5.1 THE RULE

In a company's affairs the maxim 'majority rules' prevails. This means that dissatisfied shareholders rarely can act if they feel the company is badly managed to their detriment, e.g. if they feel they are getting a poor return on their investment through the incompetence of the directors. The rule is formulated to prevent a multiplicity of such actions. The case of *Foss* v *Harbottle* (1843) 2 Hare 461 clearly indicated that if a wrong is done to a company then the company is the proper claimant to right that wrong.

This rule stems from the court's reluctance to interfere in the management of a company (*Carlen* v *Drury* (1812) 1 Ves & B 154 — 'This court is not to be required on every occasion to take the management of every brewhouse and playhouse in the kingdom'). In *Foss* v *Harbottle* (1843) 2 Hare 461 two shareholders brought an action against five directors alleging misappropriation of property by them. The court held that as the injury was to the company, the company was the proper claimant and the shareholders were not competent to bring the action. It did acknowledge that this rule could be departed from but only if there were reasons of a very urgent character. In *Mozley* v *Alston* (1847) 1 Ph 790 two shareholders sought an injunction to restrain the board from acting until four of the directors who ought to have retired by rotation to allow four others to be elected did so. It expressly alleged that a majority of the shareholders supported the action and the court commented that if that was so there was obviously nothing to prevent the company from instituting an action. Such an action would be free from objection as it would be by a body legally authorised to represent the shareholders generally. In *MacDougall* v *Gardiner* (1875) 1 ChD 13, the articles of the company provided for the taking of a poll at a general meeting if five shareholders demanded one. The chairman, in breach of the articles, refused to take a poll on the question of adjournment and MacDougall brought an action seeking a declaration and an injunction to restrain the directors from taking further action. The court emphasised that the rule in *Foss* v *Harbottle* and *Mozley* v *Alston* must always be adhered to, that nothing connected with internal disputes can be made the subject of an action by one shareholder on behalf of himself and others unless there was something illegal, oppressive or fraudulent. The nature of companies meant that there was nothing more likely than that there would be something more or less irregular done at company meetings and if every member had a right to take action everything would be litigated whereas if actions had to be taken in the name of the company then, unless the majority really wished for litigation, it would not go on. Thus there is no point in having litigation in respect of a thing which in substance the majority of the company are entitled to do as the ultimate end is that a meeting is called and the majority gets its wish. In *Edwards* v *Halliwell* [1950] 2 All ER 1064 where members of a trade union sought a declaration that an increase in union dues was invalid on the ground that a rule which required a two-thirds vote on a ballot had not been followed, the rule in *Foss* v *Harbottle* was analysed as having two aspects, first the proper claimant principle (the company as the wronged person is the proper claimant) and secondly the majority rule principle (where the transaction is one which a simple majority may resolve to do and bind the company, an action by an individual shareholder cannot be maintained). The reasons for and exceptions to the rules are the subject of much academic debate.

The decision to sue must therefore be made by the company and this means either a decision of the board or a decision of the members in general meeting. (It is open to debate whether the members may resolve to sue if the general management powers have been delegated to the board: see *Marshall's Valve Gear Co. Ltd* v *Manning Wardle & Co. Ltd* [1909] 1 Ch 267 and *John Shaw & Sons (Salford) Ltd* v *Shaw* [1935] 2 KB 113.) One view is that it is a shared power. The clear rule laid down in *Foss* v *Harbottle* (1843) 2 Hare 461 is that a single shareholder, or indeed minority shareholders, may not sue.

Given the multitude of cases, complexity and differing views of the law, the following can be no more than a broad overview of the generally accepted exceptions. However, before setting out the exceptions it is necessary to set out in outline the different types of action which may be commenced.

11.5.2 TYPES OF ACTION

11.5.2.1 Personal

This is an action by a member to enforce personal rights arising from the section 14 contract or under the general law. It is commenced by the member as claimant in the same way as any other action to enforce a right, with the company and wrongdoer as defendants.

11.5.2.2 Representative

An action by a member on behalf of a group of shareholders to enforce a common right. RSC 1965, O. 15, r. 12 (preserved in the CPR, sch. 1), will apply to the proceedings which may be brought where:

(a) all members on whose behalf the action is brought have a separate cause of action and the relief claimed would not confer a right of action where none previously existed; and

(b) all members of the class represented share an interest which is common to all of them; and

(c) the court is satisfied that it is for the benefit of the class that the claimant should be permitted to sue in such a representative action (*Prudential Assurance Co. Ltd* v *Newman Industries Ltd* [1981] Ch 229).

The nature of representative actions is considered in the ***Civil Litigation Manual*, 8.4**.

Representative actions are used in a variety of circumstances, e.g., challenging administrative decisions and litigation by or against unincorporated associations as well as in the context of company law.

11.5.2.3 Derivative

This is an action by a member to enforce a right of the company (the rights are derived from the company). This is a type of action unique to company law, based on the legal concept that a company is a legal person separate from its members. The procedural rule is contained in RSC 1965, O. 15, r. 12A (preserved in the CPR, sch. 1). The member issues proceedings on behalf of all the other members against the alleged wrongdoers. However, as the action is brought on behalf of the company any award will be in its favour and not in favour of the member who actually instituted the proceedings. If the defendant in a derivative action has responded to the claim, the claimant must apply to the court for permission to continue the action. At the hearing the court may grant permission, dismiss the action or adjourn the application and give directions. To obtain permission to continue, it would appear that the claimant should establish a prima facie case that the company is entitled to the relief sought and that the action falls within the proper boundaries of the exceptions to the rule in *Foss* v *Harbottle* (*Prudential Assurance Co. Ltd* v *Newman Industries Ltd (No. 2)* [1982] Ch 204; see also *Smith* v *Croft (No. 2)* [1988] Ch 114).

The member bringing the action runs the risk of having to pay both his or her own costs and the other parties' costs. However, the court may direct the company to indemnify the member for such costs. Where such an indemnity is sought it must be joined with the application for permission to continue (RSC O. 15, r. 12A(13) (preserved in CPR, sch. 1)). It is likely that the court will only make an order if the action stands a reasonable chance of success and would be for the benefit of the company. In *Smith* v *Croft* [1986] 1 WLR 580 an order was refused where the action stood little chance of success and the majority of shareholders were against it.

A claimant may join a personal action with a derivative action with permission of the court, which will normally be given (*Cooke* v *Cooke* [1997] 2 BCLC 28).

11.5.3 EXCEPTIONS TO THE RULE

The conventional method of dealing with the exceptions is to classify them under the four headings set out in *Edwards* v *Halliwell* [1950] 2 All ER 1064.

11.5.3.1 Personal rights

A member may take action to protect his or her own personal rights under the articles, a separate shareholders' agreement or statute. This then is not really an exception to the rule in *Foss* v *Harbottle* because it is not an attempt to enforce the company's rights (it is frequently cited as an exception nevertheless). Thus a member may bring a personal action to enforce payment of dividends which have been declared (*Wood* v *Odessa Waterworks Co.* (1889) 42 ChD 636) or to have his or her vote recorded (*Pender* v *Lushington* (1877) 6 ChD 70 where a personal action was combined with a representative one). However, the difficulty with the exception is determining what is a personal right which can be so enforced. Compare *Pender* v *Lushington* with *MacDougall* v *Gardiner* (1875) 1 ChD 13 (see **11.5.1**) where a right to demand a poll was not enforceable. Exactly what provisions in the articles will be enforced under the s. 14 contract between the company and the member is a much debated question (see **3.4** and cases referred to there). It is clear, however, that a member cannot bring a personal action for loss in value of shares which resulted from damage to the company (*Prudential Assurance Co. Ltd* v *Newman Industries Ltd (No. 2)* [1982] Ch 204). The proper remedy is for the company to take action against the person who caused the damage to recover the loss which in turn will restore the value of the shares.

11.5.3.2 Illegal or *ultra vires* acts

A member may apply for an injunction to restrain the company from doing an illegal or *ultra vires* act (*Simpson* v *Westminster Palace Hotel Co.* (1860) 8 HL Cas 712). This is preserved by CA 1985, s. 35(2) as substituted by CA 1989, s. 108(1). The injunction may be sought in a personal or a representative action (*Prudential Assurance Co. Ltd* v *Newman Industries Ltd (No. 2)* [1982] Ch 204). In this respect it is not truly an exception to the rule. However, where the act complained of has been completed and the action is brought to recover property disposed of by the transaction the proper claimant is the company. Where a minority action is brought to recover property it must be a derivative one. At common law a company could not ratify an *ultra vires* act, but CA 1985, s. 35(3), allows this by special resolution. However, a company may resolve not to pursue a claim for damages or restitution and this is binding on minority shareholders unless fraud on the minority can be shown (*Smith* v *Croft (No. 2)* [1988] Ch 114).

11.5.3.3 Special majorities

Although it was said in *MacDougall* v *Gardiner* (1875) 1 ChD 13 that where a majority are entitled to do something there is no use in litigation as ultimately the majority can just resolve to do it in general meeting, this rule does not apply where, for example, a special resolution is required. In *Edwards* v *Halliwell* [1950] 2 All ER 1064, two trade union members who challenged an increase of dues which had been made without obtaining the required two-thirds majority consent were successful. In *Quin & Axtens Ltd* v *Salmon* [1909] AC 442 the articles of association gave the two managing directors a power of veto on certain transactions. On one transaction one of the directors dissented from the board resolution. The members in general meeting resolved to authorise the transaction. However, an injunction was granted restraining the company from acting on the resolutions as they were inconsistent with the articles and alteration of the articles requires a special resolution. This exception may be extended to cover other procedural irregularities, e.g., inadequate notice of meetings because insufficient information is given (*Baillie* v *Oriental Telephone & Electric Co. Ltd* [1915] 1 Ch 503 and *Kaye* v *Croydon Tramways Co.* [1898] 1 Ch 358). However, it is not clear how far this exception will extend.

11.5.3.4 Fraud on the minority

This is the true exception to the rule and a most difficult area to establish comprehensive principles from the numerous and varied cases. However, it is clear that there are two matters which must be proved: fraud and control. Exactly what amounts to fraud is unclear but the word does have a meaning wider than fraud at common law and includes an unconscionable abuse of majority power. It will include the appropriation of assets or advantages belonging to the company to the majority who then resolve in general meeting not to recover it (*Cook* v *Deeks* [1916] 1 AC 554, but note the contrast with *Regal (Hastings) Ltd* v *Gulliver* [1967] 2 AC 134 discussed in **7.4.4**). It will also include the compromising of litigation by a resolution of the majority to benefit themselves and disadvantage the company (*Estmanco (Kilner House) Ltd* v *Greater London Council* [1982] 1 WLR 2). In *Pavlides* v *Jensen* [1956] Ch 565 it was held that mere negligence on the part of directors who controlled the majority of the shares in the company was not sufficient. There was no allegation of fraud on the part of the directors nor of appropriation of company assets. The allegation was that company property had negligently been sold at an undervalue. Thus a resolution by the company that no action should be taken against the directors was binding on the shareholders and a minority action was not allowed. However, this case was distinguished in *Daniels* v *Daniels* [1978] Ch 406 where three minority shareholders brought an action against the two directors and majority shareholders alleging that they had caused the company to sell property at a gross undervalue to a director who was one of the majority shareholders. No fraud was alleged as the minority shareholders did not really know what had happened, only that the sale had been at an undervalue and that the director who bought had made a substantial profit. The court said that it would be monstrous, particularly as fraud is so hard to plead and prove, to restrict the exceptions to the rule in *Foss* v *Harbottle* to such an extent as to allow directors to make a profit by their negligence. A minority action was allowed on the basis that negligence may amount to fraud on the minority if it results in a benefit to the wrongdoers at the company's expense. What amounts to fraud on the minority is also often discussed in the context of the difference between a ratifiable and non-ratifiable breach.

It must be shown that the company is being prevented from bringing an action because of the control of the wrongdoer. Generally this will be shown by the fact that the wrongdoer has voting control. Thus there must be some attempt to persuade the company to sue before taking a minority action. It is not clear whether de facto control is sufficient. In *Prudential Assurance Co. Ltd* v *Newman Industries Ltd (No. 2)* [1982] Ch 204 the Court of Appeal appeared to prefer voting control but did comment that control embraced a broad spectrum from overall absolute majority of votes to a majority of votes made up of the delinquent and those voting with the directors as a result of influence or apathy. In *Smith* v *Croft (No. 2)* [1988] Ch 114 the court said that it was appropriate to have regard to the views of the shareholders, independent of the wrongdoer, who made up the majority of the minority who did not wish to continue the proceedings.

11.5.3.5 Where justice requires

There has been some discussion of whether there is a fifth exception in that the rule will be relaxed where it is necessary in the interests of justice or whether this is the basis of all the above exceptions (see *Edwards* v *Halliwell* [1950] 2 All ER 1064 and *Estmanco (Kilner House) Ltd* v *Greater London Council* [1982] 1 WLR 2). In *Prudential Assurance Co. Ltd* v *Newman Industries Ltd (No. 2)* [1982] Ch 204 the Court of Appeal commented that it was not convinced that this was a practical test.

TWELVE

JUST AND EQUITABLE WINDING UP

12.1 Introduction

As we saw at **9.3**, one of the seven statutory grounds for the compulsory winding up of a company provided for by the IA 1986, s. 122(1), is that 'the court is of the opinion that it is just and equitable that the company should be wound up'. After winding up on the ground that the company is unable to pay its debts, the 'just and equitable' ground is the most important of the grounds set out in s. 122. In the past, seeking an order for the winding up of a company on this ground served the important function of providing a practical avenue through which a minority shareholder could seek redress for overbearing conduct on the part of those in control of the company. This was particularly important given the difficulties in bringing a derivative action or for seeking relief from oppression under the (now repealed) CA 1948, s. 210.

Since 1980 this particular use of the just and equitable ground has been largely supplanted by the jurisdiction to provide relief for conduct which is unfairly prejudicial under what is now the CA 1985, s. 459. Relief for unfair prejudice is considered in **Chapter 13**. It will be seen that if unfair prejudice is established, the court is given wide powers for granting flexible relief designed to remove that prejudice. One of the drawbacks with relief on the just and equitable ground is that there is only one remedy available if it is established, namely, the winding up of the company. Obviously, in many cases this can only be regarded as a rather drastic remedy.

This chapter will consider the various types of cases where the courts have considered it appropriate to make winding-up orders on this ground, and on the interrelation between the just and equitable ground and other available forms of relief. Before doing so a number of procedural matters will be considered.

12.2 *Locus Standi*

The same categories of persons who can present ordinary winding-up petitions also have *locus standi* to present petitions on the just and equitable ground. The discussion at **9.4** therefore applies in full to these petitions. However, they are most commonly presented by shareholders. As discussed previously, to be 'contributory' a shareholder must have held the shares for at least six out of the 18 months before presenting the petition, or must have been the original allottee of the shares, or they must have devolved on the petitioner through the death of a previous owner: IA 1986, s. 124(2)(b). Further, the petitioner must have a financial interest in the winding up of the company. This will be satisfied either if the shares are partly paid (fairly rare in modern times) or if there is likely to be a surplus available for distribution to shareholders on a winding up of the company. The fact that the petitioner holds a small proportion of the issued shares is not a bar to presenting a petition if the company is likely to be solvent (see *Bryanston Finance Ltd* v *de Vries (No. 2)* [1976] Ch 63, where the petitioner held 62 out of 7,500,000 issued shares, each share being worth just a few pence).

12.3 Procedure

12.3.1 GENERAL

The petition must specify the grounds on which it is presented. On presentation the petitioner must pay the court fee and make the usual £500 deposit. There are, however, a few differences. The old *Practice Direction (Chancery Division: 10(B)(iv)(ii))* provided that contributories' petitions (as just and equitable winding-up petitions commonly are) must state whether the petitioner consents or objects to a standard-form order validating transactions during the period between presentation and determination of the petition, pursuant to the IA 1986, s. 127. As was seen at **9.7**, this is of great importance as a safeguard to persons dealing with the company and for the company itself, particularly as these petitions are rarely resolved quickly.

When a contributory's petition is presented, instead of the court appointing a return date for the final resolution of the petition (which is what happens in typical creditors' petitions), the court will fix a return date on which the Companies Court Registrar will consider the case and give directions in relation to the procedure on the petition (IR 1986, r. 4.22(2)). At the directions hearing the Registrar will consider:

(a) Giving directions for service of the petition on additional persons.

(b) Whether particulars of claim and defence should be delivered.

(c) General procedural matters, such as discovery of documents.

(d) Whether, and by what means, the petition should be advertised (creditors' petitions have to be advertised in the *London Gazette*: as advertisement can cause serious harm to a company's business, it is not uncommon for the Registrar to make an order that the petition is not to be advertised).

(e) The manner in which evidence is to be adduced at the hearing. Matters to be considered include whether the evidence can be given on affidavit, witness statement or orally, whether deponents should attend for cross-examination, and whether restrictions should be imposed on the issues to be dealt with in evidence.

(f) Other matters affecting the petition and its disposal. Such a matter is the mode and place of trial.

Notice of intention to appear needs to be given by 4 p.m. on the day before the hearing by supporting and opposing creditors, and the petitioner must compile a list of appearances.

12.3.2 ROLE OF THE COMPANY

Although the company will suffer the ignominy of being wound up if the petition is successful, the reality is that the company itself is little more than a formal party to the proceedings, which typically take the form of disputes between rival groups of shareholders. Company money must not, therefore, be used to pay the legal costs of one of the sides in the dispute (*Re A and BC Chewing Gum Ltd* [1975] 1 WLR 579), and an injunction may be sought if this is attempted by one side to the litigation (*Re Milgate Developments Ltd* [1993] BCLC 291).

12.4 Principles

At one time it was thought that the 'just and equitable' ground for winding up should be construed *eiusdem generis* with the other grounds set out in what is now the IA 1986, s. 122(1), with the effect that a petition on this ground could only be successful if the circumstances were similar to those set out in the other grounds in the section.

Since the end of the nineteenth century this idea has slowly been put to rest, and it is fair to say that today it no longer plays any part in the principles informing the courts when dealing with just and equitable winding-up petitions.

In *Ebrahimi* v *Westbourne Galleries Ltd* [1973] AC 360 the House of Lords took the view (particularly Lord Wilberforce at pp. 374–5) that the just and equitable ground should be applied flexibly and was a concept that could be adapted in suitable cases, and criticised previous attempts to categorise the situations in which relief under the section could be granted. Despite this, it is helpful for the purposes of exposition to attempt a classification of the circumstances where winding-up orders on the just and equitable ground have been made in the past, and this will be attempted at **12.6** below. It should simply be borne in mind that these categories are not set in stone, and that the court can approach individual cases in a flexible manner. The categories should perhaps be seen more as examples or illustrations of situations where winding up on this ground may be appropriate.

In a helpful general statement of principle, Lord Shaw of Dunfermline in *Loch* v *John Blackwood Ltd* [1924] AC 783 said:

> It is undoubtedly true that at the foundation of applications for winding up, on the 'just and equitable' rule, there must lie a justifiable lack of confidence in the conduct and management of the company's affairs. But this lack of confidence must be grounded on conduct of the directors, not in regard to their private life or affairs, but in regard to the company's business. Furthermore the lack of confidence must spring not from dissatisfaction at being outvoted on the business affairs or on what is called the domestic policy of the company. On the other hand, wherever the lack of confidence is rested on a lack of probity in the conduct of the company's affairs, then the former is justified by the latter, and it is under the statute just and equitable that the company be wound up.

As was mentioned in **12.1** winding up on the just and equitable ground suffers from the drawback that only one form of relief can be granted if the petition is successful. There is judicial reluctance to winding up successful companies, which is reflected in stronger cases being required where the company is successful than if it were struggling. As Nicholls LJ said in *Re Walter L. Jacob and Co. Ltd* [1989] BCLC 345, the compulsory winding up of an active company is a serious step, and a petitioner asking the court to do this must put forward and establish reasons which have a weight justifying this remedy being granted.

12.5 Quasi-partnership

In addition to the success (or otherwise) of the company, another factor that clearly influences the courts when considering just and equitable petitions is whether the company can be described as a 'quasi-partnership'. These are businesses which are, as said by Lord Cozens-Hardy MR in *Re Yenidje Tobacco Co. Ltd* [1916] 2 Ch 426, in substance partnerships but existing in the form of limited companies. They will typically be private companies with small numbers of members and formed on the basis of personal relationships between the members involving mutual confidence and on the understanding that the shareholders will participate in managing the business by being directors. The courts find it far easier to, or will only, grant relief on the basis of deadlock, loss of substratum and exclusion from management if the company is a quasi-partnership.

The leading case on this concept is *Ebrahimi* v *Westbourne Galleries Ltd* [1973] AC 360. When the company was formed it took over a business previously carried on in partnership between a Mr Ebrahimi and a Mr Nazar, who were allotted all the shares in the new company and were its first directors. Later, Mr Nazar's son was brought into the company as a director, at which stage the Nazars held 60 per cent of the shares and Mr Ebrahimi the other 40 per cent. No dividends were ever declared in favour of the shareholders, with profits being distributed in the form of directors' remuneration.

Nine years after the company was formed the Nazars used their voting power to remove Mr Ebrahimi from his post as a director under what is now the CA 1985, s. 303 (see **7.6.1**). From a strict legal point of view the Nazars were acting within their rights in exercising their votes in this way. Mr Ebrahimi petitioned for the winding up of the company on the just and equitable ground, basing his petition on his removal from the management of the company and his loss of a share in the company's profits as he was no longer being paid as a director.

Lord Wilberforce said the jurisdiction to wind up on the just and equitable ground is:

> . . . a recognition of the fact that a limited company is more than a mere legal entity, with a personality in law of its own: that there is room in company law for recognition of the fact that behind it, or amongst it, there are individuals, with rights, expectations and obligations *inter se* which are not necessarily submerged in the company structure. That structure is defined by the Companies Act and by the articles of association by which shareholders agree to be bound. In most companies and in most contexts, this definition is sufficient and exhaustive, equally so whether the company is large or small. The 'just and equitable' provision does not, as the respondents suggest, entitle one party to disregard the obligation he assumes by entering a company, nor the court to dispense him from it. It does, as equity always does, enable the court to subject the exercise of legal rights to equitable considerations; considerations, that is, of a personal character arising between one individual and another, which may make it unjust, or inequitable, to insist on legal rights, or to exercise them in a particular way.
>
> It would be impossible, and wholly undesirable, to define the circumstances in which these considerations may arise. Certainly the fact that a company is a small one, or a private company, is not enough. There are very many of these where the association is a purely commercial one, of which it can safely be said that the basis of association is adequately and exhaustively laid down in the articles. The superimposition of equitable considerations requires something more, which typically may include one, or probably more, of the following elements: (i) an association formed or continued on the basis of a personal relationship, involving mutual confidence — this element will often be found where a pre-existing partnership has been converted into a limited company; (ii) an agreement, or understanding, that all, or some (for there may be 'sleeping' members), of the shareholders shall participate in the conduct of the business; (iii) restriction upon the transfer of the members' interest in the company — so that if confidence is lost, or one member is removed from management, he cannot take out his stake and go elsewhere.
>
> It is these, and analogous, factors which may bring into play the just and equitable clause.

Although Lord Wilberforce in the second of the paragraphs quoted above said a quasi-partnership would typically have one or more of the three elements he then described, subsequent cases, such as *O'Neill* v *Phillips* [1999] 1 WLR 1092, HL, have tended to look for all three elements before deciding whether a company can be categorised as a quasi partnership. The following matters may be relevant when considering whether a company can be described as a quasi-partnership:

(a) Restrictions in share transfers may be by way of express provision in the articles of association or a shareholders' agreement, but can also be established if there is no practical market for the petitioners' shares (as is often the case with minority share interests in small private companies).

(b) The number of shareholders is important, but not determinative. Generally, the smaller the number of shareholders, the more likely the company is to be a quasi-partnership. If the other factors are strong enough, the fact a company may have eight, 10 or 12 members will not necessarily prevent it from being a quasi-partnership.

(c) There may be indications one way or the other in the articles or shareholders' agreement. For example, provisions aimed at ensuring named founders remain in post as directors points towards a quasi-partnership. A provision stating a members' agreement is not to be construed as creating a partnership tends the other way, but again is not determinative (*Re a Company (No. 003028 of 1987)* [1988] BCLC 282).

(d) Changes in the membership or ethos of a company may change its status (or may mean that some members remain as quasi-partners, while others are not). For example, the acceptance of service contracts by the petitioning shareholders after a change in shareholders (which resulted in the emergence of a new majority shareholder) terminated the company's status as a quasi-partnership in *Third* v *North East Ice and Cold Storage Co. Ltd* [1998] BCC 242.

(e) A member who was not a quasi-partner when he or she first acquired shares in the company may become a quasi-partner at a later stage. For example, the member may have received shares in an existing company as a gift or by inheritance, so that initially they were not a quasi-partner. Over time, their relationship with the other members may change, by, for example, participation in management, making personal investments in the business, or charging their home to secure the company's overdraft and there may come a point where they will be regarded as a quasi-partner (*O'Neill* v *Phillips* [1999] 1 WLR 1092, HL).

(f) Equal shareholdings point towards a quasi-partnership. Again this is not determinative one way or the other.

(g) The fact that all the members are individuals and all are to play a part in management points towards a quasi-partnership. However, it is possible for shareholders who are themselves limited companies to be quasi-partners.

12.6 Grounds

12.6.1 EXCLUSION FROM MANAGEMENT OF A QUASI-PARTNERSHIP

Directors cannot always expect that they will be directors for life. In general they are subject to removal by the shareholders under CA 1985, s. 303, and may be subject to retirement on reaching the age of 70 (CA 1985, s. 293) and by rotation after three years (see Table A, regs 73 and 74). However, there are cases where shareholders will have legitimate expectations (which may never have been expressed in writing whether in the articles of association or elsewhere) that they will be actively involved in managing the company's affairs. In *Ebrahimi* v *Westbourne Galleries Ltd* [1973] AC 360 Lord Wilberforce said:

> The just and equitable provision nevertheless comes to [the petitioner's] assistance if he can point to, and prove, some special underlying obligation of his fellow members in good faith, or confidence, that so long as the business continues he shall be entitled to management participation, an obligation so basic that, if broken, the conclusion must be that the association must be dissolved.

Typically, cases where winding-up orders are made on this basis will involve quasi-partnership companies where little or nothing has been paid to shareholders by way of dividends, and where the shareholders have also been the directors and making their livings from their salaries as directors. Often the articles or a shareholders' agreement will name the people who are to serve as directors, and will provide that they are all to use their votes to ensure that each of them will remain in post. In such cases it is very unfair if minority shareholders are later excluded from management, with the result that their investments are retained in the company, but they are deprived of day-to-day control and of any meaningful return on their investment. Nowadays such cases are usually resolved under the unfair prejudice jurisdiction in CA 1985, s. 459.

12.6.2 IRRETRIEVABLE BREAKDOWN OF BUSINESS RELATIONSHIP

The leading case on this is *Re Yenidje Tobacco Co. Ltd* [1916] 2 Ch 426. There were two shareholders, each with equal numbers of shares (a very common situation, and one which very often leads to conflict at some stage in the life of the company). The company was very successful, making large profits, which apparently increased after the shareholders fell out with each other. They refused to speak to each other. A dispute concerning the dismissal of an employee was referred to arbitration at great cost, and the loser refused to accept the decision of the arbitrator. There were further disputes about most aspects of the running of the company, ranging from the fundamental to the extremely trivial. Board and shareholders' meetings were deadlocked as neither party had a casting vote. The Court of Appeal affirmed the decision to wind up the company, holding that similar principles as apply when considering whether to decree a dissolution of a true partnership (for which see the Partnership Act 1890, s. 35(d)) should apply in relation to the breakdown of the business relationship between quasi-partners in a limited company. What is required to justify winding up is a situation (which is unlikely to be retrieved) in which it is impossible for the members to place necessary business confidence in each other, the situation not having been caused by the person seeking to take advantage of it. A recent example is *Re Worldhams Park Golf Course Ltd* [1998] 1 BCLC 554, where one of the directors had misappropriated company money. In the absence of any condonation of this misconduct by the co-director and other shareholder, it was held that the relationship between the two shareholders had irretrievably broken down, and the misconduct of itself justified the making of a winding-up order.

12.6.3 FAILURE OF SUBSTRATUM

Where a company was formed for specific purposes which are completed or become impossible to achieve, it is likely to be just and equitable for the company to be wound up. The simple justification is that the shareholders will have invested their money with a view to achieving those purposes, and should not have their money locked into a company that will not, or will no longer, be seeking to achieve those purposes. The money should be released so the shareholders can invest elsewhere. In these cases it is first necessary to determine what the substratum of the company is. This is done primarily by considering the objects clause in the memorandum of association of the company. For recently incorporated companies this will typically say simply that the company is to carry on business as a general commercial company (CA 1985, s. 3A). For these companies there is little scope for saying there has been a failure of substratum, unless a common understanding about what business a quasi-partnership company would engage in can be proved by other means. Older companies tend to have very detailed objects clauses. The approach in these cases is to find what the main objects of the company are. As it was put by Salmon J in *Anglo-Overseas Agencies Ltd* v *Green* [1961] 1 QB 1, the court will usually take the first, or the first two or three, sub-paragraphs of the objects clause as the main object of the company, and will treat the other sub-paragraphs (often there will be 15 or 20 more) as merely ancillary to this main object. Other companies are formed with a specific project or particular business in mind. In these cases finding the substratum of the company is reasonably straightforward.

Examples of cases where there might be a failure of substratum include:

(a) A company was formed to run a particular mine, but was unable to acquire the mine: *Re Haven Gold Mining Co.* (1882) 20 Ch D 151.

(b) A company formed to build a theatre on a particular site, which proved to be too small: *Re Varieties Ltd* [1893] 2 Ch 235.

(c) A company formed to provide facilities connected with Queen Victoria' s jubilee in 1897, once the celebrations were over: *Re Amalgamated Syndicate* [1897] 2 Ch 600.

(d) A quasi-partnership company's business was running a nightclub. Its objects clause was not limited to any particular club, but allowed the company to engage in just about any activity in the leisure industry. It was alleged there was an understanding at the time it was formed that the company would not involve itself in any business other than the particular nightclub. After running the nightclub for some time the business was sold. It was regarded as arguable that the company's substratum had gone: *Virdi* v *Abbey Leisure Ltd* [1990] BCLC 342.

12.6.4 LACK OF PROBITY ON THE PART OF THE DIRECTORS

Irretrievable breakdown in business relations cases (**12.6.2** above) can arise through a clash of personalities rather than through any misconduct on the part of the other side. The breakdown in business relations cases are restricted to quasi-partnership companies. Winding-up petitions based on a lack of probity by the directors do not depend on the company being a quasi-partnership. In *Baird* v *Lees* 1924 SC 83, Lord President Clyde made the point that shareholders invest in companies, among other things, on the basis that the business of the company will be conducted in accordance with established principles of commercial administration. These are mainly defined by the Companies Act and well-known principles of good faith and honesty, and are intended to provide some guarantee of probity and efficiency. Lord Clyde went on to say:

> If shareholders find that these conditions or some of them are deliberately and consistently violated and set aside by the action of a member and official of the company who wields an overwhelming voting power, and if the result of that, for the extrication of their rights as shareholders, they are deprived of the ordinary facilities which compliance with the Companies Acts would provide them with, then there does arise, in my opinion, a situation in which it may be just and equitable for the court to wind up the company.

12.7 Clean Hands

In *Ebrahimi* v *Westbourne Galleries Ltd* [1973] AC 360, Lord Wilberforce said:

> A petitioner who relies on the 'just and equitable' clause must come to court with clean hands, and if the breakdown in confidence between him and the other parties to the dispute appears to have been due to his misconduct he cannot insist on the company being wound up if they wish it to continue.

Causation is important. Thus, in *Re Yenidje Tobacco Co. Ltd* [1916] 2 Ch 426 it was clear that both shareholders had participated in the breakdown of relations, but winding up was ordered as it could not be said that the breakdown was created by the petitioner. The way it was put by Plowman J in *Re Lundie Brothers Ltd* [1965] 1 WLR 1051 was that the petitioner's misconduct could be a bar to relief if it is shown that the breakdown in business relations was caused exclusively by the person seeking to take advantage of it.

12.8 Alternative Remedy

12.8.1 STATUTORY RESTRICTION ON JUST AND EQUITABLE WINDING UP

IA 1986, s. 125(2), provides:

> *If the petition is presented by members of the company as contributories on the ground that it is just and equitable that the company should be wound up, the court, if it is of the opinion—*
> *(a) that the petitioners are entitled to relief either by winding up the company or by some other means, and*

> *(b) that in the absence of any other remedy it would be just and equitable that the company should be wound up,*
> *shall make a winding-up order; but this does not apply if the court is also of the opinion both that some other remedy is available to the petitioners and that they are acting unreasonably in seeking to have the company wound up instead of pursuing that other remedy.*

The proper approach under this subsection in cases where the judge is of the opinion that the petitioner is entitled to some form of relief, was considered by Vinelott J in *Re a Company (No. 002567 of 1982)* [1983] 1 WLR 927. The first stage is for the judge to ignore the possibility of other forms of relief, and to decide whether it is just and equitable for the company to be wound up. Secondly, if the judge concludes that in the absence of any other remedy the company should be wound up on the just and equitable ground, such an order must be made unless the petitioner is acting unreasonably in seeking to wind up instead of pursuing some other remedy.

12.8.2 ALTERNATIVE REMEDIES

Alternative remedies typically are:

(a) Seeking relief for unfair prejudice.

(b) Seeking a voluntary winding up of the company.

(c) Seeking relief by way of derivative proceedings or otherwise in respect of any breach of fiduciary or other duty by the directors.

(d) Using a specific procedure laid down in the articles of association of the company dealing with the situation that has arisen (such as what should happen if any of the shareholders are excluded from management).

(e) One side (usually the petitioner) selling its shares to the other, either pursuant to machinery contained in the articles or a shareholders' agreement, or pursuant to an open offer to buy or sell.

Unfair prejudice petitions are considered in **Chapter 13**. The jurisdiction under the CA 1985, s. 459, covers many of the situations formerly dealt with by winding-up petitions on the just and equitable ground, and as a result just and equitable petitions are not as common as they once were.

In practical terms, voluntary winding up can usually only be achieved on securing a 75 per cent majority vote in a shareholders' meeting (IA 1986, s. 84). Voluntary winding up will only be a realistic alternative remedy if the controlling shareholders will vote for such a resolution, so this possibility will rarely be a bar to relief to petitions which are brought in order to protect the interests of minority shareholders. However, voluntary liquidation is the obvious solution in cases of failure of a company's substratum.

As discussed in **Chapter 11**, actions for breach of fiduciary duty can only be brought if a majority in the company want this to happen, and there are significant difficulties in bringing derivative actions. For a case on articles providing a procedure to remedy the situation complained about in the petition, see *Re a Company (No. 004377 of 1986)* [1987] 1 WLR 102.

12.8.3 OFFER TO BUY SHARES

To be effective as an alternative remedy an offer to buy the petitioners' shares must be on reasonable terms. Whether the offer is based on a provision in the articles or a shareholders' agreement, or on a letter written before or after proceedings are commenced, the following points should be kept in mind:

(a) The method of valuation must be realistic. Any unusual financial circumstances of the company must be dealt with in a manner fair to both sides.

(b) The valuer should be independent of the opposing parties.

(c) If there has been any impropriety in the affairs of the company, the price must reflect the value the shares would have had if the improper conduct had not occurred.

(d) Generally, the value of minority shares should not be reduced by what is called the 'minority interest discount', as the offer is to buy the shares more or less on a forced sale basis.

If a reasonable offer to buy the petitioners' shares is refused, the respondents may, in a plain and obvious case, apply to strike out a just and equitable winding-up petition, or may seek an order for a stay, instead of waiting until the final determination of the petition before raising the point under s. 125(2).

THIRTEEN

UNFAIR PREJUDICE

13.1 Introduction

Since 1948 it has been recognised that minority shareholders need protection going above and beyond their rights under the constitution of the company and the established principles of company law. There are always risks that majority shareholders will make use of their dominant position so as to vote themselves and their nominees on to the board of directors, vote themselves large remuneration packages, and prevent the company from distributing much to the shareholders in the form of dividends on the shares. In this way the majority can ensure that most or all of the spare cash in the company goes to themselves, and that the minority shareholders see little or none of it. Where the minority shareholders own up to 49 per cent of the issued shares, this can appear very unfair, particularly as in many private companies there are restrictions on share transfers. These can often be found in the articles of such companies, and, in any event, there are always limited numbers of investors who will be prepared to pay more than nominal sums for minority shareholdings in private companies. The effect was that the minority shareholders had their capital tied into the company, with little hope of getting it back so they could invest elsewhere, and with little hope of getting a meaningful return on their investment. (The same problem does not arise in respect of shareholders in publicly quoted companies. If they do not like the way in which the company is being run they can simply sell their shares on the Stock Exchange and invest elsewhere.)

There are severe restrictions on the ability of a shareholder who is complaining about the conduct of the directors and those in control of a limited liability company in bringing an action in the courts by reason of the rule in *Foss* v *Harbottle* (see **11.5**). Prior to 1948 the most direct route open to minority shareholders in seeking relief from conduct such as that described in the previous paragraph was to petition for the just and equitable winding up of the company, a topic discussed in **Chapter 12**. The great drawback in the just and equitable jurisdiction is that there is only one form of relief available, namely the winding up of the company. While this does provide relief for the minority shareholders in that they will be able to get back their investments once the liquidation is complete, the obvious problem is that this is a very drastic remedy to impose upon the company. The company may be very profitable, but there may be fears that much of its value will be lost if it is liquidated. Unless the business is sold on as a going concern, there will also be fears that granting a winding-up order will result in the employees losing their jobs.

The CA 1948, s. 210, was enacted to enable minority shareholders to obtain relief without winding up the company. It provided that a member could complain where the affairs of the company were being conducted in a manner 'oppressive' to some part of the membership of the company, including the petitioner. If the case was made out, the section enabled the court to make such order as it thought fit with a view to bringing an end to the matters complained of, including orders regulating the future affairs of the company or for the purchase of the shares of any of the members of the company. The word 'oppressive' was construed in a very restrictive way. Relief could only be granted if the conduct was continuing, and it was necessary to show that the facts would justify the making of a winding-up order on the just and equitable ground. It was also established that where the petitioner was in reality complaining about being removed from the board of directors, relief would be refused on the ground that the petitioner had not suffered oppression 'qua member'. The result was that very few cases succeeded.

A fresh start was made with the enactment (originally in the CA 1980, s. 75) of what is now the CA 1985, s. 459, which provides the court with jurisdiction to grant relief for unfairly prejudicial conduct. Courts dealing with petitions under the new provision have not regarded themselves as bound by the restrictions imposed under the now repealed CA 1948, s. 210. If a petition under s. 459 is successful, the court is given by s. 461 wide powers to act as it thinks fit for granting relief against the matters complained of. The most common form of relief is to provide for the purchase of the shares of the minority shareholders by the majority at a fair valuation.

13.2 Jurisdiction

The key provisions are to be found in the CA 1985, s. 459(1) and (2), which, in their current form, provide as follows:

> *(1) A member of a company may apply to the court by petition for an order under this part on the ground that the company's affairs are being or have been conducted in a manner which is unfairly prejudicial to the interests of its members generally or of some part of its members (including at least himself) or that any actual or proposed act or omission of the company (including an act or omission on its behalf) is or would be so prejudicial.*
>
> *(2) The provisions of this part apply to a person who is not a member of a company but to whom shares in the company, have been transfered or transmitted by operation of law, as those provisions apply to a member of the company; and references to a member or members are to be construed accordingly.*

Section 460 empowers the Secretary of State to apply where, having received a report, it appears to him that there is unfair prejudice.

An application under s. 459 may be made by a member, or by a person to whom shares have been transferred or transmitted even though that person's name does not yet appear on the register. However, a mere agreement to transfer will not suffice (*Re a Company (No. 003160 of 1986)* [1986] BCLC 391). The question of standing should be settled first.

A petition under s. 459 must allege that a company's affairs are being, or have been, conducted in a manner unfairly prejudicial to the interests of its members generally or some part of its members (including the petitioner). The original wording did not contain the words 'members generally' and in *Re a Company (No. 00370 of 1987)* [1988] 1 WLR 1068 it was held that if the conduct complained of affected all members in the same way it could not be the subject of a petition as it was not unfairly prejudicial to some part of the members. However, the amendment by CA 1989 in adding the words 'members generally' removes any doubt on this.

The wording of the new provision makes it clear that it is no longer necessary to show a course of conduct. Isolated acts may suffice to found a petition. The court also need no longer consider whether the facts would justify a winding up on the just and equitable ground.

13.3 Procedure

Special provision is made for the procedure on applications under CA 1985, s. 459 by the Companies (Unfair Prejudice Applications) Proceedings Rules 1986 (SI 1986 No. 2000).

The application is made by petition, and a form is set out in the schedule to the rules. A precedent can be found in **Figure 13.1**. On presentation of the petition, details of the return day are endorsed on the reverse of the form. The company and any other respondents must be served with sealed copies of the petition at least 14 days before the return day.

On the return day the Registrar gives directions on all matters affecting the procedure of the petition, but will give particular consideration to:

(a) Service of the petition on further persons.

(b) Whether particulars of claim and defence are to be delivered. In practice these statements of case are referred to as points of claim and defence.

(c) Whether and how the petition is to be advertised. Until the court has given directions concerning advertising it will be a breach of the spirit of the rules, and a prima facie abuse of the process of the court, for any party to bring the fact that a petition has been presented to the attention of anyone who is not a party to the petition (*Re a Company (No. 002015 of 1996)* [1997] 2 BCLC 1). If a party disregards this and informs someone else about the petition, the court has a discretion to make such order as might be fair and reasonable in the circumstances. If the conduct is regarded as sufficiently serious, the petition might be dismissed.

(d) The manner of adducing evidence of trial. The Registrar will consider whether evidence will be given orally or taken in whole or part by affidavit, whether deponents should be cross-examined on their affidavits, and the matters which may be dealt with in evidence.

The company is a necessary formal party to the proceedings. In most cases it will not have any direct interest in the result. Although it will therefore be named in the petition as one of the respondents, the real dispute is between the petitioners and the individuals (usually the current directors and majority shareholders) named in the petition. Company money should not usually be used by the respondents for funding the defence to the proceedings (*Re Kenyon Swansea Ltd* (1987) 3 BCC 259 and *Re Crossmore Electrical and Civil Engineering Ltd* (1989) 5 BCC 37).

At one time it used to be common to add prayers for the just and equitable winding up of the company as an alternative to the relief sought for unfair prejudice. This is regarded as undesirable, and the *Practice Direction (Companies Court: Contributory's Petition)* [1990] 1 WLR 490 provides that an alternative prayer for winding up should be included in a petition under s. 459 only if that is the relief which the petitioner prefers or if it is considered that it may be the only relief to which the petitioner may be entitled. In *Re a Company (No. 004415 of 1996)* [1997] 1 BCLC 479 there were three petitions relating to three connected companies in which minority shareholders alleged that they had been unfairly prejudiced by policies of declaring low dividends while the companies paid excessive remuneration to the majority shareholders, who were the directors of the companies. The petitions asked for winding-up orders on the just and equitable ground in the alternative. The companies had substantial accumulated assets, so there would be substantial distributions to the minority shareholders if the companies were to be wound up. Scott V-C pointed out that winding up in these circumstances was a remedy of last resort, and would only have allowed the alternative relief to remain if there was a real possibility of the trial court making winding-up orders. As share purchase orders were the most likely form of relief, the winding-up prayers were struck out. On the other hand, an alternative prayer for winding up was allowed to remain in *Re Copeland and Craddock Ltd* [1997] BCC 294, CA, where there were allegations that the respondents had by secret transactions sold company property for cash without recording the receipts in the company's books. The court felt there was a chance the petitioner might obtain an order that the majority should sell their shares to him, and that it was therefore not unreasonable to seek a winding up in the alternative.

Figure 13.1 Unfair prejudice petition under CA 1985, s. 459

IN THE HIGH COURT OF JUSTICE No. 004499 of 2000

CHANCERY DIVISION

IN THE MATTER of R. W. Mitchell & Co. Limited

AND IN THE MATTER of the Companies Act 1985

BETWEEN

ERIC PETER LYON Petitioner

and

(1) RONALD WILLIAM MITCHELL
(2) NIGEL JOHN MITCHELL
(3) JUDITH MARGARET DICKSON
(4) R.W. MITCHELL & CO. LIMITED Respondents

TO Her Majesty's High Court of Justice
The petition of Eric Peter Lyon of 89 York Road, Bradford, BD7 6TR

1. R. W. Mitchell & Co. Limited (hereinafter called 'the Company') was incorporated on 18th of March 1971 under the Companies Act 1948.

2. The registered office of the Company is at 24 High Street, Bradford BD1 4AZ.

3. The nominal capital of the Company is £20,000 divided into 20,000 shares of £1 each. The amount of the capital paid up or credited as paid up is £15,000. The petitioner is the holder of 2,000 shares of £1 each and at the date of this petition those shares are registered in the name of the petitioner.

4. The principal objects for which the Company was established are to carry on business as a building and civil engineering contractor and other objects stated in the memorandum of association of the Company.

5. The respondents Ronald William Mitchell and his son Nigel John Mitchell were the original directors of the Company. On incorporation the Company had a nominal capital of £100 divided into 100 shares of £1 each, the respondent Ronald William Mitchell being at that time the holder of 99 shares and the respondent Nigel John Mitchell being the holder of 1 share.

6. From time to time the nominal capital of the Company was increased by resolutions passed by the Company in general meeting, and further shares were allotted by the directors.

7. By a written contract of employment dated 14th of October 1979 (hereinafter 'the employment contract') the petitioner was employed by the Company as a civil engineer. At that time the Company had 10 employees.

8. Subsequently the business of the Company expanded at a considerable rate, and by August 1989 the Company employed 50 staff and in the year ending 31st of May 1989 had a turnover of £4,529,528 and pretax profits of £48,327.

9. The success of the Company was largely due to the hard work and technical skill of the petitioner. In recognition of this, the petitioner was appointed a director of the Company at the annual general meeting of the Company held on 3rd of August 1989. The other directors of the company at that time were the respondents Ronald William Mitchell, Nigel John Mitchell and Judith Margaret Dickson, the daughter of the respondent Ronald William Mitchell.

10. At a meeting of the board of directors also held on 3rd of August 1989 the petitioner was allotted 2,000 shares of £1 each in the Company. Immediately before the said allotment to the petitioner there were 6,500 issued shares of the Company. These were held as to 4,500 thereof by the respondent Ronald William Mitchell, as to 1,000 thereof by the respondent Nigel John Mitchell, and as to 1,000 thereof by the respondent Judith Margaret Dickson.

11. By a letter to the Company dated 20th of April 1997 the petitioner resigned his employment with the Company with effect from 31st of October 1997 pursuant to the terms of the employment contract.

12. At the annual general meeting of the Company held on 14th of August 1997 the petitioner was removed from his directorship of the Company on a show of hands by 3 votes to 1.

13. During the period 1989 to 1996 inclusive, dividends of 15p per share were declared each year at annual general meetings of the Company.

14. The profits of the Company in the year ending 31st of May 1997 available for distribution were at least £62,000, in the year ending 31st of May 1998 at least £78,000, and in the year ending 31st of May 1999 at least £37,000. Notwithstanding such profits being available for distribution, the Company has not declared any dividends after 1996.

15. The respondent Ronald William Mitchell's remuneration from the Company in the year ending 31st of May 1997 was £39,000, in the year ending 31st of May 1998 it was £43,000, and in the year ending 31st of May 1999 it was £50,000. The respondent Nigel John Mitchell's remuneration from the Company in the year ending 31st of May 1997 was £22,000, in the year ending 31st of May 1998 it was £27,000, and in the year ending 31st of May 1999 it was £36,000. The respondent Judith Margaret Dickson's remuneration from the company was £6,000 in each of the years ending 31st of May 1997 to 31st of May 1999.

16. The Company's accounts for the year ending 31st of May 1999 were made available to the petitioner on 3rd of February 2000. These accounts showed that during the year ending 31st of May 1999 a further 4,500 shares had been allotted to the respondent Ronald William Mitchell at par, a further 1,000 shares had been allotted to the respondent Nigel John Mitchell at par, and a further 1,000 shares had been allotted to the respondent Judith Margaret Dickson at par. No further shares at that time were or subsequently have been offered to the petitioner.

17. In the premises the actions of the respondents Ronald William Mitchell, Nigel John Mitchell and Judith Margaret Dickson as directors of the Company have been deliberately designed to damage the petitioner's interest in his shares in the Company by ensuring no dividends are paid while the respondents are able to draw remuneration as directors and by diluting the petitioner's shareholding in the Company from 23.5 per cent to 13.3 per cent of the issued share capital.

18. In these circumstances the petitioner submits that the affairs of the Company are being conducted in a manner which is unfairly prejudicial to the interests of some part of the members including the petitioner.

THE PETITIONER therefore prays as follows:

(1) that the respondents and each of them may be ordered to purchase the petitioner's shares at a fair value to be determined by the court;
(2) that the Company may be ordered to pay a dividend for the year ending 31st of May 2000 if profits are available for that purpose;
(3) that there be an inquiry ordered as to what dividends ought to have been declared by the Company in the years ending 31st of May 1997, 31st of May 1998 and 31st of May 1999;
(4) and that such other order may be made as the court thinks fit.

NOTE

It is intended to serve this petition on:
(1) Ronald William Mitchell of 18 Fairmile, Bradford, BD8 3LR
(2) Nigel John Mitchell of 92 Ellesmere Road, Bradford, BD8 2DA
(3) Judith Margaret Dickson of 41 Landhope Close, Mold, Clwyd, CH7 6RJ
(4) R.W. Mitchell & Co. Limited of 24 High Street, Bradford, BDI 4AZ.

ENDORSEMENT

This petition having been presented to the court on 20th of March 2000 let all parties attend before the Registrar in Chambers on:

Date:	29th May 2000
Time:	3 p.m.
Place:	Room 412, Thomas More Building, Royal Courts of Justice, Strand, London, WC2A 2LL

for directions to be given.

The solicitors for the petitioner are:

Name:	Messrs Dixon and Comyn
Address:	83 High Street, Bradford, BDI 4BD
Tel. No.:	01274 793692
Reference:	ALC/LYON

13.4 Interim Relief

13.4.1 INTERIM PAYMENTS

It was held in *Re a Company (No. 004175 of 1986)* (1987) 3 BCC 41 that there is no power to grant an interim payment in an unfair prejudice petition prior to the hearing. This is because it is only after judgment that the statutory criterion for granting relief under s. 461 (namely, that the court is satisfied that the petition is well founded) can be established. However, an interim payment can be ordered after judgment if the judgment is under appeal (*Ferguson* v *Maclennan* [1990] BCC 702, Court of Session).

13.4.2 INTERIM INJUNCTIONS

Interim injunctions have been granted to prevent the company from financing resistance to s. 459 petitions where it does not have an interest in the outcome of a dispute which in essence is a dispute between competing shareholders (see *Re Milgate Developments Ltd* [1991] BCC 24 and *Re a Company (No. 004502 of 1988), ex parte Johnson* [1991] BCC 234). In the two cases cited for this proposition, once the judges found they had jurisdiction to make the order they immediately went on to do so with little additional reasoning, apart from a brief reference to *American Cyanamid Co.* v *Ethicon Ltd* [1975] AC 396, because there was no real defence to the application for the injunctions.

Interim injunctions to restrain a director of the company from continuing unfairly prejudicial conduct pending the hearing of the petition were granted in *Re a Company (No. 003061 of 1993), Safinia* v *Comet Enterprises Ltd* [1994] BCC 883. It was alleged that certain agency agreements were being diverted from the company. Applying *American Cyanamid* principles, interim injunctions were granted so as to preserve commission payments alleged to be due to the company, and to prevent active diversion of assets which appeared to belong to the company. In *Re a Company (No. 00330 of 1991), ex parte Holden* [1991] BCC 241, an interim injunction was granted to prevent majority shareholders from buying out the petitioner's shares pursuant to a provision in the company's articles.

13.4.3 SECURITY FOR COSTS

It has been held that a petitioner in an unfair prejudice petition brings proceedings as a claimant for the purpose of enabling the court to make an order for security for costs (*Re Unisoft Group Ltd (No. 1)* [1993] BCLC 1292).

13.5 Principles

13.5.1 GENERAL CONCEPTS

There is no statutory definition of the term 'unfair prejudice', which has been left by the legislature as a deliberately wide concept which can be applied by the courts so as to give relief where it is just to do so. In an influential passage from an unreported decision (*Re Bovey Hotel Ventures Ltd*, 31 July 1981), which is quoted in full in *Re R.A. Noble and Sons (Clothing) Ltd* [1983] BCLC 273 at pp. 290–1, Slade J said:

> Broadly, and without prejudice to the generality of the wording of the section, which may cover many other situations, a member of a company will be able to bring himself within the section if he can show that the value of his shareholding in the company had been seriously diminished or at least seriously jeopardised by reason of a course of conduct on the part of those persons who have had de facto control of the company, which has been unfair to the member concerned. The test of unfairness must, I think, be an objective, not a subjective one. In other words it is not necessary for the Petitioner to show that the persons who have had de facto control of the company have acted as they did in the conscious knowledge that this was unfair to the Petitioner or that they acted in bad faith; the test, I think, is whether a reasonable bystander observing the consequences of their conduct, would regard it as having unfairly prejudiced the Petitioner's interests.

The central idea behind the section is that the court may intervene where the conduct of the respondents has seriously diminished the value of the petitioner's shares, or at least put the value of those shares at serious risk. In most of the cases brought to court this has been fairly self-evident from the facts, with the main areas of dispute being whether the conduct of the respondents was unfairly prejudicial; whether the petitioner was damaged as a shareholder or in some other capacity; or whether the petitioner should be refused relief because of the petitioner's own misconduct or through failing to accept a reasonable offer for the purchase of the petitioner's shares. However, it is important to establish substantial harm or potential harm to the value of the petitioner's interest in the company, or the petition will fail on this ground alone. Thus, in *Re Blackwood Hodge plc* [1997] 2 BCLC 650 the directors failed to give a proposal to merge two pension schemes the consideration it deserved, and failed to declare their interest to the board contrary to the CA 1985, s. 317. On the face of it the transaction appeared to involve giving away a substantial funding surplus under the company's pension to the merged scheme and receiving nothing in return. On analysis of the evidence, however, the judge found (after a four-week trial) that the transaction was neutral, so the company lost nothing in the merger. That finding meant, despite the failures of the directors, that the petition had to be dismissed.

The references in the passage quoted above from *Re Bovey Hotel Ventures Ltd* to 'a course of conduct' and 'to the member concerned' must be regarded as being more restrictive than the present law: the former phrase is too restrictive because subsequent decisions have made it plain that isolated incidents may be unfairly prejudicial, and the latter phrase is also too restrictive because of the change of wording in the section in 1989. Nevertheless, six basic propositions can be derived from this decision and that in *Re DR Chemicals Ltd* (1989) 5 BCC 39:

(a) The test of unfair prejudice is objective.

(b) It is not necessary for the petitioner to show bad faith.

(c) It is not necessary for the petitioner to show a conscious intention to cause prejudice.

(d) The test is one of unfairness, not unlawfulness.

(e) The alleged conduct must affect the petitioner as a shareholder.

(f) Laches (i.e., delay) may bar relief under s. 459.

In *Re Saul D. Harrison and Sons plc* [1994] BCC 475, CA. Hoffmann LJ pointed out that it is important to bear in mind that the word 'unfairness' in the section has to be applied in the context of a commercial relationship. Conduct may be technically unlawful without being unfair, and it may be unfair without being unlawful. For example, a technical breach of the statutory requirements regarding issuing shares might not amount to unfairly prejudicial conduct (*Re D.R. Chemicals Ltd* (1989) 5 BCC 39). Nevertheless, Hoffmann LJ said the starting point in a s. 459 case is to consider whether the conduct complained about was in accordance with the articles of association of the company. Even if the letter of the articles has been complied with by the majority, their conduct may be unfairly prejudicial if either:

(a) the majority have failed to use their fiduciary powers as directors for the benefit of the company as a whole; or

(b) the petitioner can show that some legitimate expectation not formally expressed in the constitution of the company has been infringed (see **13.5.2**).

In *O'Neill* v *Phillips* [1999] 1 WLR 1092, Lord Hoffmann said that the concept of fairness had to be applied in the context of the case in hand. Conduct which might be perfectly fair between competing businessmen might not be fair between members of a family. The court has to apply two principles. One is that the articles and other express terms on which the shareholders have become associated must be respected. The other is that equity will intervene where the respondents have not acted in good faith. It is for this reason that successful unfair prejudice petitions are those based either on breach of the terms on which the parties became associated, or where those terms are used in a manner which equity would regard as contrary to good faith.

A successful petition will have to be based either on continuing unfairly prejudicial conduct, or on past conduct which has a continuing unfairly prejudicial effect. Where past unfairly prejudicial conduct has been remedied, the petition should be dismissed (*Re Legal Costs Negotiators Ltd* (1998) *The Times*, 15 July 1998).

13.5.2 LEGITIMATE EXPECTATIONS

In most cases the basis on which the parties became associated will be adequately and exhaustively laid down by the articles of association (see Lord Wilberforce in *Ebrahimi* v *Westbourne Galleries Ltd* [1973] AC 360). The superimposition of equitable considerations requires 'something more', or 'some special circumstances' (see *Re Posgate and Denby (Agencies) Ltd* (1986) 2 BCC 99,352). Although it is just about possible for parties to have legitimate expectations going beyond the terms of the articles in a public company, such cases will be rare (Re *Leeds United Holdings plc* [1996] 2 BCLC 545). In *O'Neill* v *Phillips* [1999] 1 WLR 1092, Lord Hoffmann said the concept of 'legitimate expectations' is a consequence, not a cause, of the equitable restraint of unconscionable conduct, and the concept should not be given an unrestrained life of its own. In practical terms the concept is restricted to smaller, quasi-partnership, companies. To be recognised by the court the alleged legitimate expectation has to relate to the conduct of the company's affairs. The most obvious and common example is an expectation of being able to participate in decisions relating to the conduct of the company's affairs. An expectation that another shareholder will not sell his shares without the consent of some or all of the other shareholders was held in *Re Leeds United* not to relate to the conduct of the company's affairs, and was not capable of being protected under s. 459.

Although the courts will act to protect the shareholders' legitimate expectations, it is established that the court is not able to rewrite the terms and understandings on which the members became associated (*Re Posgate and Denby (Agencies) Ltd* (1986) 2 BCC 99,352). Where the parties have spelt out their arrangements in detailed documentation (such as in a full shareholders' agreement and/or by detailed provisions in the articles tailored to their particular company), there may be limited scope, if any, for suggesting that the shareholders might have some legitimate expectations over and above what they have agreed in writing. However, there have been cases, such as *Re Elgindata Ltd* [1991] BCLC 959 and *Re a Company (No. 002015 of 1996)* [1997] 2 BCLC 1, where the possibility of finding the necessary 'something more' was not ruled out despite voluminous documentation between the parties.

In *O'Neill* v *Phillips* [1999] 1 WLR 1092 the petitioner had worked his way up in the company. There came a point when the majority shareholder handed over the running of the company to the petitioner and agreed in principle, and subject to certain business objectives being satisfied and the execution of formal documents, to increase the petitioner's share holding to 50 per cent. However, the fact there was no formal agreement to do so was held to be fatal to a petition based on what was alleged to be a legitimate expectation that his share holding would be increased. Similarly, in the same case it was held that the petitioner did not have an enforceable 'legitimate expectation' that the share in the company's profits that he had been receiving when he was running the company would not be reduced when the majority shareholder resumed running the company at a later date.

13.5.3 CLEAN HANDS

Although the jurisdiction under s. 459 is equitable in character, the fact that the petitioner may not come to the court with clean hands will not of itself bar relief. It may, however, have an effect on the remedy that the court may grant (*Re London School of Electronics Ltd* [1986] Ch 211).

13.5.4 INTERESTS AS A MEMBER

As mentioned in **13.1**, under the old CA 1948, s. 210, a petitioner had to show that the oppression complained about had been suffered in the petitioner's capacity as a shareholder. Being removed from office as a director was regarded as conduct affecting the petitioner as a director, not as a shareholder. An early case under the present provision, *Re a Company (No. 004475 of 1982)* [1983] Ch 178, applied the same principle to unfair prejudice petitions. However, later cases have applied the concept of petitioning as a shareholder in a more flexible way. In *Re a Company (No. 00477 of 1986)* [1986] BCLC 376 Hoffmann J said the exclusion from management of a managing director of a large public limited company who happens to hold a few shares (perhaps as a share qualification for being a director) would not be able to petition for relief under s. 459 in the event of being removed from his office as a director. On the other hand, the same is not true of small private companies in which two or three members have invested their capital on the footing that dividends were unlikely to be declared, but that each would earn a living by working for the company and drawing remuneration as a director. In such cases, if it can be said that the members had a legitimate expectation of continued employment as a director by the company, dismissal from office may constitute unfairly prejudicial conduct.

Exclusion from management resulting in loss of control over capital invested in a company by a person connected with the excluded director may, in appropriate circumstances, affect the excluded director as a shareholder. Thus, in *R and H Electric Ltd* v *Haden Bill Electrical Ltd* [1995] 2 BCLC 280 a company effectively controlled by the petitioner had made a loan of £200,000 in order to provide working capital for a quasi-partnership in which the petitioner held 25 per cent of the shares and was the chairman. Later, problems arose between the petitioner and the other directors, who then summarily dismissed him without consultation and without any discussion about the future of the loan capital. It was held that the petitioner had a legitimate expectation of being able to participate in the management of the quasi-partnership company for at least as long as the lending company and the petitioner were closely associated with it. Accordingly, even though the petitioner's conduct was open to criticism his removal was held to be unfairly prejudicial to his interests as a member.

Other forms of conduct complained about by petitioners may also fall outside s. 459 on the basis that they do not affect the petitioner as a shareholder. An example is *Re J.E. Cade and Sons Ltd* [1991] BCC 360, where the minority shareholder had granted a licence to the company over a farm. In his petition he claimed the business relationship between the members had irretrievably broken down, that he had been unfairly prejudiced, and as part of the relief sought he asked for an order that the company should give up possession of the farm. It was held that this head of relief had to be struck out, because the petitioner's interests as the freeholder were in fact adverse to his interests as a shareholder in the company.

13.5.5 MATTERS AMOUNTING TO UNFAIR PREJUDICE

13.5.5.1 Exclusion from management

This has already been discussed in **13.5.4**. This is one of the most common forms of complaint under this section. As discussed above, it is most likely to be successful if the company is a small, quasi-partnership company (a concept discussed at **12.5** above). However, there must be an exclusion from management, not merely an alteration in the capacity in which the Petitioner is managing (see *O'Neill* v *Phillips* [1999] 1 WLR 1092, where the Petitioner failed despite being reduced from running the company to being a director).

13.5.5.2 Payment of inadequate dividends

This is commonly combined with exclusion from management and/or with allegations that the directors have paid themselves excessive remuneration. In *Re Sam Weller and Sons Ltd* [1990] Ch 682 the ground said to amount to unfair prejudice was that the company had paid 'the same derisory dividend' of 14p per share for the past 37 years, and that the most recent accounts showed that net profits had covered the dividend declared by 14 times. On an application to strike out the petition as disclosing no reasonable grounds for bringing a claim it was held that the allegation could amount to unfair prejudice.

13.5.5.3 Improper allotments of shares

Re D.R. Chemicals Ltd (1989) 5 BCC 39 was regarded as a blatant case of unfairly prejudicial conduct. This was a company with two shareholders, one holding 60 shares and the other 40 shares. The shareholders split up, with the majority shareholder continuing the business. The majority shareholder then used his position as director and majority shareholder to allot himself a further 900 shares at par without informing the petitioner of what he was doing. It was found that he did this for the wholly improper purpose of diluting the shareholding of the petitioner (reducing his interest to 4 per cent).

13.5.5.4 Discriminatory rights issue

A rights issue operates by the company offering to sell new shares to the existing shareholders in proportion to the number of shares they hold at the time of the offer. If any shareholders do not take up the offer, it is commonly provided that the company can sell the shares that have not been bought by the original offerees to the other shareholders. Normally there is nothing wrong in making a rights issue. Occasionally, however, this can operate unfairly. In *Re a Company (No. 007623 of 1986)* [1986] BCLC 362, Hoffmann J said:

> If the majority know that the petitioner does not have the money to take up his rights and the offer is made at par when the shares are plainly worth a great deal more than par as part of a majority holding (but very little as a minority holding), it seems to me arguable that carrying through the transaction in that form could, viewed objectively, constitute unfairly prejudicial conduct.

13.5.5.5 Diverting business opportunities

Breach of fiduciary duty on the part of the directors can amount to unfairly prejudicial conduct even in the absence of any breach of the terms of the articles of association. One of the most common complaints is that directors in control of one company have diverted business opportunities away from a company in which the petitioner holds a minority interest to another company where the directors (or those appointing the directors) hold all the shares. Where this can be proved it will clearly amount to unfair prejudice (*Re London School of Electronics Ltd* [1986] Ch 211).

13.5.5.6 Preventing the company recovering its property

An example of this is *Whyte, Petitioner* (1984) 1 BCC 99,044 (Court of Session). The petitioner held 49 per cent of the shares in the company, the other 51 per cent being held by the subsidiaries of R Ltd. The company had six directors, who resolved at a board meeting to bring proceedings against R Ltd. The majority shareholders then requisitioned a meeting (see **6.5.5**) for the purpose of removing two of the existing directors and appointing a further nominee director, which would have the result of nominee directors forming the majority on the board of the company. The nominee directors would then be able to stop the litigation against R Ltd. It was held that this amounted to unfair prejudice of the petitioner, and an injunction was granted.

13.5.5.7 Mismanagement

Allegations of mismanagement on the part of those in control of a company will not, on their own, generally amount to unfair prejudice. The reason, as stated by Roger Kaye QC in *Re a Company (No. 002015 of 1996)* [1997] 2 BCLC 1, is that managerial decisions are just as they imply, decisions by management. The courts are ill-equipped to resolve disputes about whether given management decisions were or were not proper, let alone to characterise them as amounting to unfair prejudice. Nevertheless, in suitable cases allegations of this nature will be allowed to remain in unfair prejudice petitions as forming part of the context of the case, and perhaps lending weight to other, more obvious, allegations of unfairly prejudicial conduct. However, serious mismanagement can constitute unfair prejudice (*Re Elgindata Ltd (No. 2)* [1992] 1 WLR 1207).

13.5.5.8 Totality of conduct

In some cases a number of complaints, none of them in themselves sufficient to amount to unfairly prejudicial conduct, may, when taken together, be held to satisfy the test in s. 459. An example is *Re a Company (No. 00314 of 1989)* [1990] BCC 221, where the respondents had made proposals for removing the petitioner as a director, proposed the appointment of new directors, proposed altering the memorandum and articles of association, and had offered to purchase her shares without providing her with information relevant to ascertaining their value, in total constituted unfairly prejudicial conduct.

13.6 Remedies

If the court is satisfied that the petitioner's interests have been unfairly prejudiced by the conduct of the company's affairs, it has wide powers for granting relief under s. 461. Subsections (1) and (2) provide:

> *(1) If the court is satisfied that a petition under this part is well founded, it may make such order as it thinks fit for giving relief in respect of the matters complained of.*
>
> *(2) Without prejudice to the generality of subsection (1), the court's order may—*
>
> *(a) regulate the conduct of the company's affairs in the future,*
>
> *(b) require the company to refrain from doing or continuing an act complained of by the petitioner or to do an act which the petitioner has complained it has omitted to do,*
>
> *(c) authorise civil proceedings to be brought in the name and on behalf of the company by such person or persons and on such terms as the court may direct,*
>
> *(d) provide for the purchase of the shares of any members of the company by other members or by the company itself and, in the case of a purchase by the company itself, the reduction of the company's capital accordingly.*

Subsections (3) to (5) of s. 461 deal with orders requiring alterations to the company's memorandum or articles.

13.6.1 SHARE PURCHASE ORDERS

By far the most common order made on a successful s. 459 petition is an order for the purchase of the shares of one side by the other. Most unfair prejudice cases are brought by shareholders in small private companies. Often there will be express restrictions on share transfers set out in the articles of association, or major practical difficulties in selling shares at realistic prices. If an unfair prejudice case is made out, the probability is that the shareholders are no longer able to continue doing business with each other, and the best solution is that the company should be left in the hands of one side or the other, with the outgoing party having their capital returned to them so they can invest elsewhere.

13.6.1.1 Who goes?

Although s. 461 provides that either party may be ordered to buy the other side out, usually it is clear that it will be the majority who will be ordered to buy out the minority. Often it will be the majority who will have been running the business in the period leading up to the final disposal of the proceedings (so there will be continuity of management), and generally they will find it easier to buy out the smaller number of shares owned by the minority rather than the other way around. However, the usual position can be displaced by other factors, with each case turning on its own facts. Factors can include who founded the business, the respective roles of the parties in building up the company's business, any special qualifications needed for running the business successfully, and any dishonesty or breach of fiduciary duty established against either side. The purpose behind s. 461 is to grant relief in respect of the matters complained about in the petition (*Re a Company (No. 00836 of 1995)* [1996] BCC 432). Its purpose is not to expropriate the shares of the majority. In cases where there are majority shareholders in control of the business it will therefore be very rare for the court to order them to sell their shares to the minority. The most difficult cases are those where both sides hold an equal number of shares, an example being *Re a Company (No. 003096 of 1987)* (1988) 4 BCC 80.

13.6.1.2 Who buys?

Usually this simply follows from the previous paragraph. In exceptional cases, however, someone who is not a shareholder and not a director may be joined as a party and ordered to buy out the petitioner's shares, see *Supreme Travels Ltd* v *Little Olympian Each-Ways Ltd* [1994] BCC 947.

13.6.1.3 Share valuation

The general principle is that the shares must be valued at a price that is fair on the facts of the particular case (*Re London School of Electronics Ltd* [1986] Ch 211). Outside the area of unfair prejudice it is clear that a fair valuation of shares representing a minority interest in a private company will have to take into account the fact that such a holding does not carry with it control of the company and that the minority shareholder is therefore subject to the whims of the majority regarding dividend policy and management decisions. There will therefore be a substantial minority interest discount when determining the value of minority shares (*Howie* v *Crawford* [1990] BCC 330).

A different approach is often taken in unfair prejudice cases. In *Re Bird Precision Bellows Ltd* [1986] Ch 658, the Court of Appeal, approving the judgment of Nourse J at first instance (reported at [1984] Ch 419), said a different approach was required where a minority shareholder's shares were ordered to be bought after a finding of unfair prejudice, because the minority shareholders could not be regarded as voluntary sellers. Instead, the general rules are:

(a) The shares held by a quasi-partner should not be discounted for minority interest, but should be valued on a pro-rata basis according to the value of the shares as a whole.

(b) If the minority shareholder had acted so as to deserve his exclusion from the company, the price should be appropriately discounted to reflect that fact.

(c) In cases where delinquent majority shareholders in a quasi-partnership company are ordered to sell their shares to the minority the price should not generally include a premium to reflect the fact their shares carry majority control.

(d) Where shares in a quasi-partnership company were acquired by the petitioner as an investment at a price which was discounted because they represented a minority holding, any sale order would most probably be at a price incorporating a minority interest discount.

13.6.1.4 Date of valuation

Usually the shares should be valued as at the date the petition was presented. This prima facie rule will be displaced where it is necessary to find some other date in order to ensure the valuation is fair. This might be the case where the unfairly prejudicial conduct has had an effect on the value of the assets of the company. In such a case a date for the valuation might be a date just before the unfairly prejudicial conduct started (*Re O.C. (Transport) Services Ltd* [1984] BCLC 251). Another alternative is the company's usual year-end immediately preceding the date of the trial, a solution adopted in *Quinlan* v *Essex Hinge Co. Ltd* [1997] BCC 53.

13.6.2 LOANS

In *Re Nuneaton Borough AFC Ltd (No. 2)* [1991] BCC 44 it was held that s. 461 was wide enough for the court to make an order for the transfer of shares to be made conditional on the party buying the other side out repaying loans made by the outgoing shareholders to the company. On the facts it was held that it would have been unjust to allow the company to retain the loans after the outgoing shareholder had been bought out.

13.6.3 CIVIL PROCEEDINGS

The power contained in s. 461(2)(c) to authorise civil proceedings to be brought in the name and on behalf of the company by such persons as the court may direct is a way of getting around the problems caused by the rule in *Foss* v *Harbottle* (see **11.5**). It is not always necessary to go through a two-stage process on this, with the unfair prejudice petition being the first stage, granting as relief the authorisation of the second stage, namely, proceedings brought on behalf of the company. Where the alleged unfairly prejudicial conduct involves the diversion of company funds it has been held (*Re Fahey Developments Ltd* [1996] BCC 325) that the petitioner is entitled to seek an order under s. 461 for payment to the company from the members, former members and directors allegedly involved in the diversion of assets and also from third parties who may be proved to have knowingly received or improperly assisted in the wrongful diversion.

13.6.4 NO APPROPRIATE RELIEF

In *Antoniades* v *Wong* [1997] 2 BCLC 419, CA, the petition succeeded, and investigations were made into ascertaining the net assets of the company for the purpose of a share sale order, taking into account all the wrongs done to the company. This proved so complicated that the judge described it as an impossible task. The Court of Appeal approved the judge's finding that there was no practical relief that he could grant under s. 461, and approved the judge's offer to the petitioner of amending the petition so as to provide for the winding up of the company on the just and equitable ground.

13.7 Striking Out

Striking out was discussed in some detail in the ***Civil Litigation Manual*** at **28.2**. It is very much a live issue in unfair prejudice proceedings. Striking-out applications in this context broadly fall into two categories. One is where it is argued by respondents that the proceedings (or parts of them) or the relief sought falls outside the scope of ss. 459 and 461, and hence should be struck out as disclosing no reasonable grounds for bringing the claim. Like general striking-out cases, s. 459 petitions will only be struck out if they are plainly and obviously unsustainable. Applications in the first category are based on the principles described in the previous sections, and do not call for further comment here.

In the second category are cases where it is argued that the petition is an abuse of process on the ground that the petitioner should have sought the remedy prayed for in the petition by adopting a remedy readily available under the articles of association, or should have accepted an open offer made by the respondents giving the petitioner all the relief that could realistically be obtained on the petition. In *Re a Company (No. 004377 of 1986)* [1987] 1 WLR 102 Hoffmann J pointed out that for small companies the legal costs and the loss of management time incurred in defending unfair prejudice claims can be overwhelming. His lordship therefore stated the view that a member seeking a share sale order should not present a petition until after an attempt has been made to sell the shares under the provisions in the articles of association of the company (which often have provisions dealing with proposed sales of shares by members). His lordship also pointed out that the common form of wording of such provisions in articles of association that the auditors of the company should fix the price at a 'fair value' gives the auditors the same function as the court has to perform under s. 461. This procedure for first seeking an agreed sale under the articles was recognised as being inappropriate where either:

(a) the respondents have been guilty of bad faith or plain impropriety; or

(b) if the articles provide for some arbitrary or artificial method of valuation.

Hoffmann J went further in *Re a Company (No. 006834 of 1988)* [1989] BCLC 365, where he said that where it is plain that the court would make a share sale order on a petition under s. 459 and the articles provide machinery for determining the fair price for the petitioner's shares, an unfair prejudice petition would ordinarily be struck out as an abuse of process unless an attempt to sell under the terms of the articles had been made. This was so even if there was no guarantee that the valuer would not apply a minority interest discount on a valuation under the articles even though no such discount would be applied by the court (following the reasoning in *Re Bird Precision Bellows Ltd* [1984] Ch 419, see **13.6.1.3**).

Some doubt about whether the *Re a Company (No. 004377 of 1986)* line of cases should continue to apply was caused by the decision in *Virdi* v *Abbey Leisure Ltd* [1990] BCLC 342, CA. This was a petition for winding up on the just and equitable ground. The company had sold its business, and its only asset was cash. It was held that the petitioner was not obliged to use the machinery in the articles before presenting the petition because the valuer might have applied a minority interest discount and also might have reduced the valuation by too much to reflect certain disputed claims. The *Abbey Leisure* decision was applied at first instance in the unfair prejudice case of *Re a Company (No. 00330 of 1991), ex parte Holden* [1991] BCC 241, where the facts were very similar to *Abbey Leisure*. Although the *Abbey Leisure* approach applies to cases where the company has ceased trading (where the petitioner has real grounds for expecting the valuation to be proportionate to the net assets of the company as on a winding up), the better view is that it does not apply to cases where the company is still a going concern. Where the business is still in operation, the petitioner should still, in general, seek a remedy first under the articles, and only if that is unsuccessful should a petition be presented (*Re J.E. Cade and Sons Ltd* [1991] BCC 360).

If a striking-out application is to be made on the basis that an open offer has been made after proceedings were commenced which has been unreasonably refused, great care has to be taken in formulating the offer to ensure that it gives the petitioner all the relief that could reasonably be expected if the matter had been dealt with by the court.

The following principles were laid down by Lord Hoffmann in *O'Neill* v *Phillips* [1999] 1 WLR 1092 where an offer to buy is relied upon in a striking out application:

(a) The offer must be to purchase the shares at a fair value. This will ordinarily be a value representing an equivalent proportion of the total issued share capital, without a discount for the shares being a minority holding. Although there may be special circumstances justifying applying a discount, it will seldom be possible to say that a discounted offer is plainly reasonable for the purposes of striking out.

(b) The value, if not agreed, should be determined by a competent expert. Appointing an expert to be agreed by the parties, or, in default of agreement, an expert nominated by the president of the Institute of Chartered Accountants (or some similar mechanism) would suffice.

(c) The offer should be to have the value determined by the expert as an expert, in order to promote speed and economy.

(d) Both parties should be treated equally, such as by having equal access to information about the company having a bearing on the value of the shares, and both having the right to make written or oral submissions to the expert.

(e) It may be necessary for the offer to include payment of the petitioner's costs. Whether this is necessary depends on the circumstances. There would be no need to offer to pay the petitioner's costs if the petition was presented before the respondents had a reasonable time to formulate an offer. If the offer is made some years into proceedings, an effective offer will almost certainly need to include payment of the petitioner's costs.

There will be some cases where even if the above guidelines are followed, an unfair prejudice petition will still not be struck out. One example is *North Holdings Ltd* v *Southern Tropics Ltd* (unreported, 17 June 1999, CA), where there were grounds for believing that the respondents had diverted business opportunities to another company, so valuing the petitioner's shares involved mixed questions of fact and law which were better resolved by a court than an expert valuer.

FOURTEEN

WORKED EXAMPLE

14.1 Introduction

The papers in this chapter were the formal assessment for the Company Law Module a few years ago. The case, *Re Beadnell Bay Petroleum Limited*, is set in the context of a company engaged in the exploration of oil in the North Sea. Counsel has been asked to advise the company on the merits of a possible claim against its former managing director, Mr Gallagher, and to settle proceedings. No knowledge of oil exploration law is required beyond the information given in the papers. The Instructions to Counsel have an express statement that there is no need for an application for a freezing injunction (which would otherwise have been something that ought to have been considered), thereby allowing Counsel to concentrate on the company law issues raised.

The background is that the company had incurred expense in conducting various geological investigations in the North Sea, and had identified a location that had some promise as the site of a possible oilfield. Instead of applying for a Department of Energy production licence in the name of the company it appears Mr Gallagher applied for and was granted a production licence for the relevant site in his own name. Oil was subsequently confirmed at the site, which is now being exploited by a rival company. It is thought that Mr Gallagher is making substantial sums in the form of royalties from oil produced from the site.

The Instructions to Counsel are set out at **14.2**. The extracts from the articles of association of the company at the end of the papers are based loosely on the 1948 Act version of Table A. Regulation 94 is the same as reg. 80 of the 1948 Table A, and regs 99 and 100 correspond to reg. 84(1) and (2).

The assessment criteria for the Opinion and Particulars of Claim are set out at **14.3**. Similar (though not always identical) formulations for assessment criteria have always been used for Company Law assessments. At **14.4** and **14.5** are the suggested Opinion and Particulars of Claim. Some brief comments appear at **14.6**.

14.2 *Re Beadnell Bay Petroleum Limited:* Instructions to Counsel

Re: BEADNELL BAY PETROLEUM LIMITED

INSTRUCTIONS TO COUNSEL TO
ADVISE AND SETTLE
PARTICULARS OF CLAIM

Counsel will find herewith:

1. Statement of Mr Keith Symons;
2. Statement of Mr William Knight;
3. Extracts from Exploration Licence;
4. Extracts from Production Licence;
5. Extracts from Board Minutes;
6. Correspondence;
7. Extracts from Articles of Association.

Counsel is instructed on behalf of Beadnell Bay Petroleum Limited ('the Company') following a board resolution on 10th February 2000 to seek legal redress against its former Managing Director, Mr Michael Gallagher. In essence, it is alleged that Mr Gallagher has dishonestly taken the Production Licence (enclosure 4) in his own name instead of the name of the Company, and is pocketing the extremely large royalties derived from it.

The Company is in the business of oil and petroleum exploration and production. Throughout its existence it has been principally engaged in the North Sea area. An Exploration Licence (enclosure 3) was granted in its favour in 1991. Over the next two years it conducted various geological investigations of the seabed in an area about 60 miles off the Northumberland coast. In 1993 certain financial problems were encountered by the Company, as set out in the statement of Mr Symons (enclosure 1). About the same time applications were invited by the Department of Energy for Production Licences in respect of a number of blocks of the seabed, including part of the area surveyed by the Company. One particular block was felt by the Board of the Company to have real promise as a potential oil field.

At that time Mr Gallagher was the Company's Managing Director, but was not employed by the Company. Instead of applying for a Production Licence in the name of the Company, he lodged an application in his own name. As Counsel will see, the Production Licence granted in relation to block 79452 on 18th September 1993 is in Mr Gallagher's name.

In October 1994 substantial petroleum reserves were discovered in block 79452. This is now known as the Ólen Horst field. Instructing Solicitors are aware that in February 1996 the Secretary of State gave written consent to the assignment of the Production Licence from Mr Gallagher to Earlsferry Oil and Gas Public Limited Company ('Earlsferry'), a large and established oil production company. Commercial production of the Olen Horst field commenced in March 1999. Although the Company is not privy to the terms of Mr Gallagher's arrangement with Earlsferry, nor of the production figures for the field, the published estimate is that there are reserves of 100 million barrels in the field. It is anticipated that Mr Gallagher will be paid very large sums by Earlsferry over a period of some years.

It seems to those Instructing that the Company should be able to claim against Mr Gallagher, and the Company is anxious to commence proceedings as soon as possible. There has been correspondence with Mr Gallagher, but he is unwilling to negotiate. Counsel should know that Mr Gallagher has substantial business interests in this country in addition to his interest in the Olen Horst field, so those Instructing have advised the Company that it would be inappropriate at this stage to apply for a freezing injunction.

Counsel is asked to advise on the merits of an action against Mr Gallagher, and to settle Particulars of Claim.

STATEMENT OF KEITH HARVEY SYMONS

I am Keith Harvey Symons of Watermill House, Billings Lane, North Kyme, Lincolnshire. The contents of this statement are true to the best of my knowledge and belief.

I am the Chairman of the Board of Directors of Beadnell Bay Petroleum Limited ('the Company'), and have been since 1992. I graduated from Aston University in 1975 with a degree in Business Studies and Financial Management and have spent my entire working life in management roles in the Theobald group.

At present the Company has two directors in addition to myself: Mr William Knight, who is the present Managing Director, and who became a director of the Company for the first time in May 1995; and Mr Trevor Alan Walsh, who was appointed in 1989. Mr Walsh has expertise in interpreting seismic readings in connection with oil exploration. He has attended no more than two or three Board meetings since I was appointed.

The Company was incorporated on 7th July 1988. It was originally a £100 company, but its nominal capital was increased to 10,000 £1 ordinary shares in 1992. Of these shares 3,000 have been issued to North Sea Shelf Drilling Limited ('Shelf Drilling') and 2,900 have been issued to Howdenbury (UK) Limited ('Howdenbury'), the remainder being unissued. Shelf Drilling is a company controlled by Theobald International Holdings PLC, the principal holding company of the Theobald family. I have been a director of Shelf Drilling for the last 10 years.

Howdenbury has always been almost wholly owned by Mr Michael Gallagher. Before 1992 the Company was almost wholly owned by Howdenbury. Mr Gallagher is a geologist and has been involved in oil exploration for all his working life. He is 52. In its early years the Company was funded by an American oil company. It had obtained an Exploration Licence from the government, and had been conducting geological surveys of the area off the Northumberland coast. In about August 1992 Mr Gallagher approached Mr Theobald with a proposal for participation in the Company's activities in the North Sea. At that time Mr Theobald had no interests in the North Sea, but was attracted to the prospect of moving into oil. I have since that time discovered that the American finance was about to be withdrawn. The end result of quite intensive negotiations was that in December 1992 the Theobald group made a substantial investment of capital in the Company, was allocated additional shares, and I was appointed Chairman of the Board of Directors. Mr Gallagher continued as Managing Director.

I have fairly substantial commitments elsewhere in the Theobald group, and the only member of the Board engaged full time in running the day-to-day affairs of the Company was Mr Gallagher. My position as Chairman and Mr Gallagher's as Managing Director were confirmed at the Company's AGM in January 1993.

The arrangements made between the Company, Shelf Drilling and Howdenbury in December 1992 were as follows:

(a) The Company would complete the programme of testing and investigation of the strata under the seafloor it had commenced in 1991 as set out in documents (including estimates for costs) provided by Mr Gallagher at that time.

(b) The costs of the programme, which were estimated at £7 million, would be met by Shelf Drilling.

(c) In the event that commercially exploitable oil reserves were discovered by the Company:

  (i) Shelf Drilling would have first call on profits made for reimbursement of its costs of the exploration programme;

(ii) After paying costs, further distributions of profits would be 70 per cent to Shelf Drilling and 30 per cent to Howdenbury.

(d) To give effect to the agreement a further 3,883 ordinary shares would be issued to Shelf Drilling at that time at par.

Board meetings were held monthly. Mr Gallagher would always report on the progress of operations in the North Sea. From April or May 1993 he indicated that one particular area off the Northumberland coast was showing every sign of containing a reasonably sized oil deposit. This area was subsequently incorporated in block 79452 as designated by the Department of Energy. In June 1993 the Department of Energy advertised inviting applications for Production Licences for a number of blocks or areas in the North Sea, including block 79452.

Payments totalling £5.24 million were made by Shelf Drilling to the Company in the period from December 1992 to July 1993 for drilling etc. operations. This sum, together with compound interest at 2 per cent above Barclays Bank base rate, at present stands in the Company's books as a debt owed to Shelf Drilling.

In the second week of July 1993 the Theobald group suffered a wholly unconnected serious cash flow problem following the collapse of its restaurant division in Canada. From July 1993 I was fully engaged trying to shore up the financial crisis facing the group. Mr Gallagher was informed of the group's difficulties at about that time. In any event they were widely reported in the financial press. As there was no money available I told Mr Gallagher not to allow the Company to incur any further expense until further notice.

I am aware that on 6th August 1993 there was a meeting between Mr Theobald and Mr Gallagher concerning their future operations in the North Sea. My understanding is that they discussed the possibility of a new company being formed to make an application for a Production Licence in respect of block 79452, but so far as I am aware nothing concrete was agreed.

Mr Gallagher orally tendered his resignation as a director and as Managing Director of the Company at the Board meeting on 2nd September 1993 to take effect immediately. Although I was reluctant to accept he was adamant he wanted to go, and as he was not an employee I could not insist on any notice being given to the Company.

I was never told by Mr Gallagher that he intended to apply for a Production Licence in respect of block 79452. I was not invited to the so-called Board meeting on 6th August 1993. Questions relating to the Production Licence have never been raised or voted upon at meetings of the shareholders of the Company. The Company has been dormant since the summer of 1993.

It is a matter of record that substantial oil reserves were confirmed to exist in block 79452 in October 1994. This deposit is now known as the Olen Horst oilfield.

Signed:

Dated: 10th May 2000

STATEMENT OF WILLIAM KNIGHT

I am William Knight of 35 Beresford Road, Wallsend, Newcastle upon Tyne. The contents of this statement are true to the best of my knowledge and belief.

I am the Managing Director of Beadnell Bay Petroleum Limited ('the Company'), and have been since my appointment in May 1995. I graduated from Portsmouth Polytechnic in 1981 with a Master's Degree in Mining Engineering, where I wrote a dissertation on the problems in extracting oil shale. I have spent my entire working life in the mining industry, originally with the National Coal Board, but since 1988 with drilling operations in the North Sea.

Persons intending to prospect for oil in the North Sea have to apply for licences from the Secretary of State for Energy. This the Company did in 1990. A small fee (£500) is payable. An Exploration Licence was granted to the Company in February 1991. Various exploratory operations were then conducted by the Company under an arrangement with an American oil company.

I have a good relationship with the present Managing Director of Earlsferry Oil and Gas PLC ('Earlsferry'), and have made a number of inquiries as to what happened in relation to the granting of the Production Licence relating to block 79452. The application was made by Mr Gallagher in his own name on 27th July 1993. Apparently the fee of £3,700 was paid by Mr Gallagher himself. There was some correspondence between Mr Gallagher and the Department of Energy, and I have been given a copy of one letter from Mr Gallagher dated 15th August 1993.

In February 1996 the Secretary of State gave written consent to the assignment of the Production Licence to Earlsferry. My understanding is that Earlsferry are paying Mr Gallagher royalties on the price of sales of oil related products from the Olen Horst field at a rate of 1 per cent.

Signed:

Dated: 10th May 2000

EXPLORATION LICENCE

This exploration licence is made this 8th day of February 1991 between the Secretary of State for Energy of Thames House South, 1 Palace Street, London SW1 of the one part and Beadnell Bay Petroleum Limited whose registered office is situate at 62 Westgate Road, Newcastle upon Tyne, NE1 4YG of the other part.

Interpretation
1. (1) In the following clauses the following expressions have the meanings hereby respectively assigned to them, that is to say:
'the Act of 1934' means the Petroleum (Production) Act 1934;
'the Act of 1964' means the Continental Shelf Act 1964;
'the exploration area' means the area for the time being in which the Licensee may exercise the rights granted by this licence;
'the Licensee' means the person or persons to whom this licence is granted, his personal representatives and any person or persons to whom the rights conferred by this licence may lawfully have been assigned;
'the Minister' means the Secretary of State for Energy;
'petroleum' includes any mineral oil or relative hydrocarbon and natural gas existing in its natural condition in strata, but does not include coal or bituminous shales or other stratified deposits from which oil can be extracted by destructive distillation;
'well' includes borehole. . . .

Right to search for petroleum
2. In consideration of the payments hereinafter provided and the performance and observance by the Licensee of all the terms and conditions hereof, the Minister, in exercise of the powers conferred upon him by the Act of 1934 and the Act of 1964, hereby grants to the Licensee LICENCE AND LIBERTY in common with all other persons to whom the like right may have been granted or may hereafter be granted during the continuance of this licence and subject to the provisions hereof to search for petroleum in the strata in the islands and in the seabed and subsoil:

(a) comprised in the seaward areas defined by Regulation 3(1) of the Petroleum (Production) (Seaward Areas) Regulations 1988; and

(b) where the lines drawn in accordance with Schedule 1 to the said Regulations dividing landward areas from seaward areas are not the low-water line, in the areas between that line and the said dividing lines:

Provided that no rights conferred by this licence shall be exercisable in any area in respect of which a licence (not being a methane drainage licence) is for the time being in force, entitling the grantee thereof to search and bore for and get petroleum, except with the agreement of the holder of that licence to the exercise in any such area of any such rights.

Prospecting methods
3. The right to search for petroleum conferred by this licence shall include prospecting and carrying out geological surveys by physical or chemical means and drilling for the purpose of obtaining geological information about strata in the exploration area but shall not include any right to get petroleum or any right to drill wells for production of petroleum or any other well of a depth exceeding three hundred and fifty metres below the surface of the seabed or such greater depth as the Minister may from time to time approve either generally or in relation to a particular well or in relation to a class of wells to which that well belongs.

Term of licence
4. This licence unless sooner determined under any of the provisions hereof shall be and continue in force for the term of three years from 8th February 1991 but may, if the Minister sees fit and the Licensee has at least three months before the expiry of the said term made a written request for its extension, be continued for a further period of three years. . . .

Payment of consideration for licence
6. (1) The Licensee shall pay to the Minister during the term of this licence the consideration for the grant of this licence specified in Schedule 1 to this licence at the times and in the manner so specified. . . .

Avoidance of harmful methods of working
9. (1) The Licensee shall maintain all apparatus and appliances and all wells which have not been abandoned and plugged as provided by clause 7 of this licence in good repair and condition and shall execute all operations in or in connection with the exploration area in a proper and workmanlike manner in accordance with methods and practice of exploration customarily used in good oilfield practice and without prejudice to the generality of the foregoing provision the Licensee shall take all steps practicable in order

(a) to prevent the escape or waste of petroleum discovered in the exploration area;

(b) to conserve the exploration area for productive operations;

(c) to prevent damage to petroleum bearing strata;

(d) to prevent the entrance of water through wells to petroleum bearing strata; and

(e) to prevent the escape of petroleum into any waters in or in the vicinity of the exploration area. . . .

Returns
13. (1) The Licensee shall furnish to the Minister on or before the fifteenth day of each month in which this licence is in force a return in a form from time to time approved by the Minister of the progress of his operations in the exploration area. Such return shall contain

(a) a statement of the areas in which any geological work, including surveys by any physical or chemical means, has been carried out;

(b) the number assigned to each well, and in the case of any well the drilling of which was begun or the number of which was changed in that month, the site thereof;

(c) a statement of the depth drilled in each well; and

(d) a statement of any petroleum, water, mines or workable seams of coal encountered in the course of the said operations.

Power to execute works
18. If the Licensee shall at any time fail to perform the obligations arising under the terms and conditions of any of clauses 7, 9 and 11 of this licence then and in any such case the Minister shall be entitled, after giving to the Licensee reasonable notice in writing of such his intention, to execute any works and to provide and install any equipment which in the opinion of the Minister may be necessary to secure the performance of the said obligations or any of them and to recover the costs and expenses of so doing from the Licensee. . . .

Schedule 1

1. The Licensee shall pay to the Minister yearly in advance during the first three years of the term of this Licence the sum of EIGHT THOUSAND POUNDS payable on the 8th day of February in every year.

2. If the period of this Licence is extended in accordance with clause 4 hereof, the Licensee shall pay to the Minister yearly in advance during the term of such extension the sum of TEN THOUSAND POUNDS payable on the 8th day of February in every year commencing on 8th February 1994.

IN WITNESS whereof etc.

PRODUCTION LICENCE

This production licence is made this 18th day of September 1993 between the Secretary of State for Energy of Thames House South, 1 Palace Street, London SW1 of the one part and Michael Ryan Gallagher of Marigold House, Lower Wynd, Aylesbury, Buckinghamshire, HP20 6DN of the other part.

Interpretation
1. (1) In the following clauses, the following expressions have the meanings hereby respectively assigned to them, that is to say
'the Act of 1934' means the Petroleum (Production) Act 1934;
'the Act of 1964' means the Continental Shelf Act 1964;
'appropriate percentage' has the meaning assigned thereto by clause 10;
'block' means an area comprised in this licence which is delineated on the reference map deposited at the principal office of the Department of Energy and to which a reference number was assigned at the date of this licence;
'chargeable period' has the meaning assigned thereto by clause 10;
'development scheme' has the meaning assigned thereto by clause 28;
'half year' means the period from 1st January to 30th June in any year and the period from 1st July to 31st December in any year;
'initial term' has the meaning assigned thereto by clause 3 and 'second term' has the meaning assigned thereto by clause 4(4);
'the licensed area' means the area for the time being in which the Licensee may exercise the rights granted by this licence;
'the Licensee' means the person or persons to whom this licence is granted, his personal representatives and any person or persons to whom the rights conferred by this licence may lawfully have been assigned;
'the Minister' means the Secretary of State for Energy;
'oilfield' has the meaning assigned thereto by clause 28;
'petroleum' includes any mineral oil or relative hydrocarbon and natural gas existing in its natural condition in strata but does not include coal or bituminous shales or other stratified deposits from which oil can be extracted by destructive distillation;
'section' means a part of a block comprising an area bounded by minute lines of latitude and longitude one minute apart respectively;
'well' includes borehole. . . .

2. In consideration of the payments and royalties hereinafter provided and the performance and observance by the Licensee of all the terms and conditions hereof, the Minister, in exercise of the powers conferred upon him by the Act of 1934 hereby grants to the Licensee EXCLUSIVE LICENCE AND LIBERTY during the continuance of this licence and subject to the provisions hereof to search and bore for, and get, petroleum in the seabed and subsoil under the seaward area comprising an area of 20 square kilometres more particularly described in Schedule 1 to this Licence being the area comprising block No. 79452 on the reference map deposited at the principal office of the Department of Energy:

Provided that nothing in this licence shall affect the right of the Minister to grant a methane drainage licence in respect of the whole or any part of the licensed area or affect the exercise of any rights so granted.

Term of licence
3. This licence unless sooner determined under any of the provisions hereof shall be and continue in force for the term of six years next after 1st October 1993 (hereinafter called 'the initial term'); but if the terms and conditions of this licence are duly performed and observed and, in particular, if the work programme described in Schedule 4 to this licence has been duly performed, it may be continued for a further term of twelve years as provided by clause 4 of this licence and, if the terms and conditions of this licence continue to be duly performed and observed, thereafter as provided by clause 5 (and subject to the provisions of clause 6) of this licence for a further maximum period of eighteen years. . . .

Payment of consideration for licence
9. (1) The Licensee shall make to the Minister as consideration for the grant of this licence

(a) payments of royalty in accordance with clauses 10 to 12 of this licence;

(b) deliveries of petroleum in accordance with clause 13 of this licence; and

(c) payments in accordance with Schedule 2 to this licence.

(2) The Licensee shall not by reason of determination of the licence or surrender of any part of the licensed area be entitled to be repaid or allowed any sum payable to the Minister pursuant to this licence before the date of determination or surrender.

Royalty payments
10. (1) Subject to paragraph (2) of this clause the Licensee shall pay to the Minister, in respect of each half year in which this licence is in force (hereafter in this clause and in clauses 11 and 12 of this licence referred to as a 'chargeable period'), a royalty of an amount equal to the percentage specified in Schedule 3 to this licence (hereinafter referred to as 'the appropriate percentage') of the value of the petroleum relating to that period. . . .

Working obligations
16. (1) The Licensee shall before the expiry of the initial term of this licence carry out such scheme of prospecting including any geological survey by any physical or chemical means and such programme of test drilling (hereinafter collectively referred to as a '*work programme*') as may be set out in Schedule 4 to this licence.

(2) If at any time the Minister serves a notice in writing on the Licensee requiring him to submit to the Minister, before a date specified in the notice, an appropriate programme for exploring for petroleum in the licensed area during a period so specified, the Licensee shall comply with the notice; and for the purposes of this paragraph an appropriate programme is one which any person who, if he

(a) were entitled to exploit rights granted by the licence; and

(b) had the competence and resources needed to exploit those rights to the best commercial advantage; and

(c) were seeking to exploit those rights to the best commercial advantage:

could reasonably be expected to carry out during the period specified in the notice, and that period must be within the term of this licence. . . .

(5) The Licensee shall carry out any programme submitted by him in pursuance of this clause as to which either

(a) the Minister serves notice in writing on the Licensee stating that the Minister approves the programme; or

(b) it is determined in consequence of any reference to arbitration in pursuance of this licence that the programme satisfies the relevant requirements;

and any programme approved by the Minister in pursuance of this paragraph shall be deemed for the purposes of this licence to satisfy the relevant requirements.

Avoidance of harmful methods of working
23. (1) The Licensee shall maintain all apparatus and appliances and all wells in the licensed area which have not been abandoned and plugged as provided by clause 19 of this licence in good repair and condition and shall execute all operations in or in connection with the licensed area in a proper and workmanlike manner in accordance with methods and practice customarily used in good oilfield practice and without

prejudice to the generality of the foregoing provision the Licensee shall take all steps practicable in order

(a) to control the flow and to prevent the escape or waste of petroleum discovered in or obtained from the licensed area;

(b) to conserve the licensed area for productive operations;

(c) to prevent damage to adjoining petroleum bearing strata;

(d) to prevent the entrance of water through wells to petroleum bearing strata except for the purposes of secondary recovery; and

(e) to prevent the escape of petroleum into any waters in or in the vicinity of the licensed area.

Restrictions on assignment, etc.
41. (1) The Licensee shall not, except with the consent in writing of the Minister and in accordance with the conditions (if any) of the consent do anything whatsoever whereby, under the law (including the rules of equity) of any part of the United Kingdom or of any other place, any right granted by this licence or derived from a right so granted becomes exercisable by or for the benefit of or in accordance with the directions of another person.

(2) An agreement permitting the carrying out of geological surveys by physical or chemical means in the licensed area otherwise than by drilling is not prohibited by paragraph (1) of this clause if the person by whom such surveys are to be carried out is

(a) the holder of a licence granted by the Minister of the right, in common with all other persons to whom the like right may have been granted, to search for petroleum in respect of an area which would include the licensed area, but for a proviso therein excluding the exercise of such rights in the licensed area without the consent of the Licensee; or

(b) the holder of a licence granted by the Minister to search and bore for, and get, petroleum in an area adjacent to the licensed area.

Schedule 1

[Technical description of block No. 79452]

Schedule 2

1. The Licensee shall pay to the Minister the sum of TWENTY THOUSAND POUNDS as an initial payment on the grant of this licence, such sum to be paid on or before 24th September 1993.

2. The Licensee shall pay to the Minister yearly in advance during the first six years of the term of this licence the sum of THIRTY THOUSAND POUNDS payable on the 1st day of October in every year.

3. If the period of this licence is extended in accordance with clause 4 hereof, the Licensee shall pay to the Minister yearly in advance during the term of such extension the sum of FIFTY THOUSAND POUNDS payable on the 1st day of October in every year commencing on 1st October 1999.

Schedule 3

The appropriate percentage shall be eight per cent.

Schedule 4

[Detailed working obligations undertaken by the Licensee]

IN WITNESS whereof etc.

BEADNELL BAY PETROLEUM LIMITED
Extracts from Board Minutes
(Each meeting was recorded on a separate page)

8.4.1993
Present: KHS; MG
3. MG reported latest seismic surveys were being analysed. Promising geological structure about 60 miles E of Seahouses being given particular attention.

7.5.1993
Present: KHS; MG
2. MG reported area E of Seahouses had all the right characteristics for oil deposit. Further test bore justified.
Agreed: Estimate to be prepared by MG of costs of further bore. To proceed on signature of KHS.

2.7.1993
Present: KHS; MG
2. It will not be possible for further bore at site off Seahouses to be undertaken before August as drilling vessel otherwise engaged until then. Confirmed go ahead when ready.
3. MG reported Department of Energy advertised for production licences for a number of areas including the Seahouses site. Discussion as to whether an application should be lodged.
4. Discussion as to the probabilities that commercial deposits exist at Seahouses site.
Agreed: MG to provide KHS with more precise assessment by 16.7.1993.

13.7.1993
Present: KHS; MG
2. MG reported no present offshore activities in progress. No firm commitments for drilling operations.
3. Discussion of Theobald group difficulties.
Agreed: No additional expenditure to be incurred until further notice. Economies to be made where possible.

6.8.1993
Present: MG; TAW
2. Discussion of Theobald group difficulties and Seahouses site (now known as Department of Energy block 79452).
Agreed: MG to apply for production licence in own name.

2.9.1993
Present: KHS; MG
1. MG tendered his resignation as director and M-D. After discussion MG's resignation accepted by KHS.

Marigold House
Lower Wynd
Aylesbury
Buckinghamshire
HP20 4RK

15th August 1993

Mrs F Creaney
Department of Energy
Thames House South
1 Palace Street
London SW1

Dear Madam,

Re: Block 79452

Further to our letter of 11th inst., I can confirm that I have been actively employed in the oil exploration industry since 1979. I have experience with offshore oil operations both in the North Sea and in the Gulf of Mexico. Since 1988 I have been the Managing Director of Beadnell Bay Petroleum Limited, which as you will know holds an Exploration Licence issued by your department on 8th February 1991 in respect of the seaward areas of the North Sea. Beadnell Bay Petroleum Limited has extensive knowledge and expertise within the oil industry, and I attach a copy of the programme of works undertaken by the company since February 1991.

Should you need to discuss further matters with me, please contact me so that a meeting can be arranged.

Yours faithfully,

Michael Gallagher

DANIELS AND AWFORD
Solicitors

73 Granger Street
Newcastle upon Tyne
NE1 3SL

Tel: 0191 201 8376
Fax: 0191 201 8272
Our Ref: 94/DGY
Your Ref:

Date: 1st March 2000

Mr M Gallagher
Marigold House
Lower Wynd
Aylesbury
Buckinghamshire
HP20 4RK

Dear Mr Gallagher,

Re: BEADNELL BAY PETROLEUM LIMITED

We are instructed by the Board of the above-named company in relation to the granting to you of a North Sea Oil Production Licence over block 79452 on 18th September 1993.

At all material times you were a director and Managing Director of the above-named company. In that capacity you owed it various fiduciary duties which prohibited you from making a personal profit at the expense of the company. Accordingly it was your duty to apply for the above-mentioned Production Licence in the name of the company rather than in your own name.

We understand that as the Licensee of block 79452 you were able to enter into an arrangement with Earlsferry Oil and Gas PLC relating to the exploitation of the oil reserves found in the Olen Horst oilfield in the North Sea. We also understand that under that arrangement you are and will continue to be in receipt of considerable royalties in respect of oil produced by that oilfield. In the circumstances you are liable to account to our client for those royalties. Please confirm that you are holding all sums received from Earlsferry Oil and Gas PLC to the account of our client Company, and will provide full facilities for the inspection of your books for the purpose of verifying the amount due to our client.

Unless a satisfactory reply to this letter is received in the next 14 days legal proceedings may be issued against you in respect of the above matters without further notice. Legal costs will then be incurred which you may be ordered by the Court to pay in addition to the sums due to our client.

This is an important letter. It may be in your interests to consult a solicitor before replying.

Yours faithfully,

Daniels and Awford

Marigold House
Lower Wynd
Aylesbury
Buckinghamshire
HP20 4RK

17th March 2000

Messrs Daniels and Awford
73 Granger Street
Newcastle upon Tyne
NE1 3SL

Dear Sirs,

Re: BEADNELL BAY PETROLEUM LIMITED

I was disappointed to receive your letter of 1st March and to read the allegations made in it on behalf of your clients. There is absolutely no truth in what you say about misconduct on my part.

As you will be aware, Beadnell Bay Petroleum Limited as originally formed eleven years ago was wholly owned by one of my other companies, Howdenbury (UK) Limited. It is now controlled by the employers of the present chairman. In the years up to 1993 it was actively engaged in the North Sea. After my resignation in 1993 it has achieved absolutely nothing.

Exploration for and recovery of offshore oil requires a sustained commitment. What happened was that in the summer of 1993 your real clients ran out of money and reneged on the 1992 investment contract between Howdenbury (UK) Limited and North Sea Shelf Drilling Limited at a very delicate time, jeopardising several years of investment by my companies.

As your clients are aware, licensees are required to enter into a large number of expensive obligations when they take production licences. After July 1993 your clients were in no position to comply with those obligations. On instructions from his employer, Mr Theobald, Beadnell Bay's chairman, Mr Symons, laid down a directive in July 1993 that no further expenditure was to be incurred by the company. It was clear at that time that there was no prospect of Beadnell Bay obtaining a production licence in its own right.

Being unable to finance a licence of its own, it was agreed that I could apply for a production licence myself. This was at my own risk and, if it proved that there was oil in the area concerned, for my own personal benefit. This was expressly agreed to at a meeting between myself and Mr Theobald at that time, and was approved by the directors of Beadnell Bay Petroleum Limited at a meeting on 6th August 1993.

I made the position clear to the Department of Energy in November 1993. The Department was fully aware of the financial problems of the Theobald group and Beadnell Bay's inability to finance the proper development of the licensed area. I made it clear that I would honour the terms of the licence from my own resources or finance that I would seek elsewhere.

Considerable expenditure (well into seven figures) was in fact incurred over the next year in test drilling, all of which came from my personal resources.

There is a great deal of being wise after the event in all this on the part of your clients. Back in 1992 I was the only person confident that there was oil at Olen Horst, and I met no end of scepticism from Mr Symons. In the light of all this I trust that you will confirm that your clients will not be taking these allegations any further.

Yours faithfully,

Michael Gallagher

Extracts from the Articles of Association of
BEADNELL BAY PETROLEUM LIMITED

Director's appointments

82. The company may by ordinary resolution appoint a person who is willing to act to be a director either to fill a vacancy or as an additional director. In addition, by ordinary resolutions one person so appointed may be appointed chairman of the board of directors and a second person may be appointed as managing director of the company.

Proceedings of directors

86. The directors may meet together for the dispatch of business, adjourn, and otherwise regulate their meetings, as they think fit. A director may at any time summon a meeting of the directors. It shall not be necessary to give notice of a meeting of directors to any director for the time being outside the United Kingdom. Questions arising at any meeting shall be decided by a majority of votes. In case of an equality of votes, the chairman shall have a second or casting vote.

87. The quorum necessary for the transaction of the business of the directors may be fixed by the directors, and unless so fixed shall be two.

91. All acts done by any meeting of the directors shall, notwithstanding that it be afterwards discovered that there was some defect in the appointment of any such director or that they or any of them were disqualified, be as valid as if every such person had been duly appointed and was qualified to be a director.

Powers of directors

94. The business of the company shall be managed by the directors, who may pay all expenses incurred in promoting and registering the company, and may exercise all powers of the company as are not by the Companies Acts 1948 to 1981 or by these regulations, required to be exercised by the company in general meeting, subject, nevertheless, to any of these regulations, to the provisions of the Companies Acts 1948 to 1981 and to such regulations, being not inconsistent with the aforesaid regulations or provisions, as may be prescribed by the company in general meeting; but no regulation made by the company in general meeting shall invalidate any prior act of the directors which would have been valid if that regulation had not been made.

Duties of directors

99. A director who is in any way, whether directly or indirectly, interested in a contract or proposed contract with the company shall declare the nature of his interest at a meeting of the directors in accordance with section 199 of the Companies Act 1948.

100. A director shall not vote in respect of any contract or arrangement in which he is interested, and if he shall do so his vote shall not be counted, nor shall he be counted in the quorum present at the meeting.

103. The directors shall cause minutes to be recorded:

(a) of all appointments of officers made by the company;

(b) of the names of directors present at each meeting of the directors; and

(c) of all resolutions and the proceedings at all meetings of the company, and of the directors;

and every director present at any meeting of directors shall sign his name on the minutes of the preceding meeting.

14.3 Assessment Criteria

In order to be graded competent or above, a student must show his or her ability to

A Write an Opinion which

(1) (i) Is written in clear grammatical English, correctly punctuated and properly and neatly laid out

(ii) Is written in language and in a style appropriate to an Opinion (5%)

(2) Shows a thorough grasp and a practical analysis of the material facts and issues and deals with each issue in a logical order, giving each its due weight and significance (10%)

(3) Shows a sound understanding and application of the relevant legal principles (10%)

(4) Adopts a practical approach to the case by

(i) addressing the needs and objectives of the client

(ii) answering all the questions expressly or implicitly raised in the instructions

(iii) expressing a definite conclusion where appropriate, alternatively explaining why there can be no definite conclusion

(iv) identifying and asking for relevant further information

(v) setting conclusions out clearly and prominently (10%)

(5) Gives sound, full and reasoned advice on the matters raised and questions asked in the instructions (15%)

B Draft Particulars of Claim which

(1) Are written in clear grammatical English, correctly punctuated and neat on the page (5%)

(2) Are structured so that the statement of case

(i) is properly headed and laid out

(ii) deals with the material issues in an appropriate order and in an appropriate number of paragraphs

(iii) tells a clear story (15%)

(3) (i) Set out succinctly the material facts

(ii) Identify or helps to identify the material issues

(iii) Accurately states the client's case and the relief sought

(iv) Omits all immaterial matters (15%)

(4) (i) Are written in language and in a style appropriate for a statement of case

(ii) Are precise and unambiguous

(iii) Do not rely excessively on precedents (10%)

(5) Serves its purpose, in that:

(i) it sets out a sustainable claim; and

(ii) it goes as far as it reasonably can in helping the client to achieve its objectives (5%)

Note that case preparation skills, as well as opinion writing and drafting skills, and knowledge of law are required in order to satisfy these criteria.

14.4 Suggested Opinion

Re: BEADNELL BAY PETROLEUM LIMITED

OPINION

1. I am instructed on behalf of Beadnell Bay Petroleum Limited ('the Company') to advise on the merits of an action against Mr Michael Gallagher for breach of fiduciary duty. The Company was formed to search for and extract petroleum, and has been engaged principally in the North Sea. Mr Gallagher was a director and the managing director of the Company from its incorporation in 1988 until his resignation on 2 September 1993.

2. Substantial investment was made by the Company in the period up to July 1993 in exploration operations under an Exploration Licence granted to it by the Department of Energy on 8 February 1991. These identified one area, block 79452, as the potential site of an oilfield. A Production Licence from the Department of Energy is required for extraction of petroleum from the North Sea. Financial difficulties were encountered by the Company in July 1993, and Mr Gallagher applied for and obtained on 18 September 1993 a Production Licence in respect of block 79452 in his own name. Substantial petroleum reserves were found in block 79452 in October 1994, and Mr Gallagher entered into an arrangement with Earlsferry Oil and Gas PLC ('Earlsferry') in February 1996 under which he appears to be in receipt of substantial royalties.

Summary of Advice
3. As a director Mr Gallagher owed a duty to the Company not to take a personal benefit through his fiduciary position without the informed consent of the Company. He could not avoid that duty by resigning just before taking the Production Licence in his own name. The real question in this case is whether there was informed consent from the Company to his taking the Production Licence in his own name. At present the evidence on this is not absolutely clear, but there is a prima facie case of breach of duty against Mr Gallagher. If it is established that Mr Gallagher breached his fiduciary duty to the Company he will hold the profits he appears to be making under the assignment of the Production Licence as a constructive trustee for the Company, and will be bound to account to it for the royalties he has and will receive.

The nature of Mr Gallagher's duty to the Company
4. It is settled law that directors owe fiduciary duties to their companies. It is also clear law that a director cannot escape the consequences of a breach of those duties by resigning his office in advance of the finalisation of the transaction in question if there has already been conduct by the director amounting to a breach of his duty to the Company: Industrial Development Consultants Ltd v Cooley [1972] 2 All ER 162. In the present case it is plain from his letter to the Department of Energy dated 15 August 1993 that Mr Gallagher applied for the Production Licence in advance of his resignation on 2 September 1993.

Fiduciary duty
5. Being a fiduciary, Mr Gallagher was not allowed to enter into transactions which may possibly have resulted in his personal interests conflicting with those of the Company. Although the duty extends to situations where there is a mere 'possibility' of a conflict of interest, this case seems to me to be one where there has been an actual conflict of interest. One aspect of this duty is that a director is not permitted to use the Company's assets, opportunities or information for his own benefit without the informed consent of the Company.

6. A strict approach is taken by the Courts. As Lord Wright said in Regal (Hastings) Ltd v Gulliver [1967] 2 AC 134, 154, '. . . if a person in a fiduciary relationship makes a secret profit out of the relationship, the court will not inquire whether the other person is damnified or has lost a profit which otherwise he would have got. The fact is

in itself a fundamental breach of the fiduciary relationship. Nor can the court adequately investigate the matter in most cases.' Liability rests on two conditions being satisfied (see Lord Macmillan at p. 153):

(a) whether the obtaining of the Production Licence was so related to the affairs of the Company that it can properly be said to have been done in the course of Mr Gallagher's management of the Company and in utilisation of his opportunities and special knowledge as a director; and

(b) whether obtaining the Production Licence in his own name resulted in a profit to himself.

Use of corporate opportunity

7. In the period leading up to Mr Gallagher's application for the Production Licence the Company had expended considerable sums in conducting geological investigations in the area including block 79452. Obviously this expenditure was incurred for the purpose of putting the Company in a position to apply for a Production Licence or Licences which it could then exploit. Mr Gallagher is a geologist and, in his capacity as Managing Director of the Company, was privy to the findings of the Company's survey work. This is clear enough from the Board minutes for April to July 1993 and Mr Gallagher's letter of 17 March 2000. If the case is defended it will be necessary to disclose the documentary records of the Company's survey work, and it may be necessary for an expert's report (perhaps by Mr Knight) to be prepared interpreting that material. Such a report should consider the strength of the evidence available in July 1993 for there being a commercially viable oilfield within block 79452.

8. When the opportunity arose in the summer of 1993 to apply for a Production Licence over block 79452 it was, given the knowledge I assume the Company's directors had about the prospects for the site, the duty of the directors to apply for such a licence on behalf of the Company. Making the application in his own name was, therefore, on the face of it a breach of Mr Gallagher's fiduciary duty to the Company.

9. In addition to making use of the Company's confidential information, it is also apparent that Mr Gallagher used the Company's name in his letter to the Department of Energy of 15 August 1993 in support of his application for the Production Licence.

The Company's financial difficulties

10. In July 1993 the Company, on account of the difficulties then being encountered by the Theobald Group, lost the source of its finances. On 13 July 1993 the Board of the Company agreed to avoid further expenditure until further notice. Certain fees have to be paid when applying for Production Licences, and a number of very onerous and expensive obligations (contained in Schedule 4 to the Licence) have to be taken on by licensees. It seems clear that in July–August 1993 the Company was not in a position to honour that level of expenditure. Although a court would almost inevitably find that there was no possibility of the Company being granted a production licence in those circumstances, that is no bar to the Company obtaining relief against a director who has allowed his personal interests to conflict with those of his Company: Regal (Hastings) Ltd v Gulliver [1967] 2 AC 134, HL.

Resulting profit

11. I am instructed that Mr Gallagher, after obtaining written permission from the Secretary of State for Energy, assigned the Production Licence to Earlsferry in February 1996. Under that assignment he is paid a royalty, believed to be 1% of the price of sales, on oil produced from block 79452.

Informed consent

12. Lord Hodson in Boardman v Phipps [1967] 2 AC 46 at 109D said that a fiduciary could justify taking a personal profit from his position as such if he had the fully informed consent of the beneficiaries. Generally, consent should be given by the shareholders rather than the directors, as the shareholders are entitled to the unbiased views of all the directors: Benson v Heathorn (1842) 1 Y & C Ch 326. I am instructed

that the shareholders were never consulted. Exceptionally, the Privy Council in Queensland Mines Ltd v Hudson (1978) 52 ALJR 379 held that where the members of the company's board:

(a) knew the full facts;

(b) decided to renounce the company's interest in the matter; and

(c) assented to the director taking it for his own benefit and at his own risk,

there was no liability to account to the company.

13. It seems from the Board minutes before me that Mr Symons was dependent on Mr Gallagher for details as to the North Sea operation being conducted by the Company. In his letter of 17 March 2000 Mr Gallagher says Mr Symons was sceptical about the prospects of block 79452 in 1992. Was this because Mr Symons did not have all the information available to Mr Gallagher? Was Mr Symons fully informed by July 1993? The reality of the situation was that there were two shareholders of the Company, ultimately owned by Mr Gallagher and Mr Theobald, with Mr Symons being Mr Theobald's representative on the Board. Was the Theobald side of the Company informed fully of the situation and Mr Gallagher's intentions when he met Mr Theobald in August 1993? Mr Theobald should be asked to provide a statement as to his conversation with Mr Gallagher, and any written record of it, and Mr Symons should be asked for the above details.

14. Whether or not the Board decision of 13 July 1993 to incur no further expense would be regarded by the Court as a decision to renounce applying for the Production Licence for block 79452 is unclear. Perhaps Mr Symons could also be asked if there was anything said as to how long the embargo on expenditure was likely to last, and whether it was contemplated at that time whether North Sea operations would resume. In the absence of evidence to the contrary, the Court will almost certainly find the Company renounced its interest in block 79452 unless it would have been possible to put in a 'holding' application.

15. The purported Board meeting of 6 August 1993 was inquorate and ineffective. A director interested in any arrangement under discussion is not, under Article 100 of the Company's Articles of Association, to be counted in the quorum, and (unless otherwise fixed), by Article 87, the quorum is two. Only Messrs Gallagher and Walsh were present at the meeting on 6 August 1993 when it was decided that Mr Gallagher should apply for the Production Licence in his own name.

16. Mr Gallagher asserts in his letter of 17 March 2000 that express permission for him to apply for the Production Licence in his own name and at his own risk was given by Mr Theobald in August 1993. Again, Mr Theobald should be asked about this.

17. Until these further inquiries are made it is impossible to say whether liability will be established. It should also be mentioned that the rather informal way of obtaining informed consent upheld in the Queensland Mines case has been criticised and it may be possible to persuade an English Court not to follow it.

Remedy

18. If liable, Mr Gallagher will hold the profits made under the Production Licence as a constructive trustee in favour of the Company, and will be liable to account to the Company for those profits.

19. In Boardman v Phipps [1967] 2 AC 46 the House of Lords allowed trustees who had allowed their personal interests to conflict with the interests of their beneficiaries a generous allowance to compensate them for the work they had undertaken in earning the profits they had to disgorge to the trust. In this case Mr Gallagher apparently expended considerable time and money in confirming the presence of oil after he obtained the Production Licence. According to Guinness plc v Saunders [1990] 2 AC

663 such an allowance cannot be made in favour of a director as to do so will interfere with the management of the company's affairs. Although this seems to be the legal position, it troubles me as the Company would inevitably have had to incur similar expenses to those incurred by Mr Gallagher. Probably the Court would regard the profits he has to return as the balance of the royalties he has and will receive after deducting the costs he has incurred.

Conclusion

20. Subject to the reservations I express regarding the Company giving its informed consent to Mr Gallagher's application for the Production Licence, this appears to be a clear case of breach of fiduciary duty. Subject to the results of the further inquiries I have suggested, it would seem appropriate to apply for summary judgment in this case if Mr Gallagher acknowledges service.

A. BARRISTER
4 Gray's Inn Place,
May 2000

14.5 Suggested Statement of Case

<u>IN THE HIGH COURT OF JUSTICE</u> CH 2000 B No.
<u>CHANCERY DIVISION</u>

BETWEEN

BEADNELL BAY PETROLEUM LIMITED <u>Claimant</u>

and

MICHAEL RYAN GALLAGHER <u>Defendant</u>

<u>PARTICULARS OF CLAIM</u>

1. The Claimant is a limited company incorporated and registered under the Companies Acts 1948 to 1981 for the purpose, among other things, of exploring for and extracting petroleum. Until his resignation on 2nd September 1993 the Defendant was a director and the managing director of the Claimant.

2. On 8th February 1991 the Claimant was granted an Exploration Licence by the Secretary of State for Energy under which it was permitted to search for petroleum in the strata in the seabed and subsoil in the seaward areas of the North Sea as defined by Regulation 3(1) of the Petroleum (Production) (Seaward Areas) Regulations 1988. A true copy of the Exploration Licence is served with these Particulars of Claim.

3. Pursuant to the said Exploration Licence the Claimant incurred expenses exceeding £5.24 million in the period from 8th February 1991 to 1st August 1993 in searching for petroleum in the said seaward areas of the North Sea, and in particular in an area approximately 60 miles east of Seahouses, Northumberland presently included in block 79452 as shown on a reference map deposited at Thames House South, 1 Palace Street, London SW1, the principal office of the Department of Energy.

4. As a result of the searches pleaded in paragraph 3 above and of analyses conducted by or on behalf of the Claimant of samples, information and data produced by such searches, the Defendant was privy to information that block 79452 was the potential site of a valuable reserve of petroleum.

5. In or about July 1993 the Defendant applied in his own name to the Secretary of State for Energy for, and on 18th September 1993 was granted in his own name, a Production Licence in respect of block 79452. The Production Licence gave the Defendant an exclusive right to search and bore for, and extract, petroleum (other than methane) in the seabed and subsoil of block 79452 for a term of 6 years from 1st October 1993, such term being capable of extension for further periods not exceeding 30 years. The Claimant will refer to the said Production Licence at trial for its full terms, and a true copy of it is served with these Particulars of Claim.

6. In applying for and entering into the said Production Licence the Defendant acted in breach of his duties as a director of the Claimant in that he:

(a) acted mala fide and against the Claimant's interests; and/or

(b) made, and is making, secret profits by virtue of the rights conferred by the Production Licence; and/or

(c) took a personal benefit through his position as a director of the Claimant without the informed consent of the Claimant; and/or

(d) allowed his personal interests to conflict with the interests of the Claimant.

PARTICULARS OF BREACH OF FIDUCIARY DUTY

The Defendant was in breach of his fiduciary duty to the Claimant in that he:

(1) Applied for the Production Licence in his own name.

(2) Failed to apply for the Production Licence in the name of the Claimant.

(3) Used the Claimant's name without its permission in making representations to the Department of Energy in support of his application for the Production Licence, in particular in a letter to the Department of Energy dated 15th August 1993, a true copy of which is served with these Particulars of Claim.

(4) Made use for his personal benefit of information obtained during his office as a director of the Claimant about the prospect of commercially exploitable petroleum deposits being present in block 79452.

(5) Failed to notify or inform fully the Claimant's board of directors or shareholders in general meeting of his actions.

7. In October 1994 substantial petroleum reserves were discovered in block 79452, and commercial extraction of those reserves began in March 1999.

8. In or about February 1996 the Defendant assigned the benefit of the Production Licence to Earlsferry Oil and Gas Public Limited Company.

9. In these circumstances the Defendant is liable to account to the Claimant for all profits he has derived and will derive directly or indirectly from his obtaining of the Production Licence.

10. Further or alternatively, by reason of the matters aforesaid the Claimant has suffered loss and damage.

PARTICULARS OF LOSS AND DAMAGE

The Claimant has by reason of the Defendant's actions been deprived of the opportunity to extract and sell the petroleum reserves in block 79452, and has thereby lost the profits on such sales.

(i)	Estimated capital costs for production facilities at block 79452	£
(ii)	Annualised cost of production facilities if costs spread over [ ] years	£
(iii)	The annual production figure for petroleum from block 79452 is estimated at [ ] barrels	
(iv)	Price of [Olen Horst] petroleum in [date]	£
(v)	Estimated annual operating and recovery costs for block 79452	£

Gross annual price of sales	£
Less annualised capital costs	£
Less annual operating and recovery costs	£
Annual loss of profit	£

Loss of profits from 1st March 1999 to the date of issue of the Claim Form in these proceedings	£
And continuing at the daily rate of	£

11. Further, the Claimant claims interest against the Defendant to be assessed pursuant to the Supreme Court Act 1981, section 35A and/or the rules of equity on the sums claimed and/or found due on the taking of the account claimed at such rate and for such period as to the Court shall seem just.

AND the Claimant seeks:

(1) Damages.

(2) An account of the profits made and to be made by the Defendant directly and indirectly from his obtaining of the Production Licence.

(3) Payment of the amount found due to the Claimant on taking the said account.

(4) Such other accounts, directions and inquiries as may be necessary.

(5) Interest under the Supreme Court Act 1981, section 35A, alternatively under the equitable jurisdiction of the Court, to be assessed.

(6) Further or other relief.

A. BARRISTER

Statement of Truth

(I believe) (The Claimant believes) that the facts stated in these Particulars of Claim are true.

I am duly authorised by the claimant to sign this statement.

Full name
Name of claimant's solicitors' firm Daniels and Awford
Signed Position or office held
(Claimant) (Litigation friend) (Claimant's solicitor) (if signing on behalf of firm or company)

DATED the day of 2000

Address for service
Daniels and Awford, 73 Grainger Street, Newcastle upon Tyne, NE1 3SL.
To: The Defendant
And to: The Court Manager.

14.6 Discussion

Opinion writing and drafting in the context of company law should follow the same approach as that recommended for the main opinion writing and drafting courses at the Inns of Court School of Law. The principles laid down and the suggestions made in the main Manuals for these skills should therefore be followed when doing the same tasks in a company law context.

The main difference is that, unless Counsel is instructed by a specialist company law firm or a firm with a company law department, the probability is that the solicitor sending the Instructions is less likely to be familiar with the finer points of law on the subject than when the Instructions relate to one of the more mainstream legal areas, such contract, tort and land law. As a result it will almost certainly be necessary to give more detail or to provide more references to primary sources than would be necessary in one of the more well-known areas. The other reason why more law tends to be discussed in company law opinions is that there is a greater prospect that one or more of the real issues in the case will be primarily issues of law, rather than issues of fact, which is the usual position in contract and tort cases.

Before starting your drafts on a final assessment you should make sure you are fully conversant with the assessment criteria for the exercise in hand, as your work will be marked using the criteria published for that assessment (and on those criteria alone). The wording adopted will have been tailored to the requirements of the exercise.

It is hoped that the Opinion at **14.4** will be fairly self-explanatory. It should be practical, identify and discuss the real issues, be legally and factually sound, ask for necessary additional information (see paragraphs 13, 14 and 16), and give reasoned answers to the issues raised by the Instructions.

One of the initial problems with drafting the Particulars of Claim in this case is the lack of a particularly helpful precedent in the usual precedent books (such as *Atkin's Court Forms* and Bullen, Leake and Jacob, *Precedents of Pleading*). However, there are a number of precedents which can be used from analogous areas (such as constructive trusts and breach of fiduciary duty of trustees), which can be used to obtain some ideas. The overall structure used in the draft at **14.5** was based on general principles as set out in the ***Drafting Manual***. Paragraph 1 pleads the fact that the Defendant was a director of the Claimant, and hence owed it the usual fiduciary duties. Paragraphs 2, 3, 5, 7 and 8 plead background facts. They appear in this sequence mainly for chronological reasons. Paragraph 4 pleads that the Defendant was privy to company information concerning the site of the oilfield. Paragraph 6 pleads the breaches of four named fiduciary duties, with particulars. Paragraphs 9 and 10 plead the injury to the Company and the liability to account, with interest being claimed in paragraph 11. The prayer sets out the remedies claimed.

INDEX